# THE ILLUSTRATED LOTUS 1-2-3 (RELEASE 2.01) BOOK

**Ralph Mylius**

**Wordware Publishing, Inc.**
**Dallas • London**

**Library of Congress Cataloging in Publication Data**

Mylius, Ralph.
   The illustrated Lotus 1-2-3 book

   Includes index.
   1. Lotus (Computer program).     2. Business—
   Data processing.       I. Title.     II. Title: The
   illustrated Lotus one-two-three book.
   HF5548.4.L67M95     1986     005.36'9     86-28217
   ISBN 0-915381-67-2

1506 Capital Ave.                                            3 Henrietta Street
Plano, Texas 75074                                 London WC2E 8LU

ISBN 0-915381-67-2

10 9 8 7 6 5 4 3 2 1

All inquiries for volume purchases of this book should be addressed to Wordware Publishing, Inc. at one of the above addresses. Telephone inquiries may be made by calling:

(214) 423-0090 in the United States
01-240 0856 in Great Britain

# Contents

# Contents Continued

# Recommended Learning Sequence

# Recommended Learning Sequence (cont.)

# Module 1

## ABOUT THIS BOOK

### INTRODUCTION

This book is about Release 2.01 of Lotus Development Corporation's Lotus 1-2-3 worksheet (spreadsheet) program. It describes how Lotus 1-2-3 can be used in your home or office and presents detailed information and useful examples for each Lotus 1-2-3 worksheet menu function. It also explains and illustrates the many information manipulation capabilities offered by Lotus 1-2-3's other powerful worksheet features.

This book is written for a varied range of users. It is for the beginner who is learning Lotus 1-2-3 for the first time and for the more advanced user who needs a quick reference guide filled with examples that work. It is also for the experienced Lotus 1-2-3, Release 1A user who is upgrading to Release 2.01 and wants to discover the new features this latest release of Lotus 1-2-3 has to offer. Finally, this book is for the classroom situation in which an instructionally designed textbook is required.

Lotus 1-2-3 is a powerful worksheet program that contains many sophisticated features. The beginner as well as the more advanced user will find that it offers them the wide flexibility to create worksheets that can range from the very simple to those that are extremely complex and involve literally thousands of operations. Yet, the techniques required to create these worksheets are not difficult to learn.

To see just how easy it is to create a worksheet using Lotus 1-2-3, you might want to turn to Module 2 and perform the steps outlined in the sample session with your computer. In a matter of a few minutes, you can have Lotus 1-2-3 doing things which would take many hours if done with pencil and paper. In fact, this is one of the most pleasurable things about Lotus 1-2-3. Worksheet details that used to take hours of dull manual work require only a few seconds to perform with Lotus 1-2-3. And this, after all, is the reason you want to learn how to use the full capabilities of the program—to save your valuable time for more interesting pursuits.

Starting in Module 2, you will be introduced to many Lotus 1-2-3 commands and menu options. Don't be frightened. At first they may not make perfect sense to you. After working with the program for a few hours, you will suddenly find yourself understanding what each feature does. So, do not worry. A little experimentation with each Lotus 1-2-3 function will make things much clearer as you go along.

## ORGANIZATION

This book is organized into short, easy-to-understand modules. Each module describes a feature of Lotus 1-2-3 and then illustrates how it is applied to typical, everyday worksheet requirements. Many examples are presented in the Description, Applications and Typical Operation sections of the modules. These examples can be easily modified for use in your own worksheets.

Module 1—this module—briefly describes the intent and structure of this book and the type of equipment you need to use Lotus 1-2-3, Release 2.01.

Module 2 is your first encounter with Lotus 1-2-3. It defines some commonly used terms in worksheet creation and walks you through the typical operations required to set up a simple Lotus 1-2-3 worksheet. This is a fun module intended to give you a "bird's eye view" of what the world of worksheets is all about.

Module 3 outlines a recommended learning sequence for the rest of this book. As you move from module to module learning about Lotus 1-2-3, you can check off your progress here. The sequence presented goes from the simple Lotus 1-2-3 functions through to the more complex and can be modified to fit any teaching situation. For teachers, this module can be used as an aid in curriculum design.

Modules 4 through 70 describe and demonstrate the many Lotus 1-2-3 functions. The commands are arranged in alphabetical order by major Lotus 1-2-3 features for easy reference.

Appendices A through C contain some summarized and concentrated information about Lotus 1-2-3 worksheet commands and menus as well as a glossary of common terms used both within the program and by computer systems in general.

Appendix D contains detailed instructions on how to install the proper configuration values for Lotus 1-2-3 so that you can use a printer, a color monitor, and other peripheral devices with the program. Configuration values are a special set of instructions that tell Lotus 1-2-3 the type of equipment you are using.

Appendix E is provided for the user and for the teacher who needs a set of exercises which test the learner's knowledge of Lotus 1-2-3 features. These questions help in determining the student's progress through the book. If you can answer the exercises, then you are ready to move on to the next module.

## HARDWARE AND SOFTWARE REQUIREMENTS

Lotus 1-2-3, Release 2.01 is used with computers having the PC-DOS or MS-DOS operating systems. It requires an IBM PC, PC/AT, PC/XT, or PC-compatible having 256 kilobytes or more of random access memory (RAM). Your system should be equipped with at least two 360-kilobyte floppy disk drives and, optionally, a printer to create a paper copy of both your worksheets and any graphs created from them.

**NOTE**

Release 2.01 of Lotus 1-2-3 corrects the hardware sensitivity of Release 2.0. Certain "PC-compatible" computers which could run the older Release 1A did not work well with Release 2.0. If your computer does not operate using Lotus 1-2-3, Release 2.0, obtain the upgrade to Release 2.01 from Lotus Development Corporation.

## WHAT YOU SHOULD KNOW

You should be familiar with your computer, its keyboard layout, and the operating system commands that allow you to list directories on your diskettes (or hard disk drive). You should also be able to use the DOS commands that allow you to copy, rename, and delete diskette files and to format a new diskette.

# Module 2

# LOTUS 1-2-3, RELEASE 2.01 OVERVIEW

## INTRODUCTION

This module defines the term *worksheet*. It presents information about how Lotus 1-2-3 is used to create, arrange, and manipulate information within an electronic worksheet. A description of the capabilities and limitations of both the old and the new releases of Lotus 1-2-3 is also presented.

Additionally, this module describes the basic keyboard skills needed to move around inside a Lotus 1-2-3 worksheet once it is created.

## THE NEW FEATURES IN RELEASE 2.01

Lotus 1-2-3, Release 2.01 contains many new features while still retaining most of the commands and functions of Release 1A. These new features include the following:

**Worksheet Size** is still 256 columns as was Release 1A, but the number of rows is expanded from 2096 to 8192. This increases the worksheet size fourfold over Release 1A.

**Memory** efficiency has been increased. You can put information in remote areas of the worksheet without using up extra memory. Also, Lotus 1-2-3 can access approximately four megabytes of extended memory if this feature is available on your system.

**Speed** of calculations is greatly increased with systems that have an 8087 or 80287 math coprocessor.

**File Utilities** have been replaced with much more convenient commands.

- You can specify a complete pathname without changing the file directory first.
- You can leave the worksheet and enter the computer's operating system without quitting Lotus 1-2-3 by using the /System command.
- The /Worksheet Status command displays a more extensive screen of information about your current status.
- The menu line displays column width and cell protection information.
- The current date and time are displayed on the screen.

**Text Manipulation** has been enhanced to allow concatenations of text labels.

**Hidden Columns** and **Hidden Formats** allow you to suppress the display of entire columns or of selected worksheet cells.

**Passwords** allow you to assign unique names to protect a worksheet from unauthorized viewing or use.

**New @ function string capabilities** can manipulate entire strings of text.

**/Range Value** copies the current values in a range of cells instead of the formulas.

**/Range Transpose** copies columns of cells to rows, and vice versa.

**/Data Matrix** multiplies and inverts matrices.

**/Data Regression** performs regression analysis.

**/Data Parse** converts a wide column of labels into several columns of labels and numbers.

In addition to these new features, Release 2.01 also provides the /Worksheet Global Default Other International command to set punctuation, currency, and date and time to various international character sets. You use the [COMPOSE] key to type characters from the Lotus 1-2-3 International Character set that you are not able to type from the keyboard.

Lotus 1-2-3, Release 2.01 has also greatly expanded the file translation capabilities of Release 1A. It is now possible to translate a worksheet into dBase III as well as dBase II. Text translations are also expanded. When modified using /Data Parse, text translations give you the ability to literally create a worksheet using a word processor and then convert it into a Lotus 1-2-3 worksheet.

## WHAT IS A WORKSHEET

A *worksheet* is defined by the dictionary as "any sheet that is used in making preliminary plans, auxiliary computations, notes or comments as a guide in doing some piece of work." While this general definition is adequate for most purposes, *worksheet* as used in the context of Lotus 1-2-3 refers to an electronic worksheet—a computerized version of what could be done manually with a pencil and paper. The major advantage to the electronic worksheet is in the ability of its user to quickly make changes in its form or to perform complicated computations using the information stored on it. In fact, this ability to make rapid changes to a worksheet has made obsolete the "preliminary" and "auxiliary" sense of the standard definition. Lotus 1-2-3 is now used by all types of people to permanently keep track of information about which they are concerned. The electronic worksheet has taken the place of what were previously called permanent records. It now supplies the information manipulation and storage means for a multitude of varied users.

## GETTING STARTED WITH LOTUS 1-2-3

Lotus 1-2-3 requires at least 256-kilobytes of random access memory (RAM) to load the program and is used on a floppy diskette or hard disk based computer system. To take full advantage of the program's many features, the computer system upon which it is used should contain the following minimum hardware items:

- An IBM AT or XT or 100% compatible computer using MS or PC DOS 2.0 and containing at least one 360-kilobyte floppy disk drive and, optionally, another floppy disk drive and/or hard disk drive.

- A computer monitor. Lotus 1-2-3 works with monochrome or color display adapters as well as monochrome monitors that operate using a color adapter (as with a COMPAQ).
- A dot matrix or letter quality printer that is compatible with the computer system used.

## MAKING A WORKING COPY OF THE ORIGINAL PROGRAM DISKETTES

Before using Lotus 1-2-3, perform the following easy steps to make a working copy of the program diskettes.

1. Insert the DOS diskette into disk drive A and close the load lever door.

2. Turn on the computer and display monitor. Respond to any DOS prompts as you would normally and then remove the DOS diskette from disk drive A.

3. Insert the original Lotus 1-2-3 System diskette into disk drive A. Close the load lever door.

4. Insert a blank, formatted diskette into disk drive B and close the load lever door.

### NOTE
For single floppy disk drive systems, a prompt displays during the copying process that indicates when to insert the blank, formatted diskette into disk drive A.

5. At the A> system prompt, type **COPY \*.\* B:/V** and then press **Return**.

### NOTE
The Return key is the same as the Enter key on some keyboards and the same as the return arrow key on an IBM PC keyboard.

The computer works for a few seconds while it copies the files on the original program diskette to the blank diskette in disk drive B. Once the copying process is complete and the A> prompt appears again, proceed as follows:

6. Remove the original program diskette from drive A and place it in its protective sleeve. Store the original program diskette in a safe place.

7. Remove the working copy of the program diskette from disk drive B and place it in its protective sleeve.

Be sure to mark and affix one of the diskette labels provided in the Lotus 1-2-3 package to the newly made backup copy.

**WARNING**

Diskettes are delicate. They should be handled with great care to ensure a long life. Never put your fingers on the exposed surface of a diskette and always protect them from extreme temperatures.

8. Repeat steps 3 through 7 to make a working copy of the four other original Lotus 1-2-3 program diskettes.

**NOTE**

The four other Lotus 1-2-3 program diskettes are the:

- Utility diskette
- A View of 1-2-3 diskette
- Printgraph diskette
- Install Library diskette

The "A View of 1-2-3" diskette is a brief tutorial and does not need to be copied, unless desired.

If a hard disk drive is used with Lotus 1-2-3, the various original program diskettes can be installed on it by using the COPYHARD (Typing COPYHARD with the Lotus 1-2-3 System diskette in drive A) program supplied on the original and backup system diskettes. Using this installation program permits the loading of Lotus 1-2-3 without the use of the original system diskette.

**NOTE**

Worksheets can be created with Lotus 1-2-3, Release 2.01 without installing the program software, but they cannot be printed nor can graphs be displayed. It is highly recommended that you follow the steps outlined in Appendix D before you proceed through the Modules in this book.

## A SAMPLE LOTUS 1-2-3 SESSION

Lotus 1-2-3 is one of the most widely used computer programs in the world. It is called a worksheet (or spreadsheet) program. It is organized in rows and columns. Text, numbers, and formulas are entered to perform numeric and financial analysis.

Use this procedure to load the Lotus 1-2-3 program into the computer's memory:

1. Insert the working copy of the Lotus 1-2-3 System diskette into disk drive A and close the load lever.

2. Type **LOTUS** and then press **Return**.

The computer works for a few seconds and then displays the following screen:

```
1-2-3  PrintGraph  Translate  Install  View  Exit
Enter 1-2-3 -- Lotus Worksheet/Graphics/Database program
```

```
                        1-2-3 Access System
                         Copyright 1986
                    Lotus Development Corporation
                        All Rights Reserved
                          Release 2.01


  The Access System lets you choose 1-2-3, PrintGraph, the Translate utility,
  the Install program, and A View of 1-2-3 from the menu at the top of this
  screen.  If you're using a diskette system, the Access System may prompt
  you to change disks.  Follow the instructions below to start a program.

  o  Use [RIGHT] or [LEFT] to move the menu pointer (the highlight bar at
     the top of the screen) to the program you want to use.

  o  Press [RETURN] to start the program.

  You can also start a program by typing the first letter of the menu
  choice.  Press [HELP] for more information.
```

This is the 1-2-3 Access System screen. It contains a menu of items shown between the double lines at the top of the screen. (Menus are lists of choices from which you make a selection.) From this menu you reach the major worksheet program sections. Note that the highlighted area on the menu is at 1-2-3. The highlight indicates the current selection within the list of choices.

3.  Notice the instructions in the body of the screen. Use the Left ( ← ) and Right ( → ) arrow keys to move the highlighter from one menu choice to another.

Also notice the up and down arrow keys on the keyboard. While these arrow keys are inoperative now, you use them later to move around inside Lotus 1-2-3 worksheets.

4.  As you move the highlighter from one menu choice to another, read the text that appears just below the row of menu choices. This information briefly describes what each menu choice does.

5.  Press **F1** and read the general information about the Lotus 1-2-3 menu choices.

**NOTE**

The F1 key is the same thing as the [HELP] key
referred to on the 1-2-3 Access Screen.

6.  Move the highlighter to the "1-2-3" menu choice and press **Return**. Read the Lotus 1-2-3 copyright and release notice.

There is no need to press any other key at this point. After a few seconds, the following screen displays:

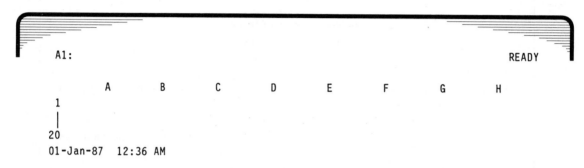

This is the Lotus 1-2-3 opening worksheet screen. Every time you load the program, this screen is displayed. All Lotus 1-2-3 menu paths start and end here. While the screen contains only 20 rows and 8 columns (A through H), Lotus 1-2-3 accepts up to 8,192 rows and 256 columns (A through IV).

There are several important items on the opening screen. In the upper right-hand corner is a highlighted block that says READY. This block always displays the operating condition of the worksheet. The READY condition (also known as *READY mode*), indicates that the worksheet is ready to accept information (numbers, text, or formulas).

Look at the highlighted area located under column A and to the right of row 1. This highlighter, commonly called the *cell pointer*, marks the information entry location within the body of the worksheet.

7.  Use the arrow keys to move the cell pointer around the worksheet.

These cell pointer locations are known as *absolute cell references*. They specify the exact position (or *coordinates*) of the highlighter by column letter and row number. Notice that as you move the pointer from cell to cell, the coordinate information displayed at the upper left-hand corner of the screen changes. This area of the screen always tells you the location of the pointer.

8.  Move the cell pointer to column D, row 10 (called cell D10) and then press **Home**.

Notice that the highlighter jumps to cell A1. No matter where you are in a worksheet, you can always return to the *Home cell* (A1) by pressing the Home key while the worksheet is in the READY mode.

Finally, look at the lower left-hand corner of the worksheet. The date and time you typed in response to the DOS prompts displays here.

From the opening worksheet screen, pressing the Slash key (/) always displays the initial Lotus 1-2-3 worksheet menu.

9.  Type **/**.

The screen displays the following:

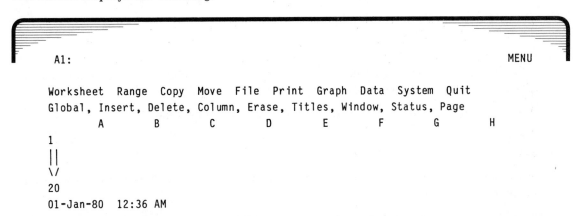

```
  A1:                                                              MENU

  Worksheet  Range  Copy  Move  File  Print  Graph  Data  System  Quit
  Global, Insert, Delete, Column, Erase, Titles, Window, Status, Page
             A        B       C       D      E       F      G      H
  1
  ||
  \/
  20
  01-Jan-80  12:36 AM
```

Notice that the operating condition block changed from READY to MENU.

Using the Lotus 1-2-3 menu system is similar to the process of traveling by car from a city in one state to a city in another state. The keyboard controls the direction the automobile takes from one destination to another. Typing a slash displays the items on the opening menu, that is, to use the analogy, the major destination points possible on a road map. A destination is selected. Once the primary menu item is chosen, secondary destination points (like cities within the states in the automobile analogy) are selected. This procedure continues until a section of the program is reached where worksheet changes are made.

Two methods are used to select worksheet menu destinations. A selection is made by typing the first letter of each menu choice in sequence, or by using the arrow keys to move the highlighter to each successive menu choice, and then pressing the Return key. Either way works, but the highlighter method is the easiest to use in the beginning. After you have a little practice with Lotus 1-2-3, typing the first letter of each choice moves through the menu selections with much greater speed.

Read the text beneath the highlighted menu item. This text briefly describes what the selection of this menu item does.

10.  Use the **Right Arrow** to move the highlighter to the next menu choice. Notice that the description line changes.

11.  Move to each menu item and read the description for each choice. Lotus 1-2-3 always gives you a description for each menu selection.

12.   Type **W**. The menu line changes to the following display:

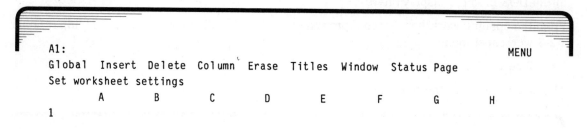

```
A1:                                                              MENU
Global  Insert  Delete  Column  Erase  Titles  Window  Status Page
Set worksheet settings
           A        B        C        D        E        F        G        H
   1
```

When the first letter of a menu choice is typed (or when the highlighted menu item is selected by pressing the Return key), Lotus 1-2-3 displays the next set of menu selections.

13.   Press **Esc** and notice that the screen returns to the opening menu.

No matter where you are in the Lotus 1-2-3 menu system, you can always press the Esc key and return to the previous menu.

14.   Press **Esc** again and notice that the menus disappear leaving only the original worksheet display.

Pressing the Esc key a number of times always moves the worksheet back through the menu system until the READY screen displays. This feature is very helpful when a menu choice is selected by mistake. You can always return to the previous display to make the correct menu choice.

Occasionally, when a command or menu choice is selected, immediate help information is required. For example, when the proper use of a command or menu selection is not clear, Lotus 1-2-3 can give you help.

15.   Type **/W**.

16.   Type **C** for the Column menu item. Notice the top of the following screen.

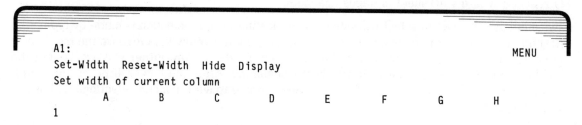

```
A1:                                                              MENU
Set-Width   Reset-Width   Hide   Display
Set width of current column
           A        B        C        D        E        F        G        H
   1
```

This is the Lotus 1-2-3 column width set/reset and hide/display screen. Use this menu path (/WC) to change the width of the current column or the width of all the columns in the worksheet or to hide columns from display or to display columns that have been previously hidden.

17.  Press **F1** to learn more about this function. The screen displays the following information.

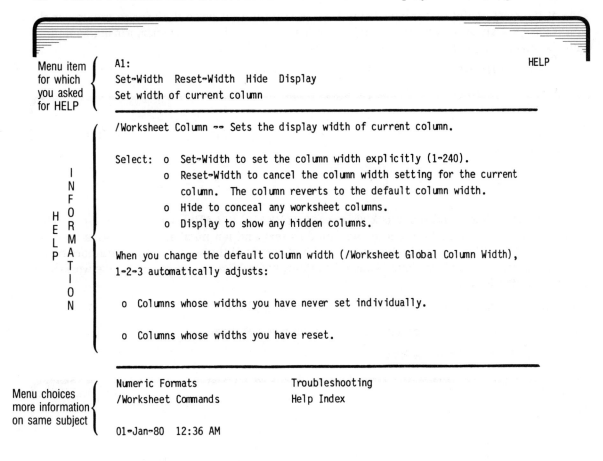

Menu item for which you asked for HELP {

```
A1:                                                       HELP

Set-Width  Reset-Width  Hide  Display
Set width of current column
```

HELP INFORMATION {

```
/Worksheet Column -- Sets the display width of current column.

Select:  o  Set-Width to set the column width explicitly (1-240).
         o  Reset-Width to cancel the column width setting for the current
            column.  The column reverts to the default column width.
         o  Hide to conceal any worksheet columns.
         o  Display to show any hidden columns.

When you change the default column width (/Worksheet Global Column Width),
1-2-3 automatically adjusts:

  o  Columns whose widths you have never set individually.


  o  Columns whose widths you have reset.
```

Menu choices more information on same subject {

```
Numeric Formats              Troubleshooting
/Worksheet Commands          Help Index


01-Jan-80  12:36 AM
```

**NOTE**
Lotus 1-2-3 always offers you help when needed. At any menu item or worksheet change (command) screen, pressing the F1 key displays information about the command or menu item in use.

Notice the area at the bottom of the screen. This area displays a menu of additional help screens designed to provide more information about the same subject. Use the arrow keys to move the highlighter to another HELP menu choice and press the Return key to display these additional information screens.

18.  Press **Esc** successively until you return to the worksheet READY screen.

One of the most useful features of Lotus 1-2-3 is the ability it gives the user to create simple worksheets quickly. A worksheet containing numbers, text, and formulas to perform mathematical calculations on the numbers can be created in a matter of minutes.

19.  Type **INVENTORY** and look at the top of the monitor.

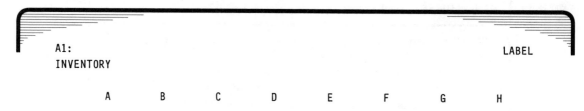

Notice the worksheet condition block changes from READY to LABEL when text is typed. This indicates that the information is to be accepted as text and not numbers. Also notice that the word "INVENTORY" displays in the upper left-hand corner of the screen. Any characters typed into a worksheet are displayed here to allow for editing before they are accepted into the worksheet by pressing the Return key.

20.  Press the **Backspace** key once; notice how it erased the Y.

21.  Type **Y** to replace the erased letter and then press **Return**.

The screen displays the following:

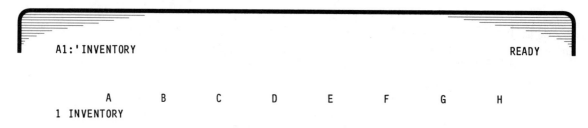

Lotus 1-2-3 inserts typed information into the current cell and the worksheet condition block returns to the READY mode. Now you can type more information into the worksheet.

Notice that the text display at the top of the screen moved up to the right of the cell position. This area is known as the *cell contents* block. The single quote mark ('), preceding INVENTORY in this block, indicates that the contents of the referenced cell is text and is left-justified. The text is displayed flush left in the cell. Some symbols used to control the position of text within a cell are as follows:

| *Operator* | *Result* |
|---|---|
| Single quote (') | Flush (justified) left |
| Double quote (") | Flush (justified) right |
| Caret ( ^ or upper case 6) | Centered |
| Backslash ( \ ) | Repeat next character across cell |

### NOTE

Remember that cell references are always expressed as column/row coordinates. These coordinates are known as the *absolute cell reference.*

22. Move the cell pointer to cell A2 (the cell below INVENTORY).

23. Type \ – (backslash hyphen) and then press **Return**.

### NOTE

Lotus 1-2-3 interprets alphabetical characters, numbers, and punctuation marks as text when preceded by a single or double quote, circumflex, or backslash. Without one of these characters, Lotus 1-2-3 interprets numbers as values and the symbols +, –, *, and / as mathematical operators.

24. Move the cell pointer to cell A4 (two rows below the dashed line). Type **Apples** and then press **Return**.

25. Continue moving the cell pointer down one row at a time and type the following information for each cell:

> **Pears**
> **Oranges**
> **Peaches**
> **Apricots**

26. Move the cell pointer to cell A10 (two rows below Apricots), type **Total**, and then press **Return**.

The screen displays the following:

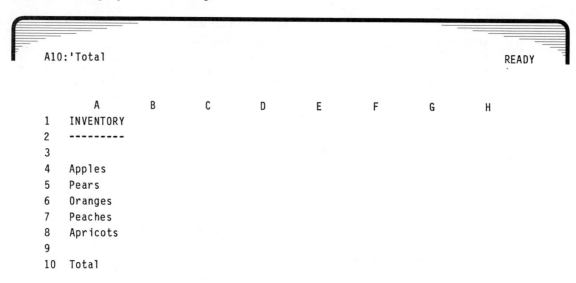

```
 A10:'Total                                                    READY


        A       B       C       D       E       F       G       H
 1   INVENTORY
 2   ---------
 3
 4   Apples
 5   Pears
 6   Oranges
 7   Peaches
 8   Apricots
 9
 10  Total
```

The worksheet now contains text and is ready for numerical information.

27. Type the following numbers starting at cell B4. Move the cell pointer down one row at a time for each number. Press **Return** after you type each number.

| Apples | 125 |
| Pears | 50 |
| Oranges | 100 |
| Peaches | 75 |
| Apricots | 25 |

Notice that as you type the numbers, the worksheet condition block changes from READY to VALUE. Just as the LABEL display indicates that you are typing text, the VALUE display in the worksheet condition block indicates that you are typing numbers into the worksheet.

Once the numbers are typed, a formula can be created to add all the numbers together.

28. Move the cell pointer to cell B10, type + (plus sign), and then move the cell pointer to cell B8 and type another + (plus sign).

Notice that the cell pointer returns to cell B10 automatically. Every time a mathematical operator is typed into a worksheet formula, the cell pointer returns to the cell where the final result of the formula is to appear in the worksheet. The following table describes Lotus 1-2-3 basic mathematical operators.

| Basic Lotus 1-2-3 Mathematical Operators | | |
|---|---|---|
| OPERATOR | DESCRIPTION | TYPICAL FORM |
| + | TO ADD TWO CELLS TOGETHER | + B8 + B25 |
| − | TO SUBTRACT ONE CELL FROM ANOTHER | + B8 − B25 |
| / | TO DIVIDE ONE CELL BY ANOTHER | + B8 / B25 |
| * | TO MULTIPLY ONE CELL BY ANOTHER | + B8 * B25 |

29. Continue moving the cell pointer up one row at a time (from cell B7 through B5) until all the cells except the final one have been typed into the formula. Be sure to type a plus sign (+) between each cell reference coordinate and after cell B5.

30. Move the cell pointer to the last cell to be included in the formula (cell B4). Since this is the final cell, do not type another plus sign. Press **Return** to accept the formula.

Notice the following screen:

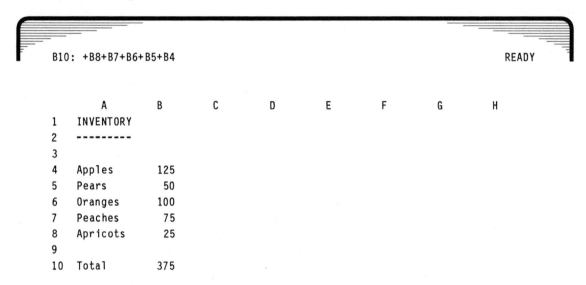

```
B10: +B8+B7+B6+B5+B4                                          READY


              A        B        C        D        E        F        G        H
    1    INVENTORY
    2    ---------
    3
    4    Apples     125
    5    Pears       50
    6    Oranges    100
    7    Peaches     75
    8    Apricots    25
    9
   10    Total      375
```

The formula added all the INVENTORY numbers and put the result into cell B10. Notice the formula displayed beside the cell reference block and that the worksheet returned to the READY mode after the total appeared in cell B10.

31. You can quit Lotus 1-2-3 by typing **/QY** and then typing **E**. If you want to experiment with this sample worksheet (for example, labeling the numbers to say what they represent— Each, Pounds, etc.), use the QUIT command later.

# Module 3

# RECOMMENDED LEARNING SEQUENCE

To properly learn how to efficiently use the power of Lotus 1-2-3, Release 2.01, study each module of this book in the following sequence:

Turn to Module 45 to continue the learning sequence.

# Module 4
## COPY

**DESCRIPTION**

Use the COPY command to copy the information contained in one or more cells, rows, or columns from one location in a worksheet to another location.

The COPY command is located and used from the worksheet READY screen by typing a / (slash) and then typing the first letter of the following menu title:

```
MENU TITLES:              USE AND USE REQUIREMENT:

Copy                      Copy from a range of cells to a range of cells Specify from/to range
```

**APPLICATIONS**

This command copies single cells and ranges of cells from one location in a worksheet to another location. The ability to copy cell information saves a tremendous amount of time and effort and helps you prevent errors that occur when typing and formatting the same information twice.

**TYPICAL OPERATION**

1. From the worksheet READY screen, create or retrieve the worksheet used in Module 47.

2. Move the cell pointer to B3 and then type **/C**. The following screen displays:

```
B3:[W20]  8                                                    POINT
Enter range to copy FROM: B3..B3

                  A            B       C       D       E       F       G
 1   SALE BY PRODUCT
 2
 3   CATTLE                    8
 4   SHEEP                    10
 5   HOGS                     15
 6
 7   TOTAL
```

Lotus 1-2-3 asks you which cell or range of cells to copy FROM. Notice that the cell pointer is located at cell B3.

3.  Move the cell pointer down to cell B5.

Notice that the cells are highlighted and that the FROM range displays B3..B5.

4.  Press **Return**; the screen changes to the following:

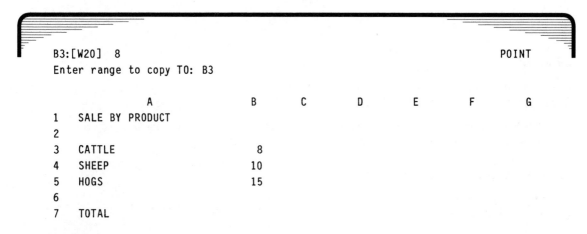

```
B3:[W20]  8                                                        POINT
Enter range to copy TO: B3

                    A              B       C       D       E       F       G
1    SALE BY PRODUCT
2
3    CATTLE                        8
4    SHEEP                        10
5    HOGS                         15
6
7    TOTAL
```

Lotus 1-2-3 asks for the range of cells to which you want to copy the information marked in cells B3 through B5. Notice the worksheet condition block. POINT is always displayed when you are indicating cell locations. When you see this word, Lotus 1-2-3 is asking for cell range information.

5.  Move the cell pointer to C3, type . (a period) and then move the cell pointer to C5.

Lotus 1-2-3 highlights the cells to which the information is to be copied.

6.  Press **Return** and study the following screen:

```
B3:[W20]  8                                                        READY

                    A              B       C       D       E       F       G
1    SALE BY PRODUCT
2
3    CATTLE                        8       8
4    SHEEP                        10      10
5    HOGS                         15      15                              .
6
7    TOTAL
```

Lotus 1-2-3 copies the information contained in cells B3 through B5 to cells C3 through C5. Notice that it did not copy the column width setting of column B (20 characters) and that the information in column B is not disturbed.

**NOTE**

Though it is always good pratice to mark the entire range that you are copying to, Lotus 1-2-3 allows you to mark only the upper left-hand corner of the "Copy To" range.

7. Quit the worksheet.

8. Turn to Module 37 to continue the learning sequence.

# Module 5

## DATA DISTRIBUTION

### DESCRIPTION

Lotus 1-2-3 provides many data manipulation commands. These range from the simple creation of a listing of numbers to the complex statistical analysis of a range of values using regression theory. One of these is the DATA DISTRIBUTION command. Use this command to create a frequency distribution of the values within a cell range.

The DATA DISTRIBUTION command is located and used from the worksheet READY screen by typing a / (slash) and then typing the first letter of the following menu title:

```
MENU TITLES:          USE AND USE REQUIREMENT:

Data Distribution     Specify values range Specify bin range
```

### APPLICATIONS

When you need to know how many times various values within a range of worksheet cells are repeated, use the DATA DISTRIBUTION command. This command is useful when you have a long list of values, for example, a long listing of the sales prices for different inventory items, and you want to know how many items there are per range of sales prices within the list.

### TYPICAL OPERATION

1.  From the worksheet READY screen, enter the following values for cells A1 through A10.

| | | | |
|---|---|---|---|
| A1 | **5** | A6 | **7** |
| A2 | **3** | A7 | **5** |
| A3 | **25** | A8 | **3** |
| A4 | **5** | A9 | **10** |
| A5 | **7** | A10 | **4** |

Before a range is evaluated for frequency distributions, an interval must be set. Intervals specify the value ranges to be evaluated as in how many values are from n to n1, from n1 to n2, from n2 to n3 . . .etc.

2. Move the cell pointer to B1 and type the following intervals:

| | | | |
|-----|-----|-----|-----|
| B1 | 3 | B6 | 18 |
| B2 | 6 | B7 | 21 |
| B3 | 9 | B8 | 24 |
| B4 | 12 | B9 | 27 |
| B5 | 15 | | |

This interval set is used to test the specifed range for frequency distributions of every three units.

3. Type **/DD**.

4. Mark cells A1 through A10 as the range to test and then press **Return**.

5. Mark cells B1 through B9 as the interval (Bin) range upon which the test is based and then press **Return**.

Notice the following screen:

```
┌─────────────────────────────────────────────────────────────────┐
│  B9: 27                                                   READY   │
└─────────────────────────────────────────────────────────────────┘
```

| | A | B | C | D | E | F | G | H |
|----|----|----|----|----|----|----|----|----|
| 1 | 5 | 3 | 2 | | | | | |
| 2 | 3 | 6 | 4 | | | | | |
| 3 | 25 | 9 | 2 | | | | | |
| 4 | 5 | 12 | 1 | | | | | |
| 5 | 7 | 15 | 0 | | | | | |
| 6 | 7 | 18 | 0 | | | | | |
| 7 | 5 | 21 | 0 | | | | | |
| 8 | 3 | 24 | 0 | | | | | |
| 9 | 10 | 27 | 1 | | | | | |
| 10 | 4 | | 0 | | | | | |
| 11 | | | | | | | | |

The results of frequency distribution tests always display in the cells immediately to the right of the interval (Bin) range. Notice that the count for each interval in column B corresponds to the number of individual values found in the range tested in column A.

**NOTE**

To test a range of values that fall horizontally, that is, that are in each column of the worksheet be sure to set up the interval range in a single column with a blank column directly to the right of it.

6. Quit the worksheet.

7. The learning sequence continues with Module 6.

# Module 6

## DATA FILL

**DESCRIPTION**

Use the DATA FILL command to create and fill in a range of cells with numbers that use a skip factor.

The DATA FILL command is located and used from the worksheet READY screen by typing a / (slash) and then typing the first letters of the following menu title:

MENU TITLES:               USE AND USE REQUIREMENT:

Data Fill              Fill a table with data Specify data range

**APPLICATIONS**

The DATA FILL command is useful when creating an interval range for the DATA DISTRIBUTION command. This command saves time because it automatically creates an interval range and eliminates the need to type each individual interval number through the keyboard.

**TYPICAL OPERATION**

1.  From the worksheet READY screen, enter the following values for cells A1 through A10.

| | | | |
|---|---|---|---|
| A1 | **5** | A6 | **7** |
| A2 | **3** | A7 | **5** |
| A3 | **25** | A8 | **3** |
| A4 | **5** | A9 | **10** |
| A5 | **7** | A10 | **4** |

Notice that these are the same values as those typed in Module 5.

2.  Move the cell pointer to B1 and type **/DF**.

3.  Mark cells B1 through B9 as the fill range.

4.  Type **3** as the starting number for the fill range and then press **Return**.

5.  Type **3** as the step and then press **Return**.

A step is defined as the number of values skipped between numbers in the fill range.

6. Type **27** as the number at which the fill range is to stop and then press **Return**. Notice the following screen:

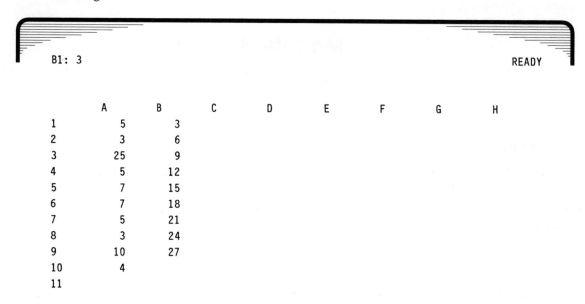

B1:  3                                                          READY

|    | A  | B  | C | D | E | F | G | H |
|----|----|----|---|---|---|---|---|---|
| 1  | 5  | 3  |   |   |   |   |   |   |
| 2  | 3  | 6  |   |   |   |   |   |   |
| 3  | 25 | 9  |   |   |   |   |   |   |
| 4  | 5  | 12 |   |   |   |   |   |   |
| 5  | 7  | 15 |   |   |   |   |   |   |
| 6  | 7  | 18 |   |   |   |   |   |   |
| 7  | 5  | 21 |   |   |   |   |   |   |
| 8  | 3  | 24 |   |   |   |   |   |   |
| 9  | 10 | 27 |   |   |   |   |   |   |
| 10 | 4  |    |   |   |   |   |   |   |
| 11 |    |    |   |   |   |   |   |   |

Notice that the fill range is exactly the same as the one you typed in Module 5. Using Lotus 1-2-3's Data Fill feature saves the effort of having to manually type an interval range.

7. Quit the worksheet.

8. The learning sequence continues with Module 7.

# Module 7
## DATA MATRIX

## DESCRIPTION

Use the DATA MATRIX commands to invert matrices formed by rows and columns. These commands must conform to the following rules:

- Only square matrices can be inverted.
- When multiplying matrices, there must be the same number of columns in the first range as there are rows in the second range.
- The largest matrix allowed is 90 rows by 90 columns.

The DATA MATRIX commands are located and used from the worksheet READY screen by typing a / (slash) and then typing the first letters of the following menu titles:

| MENU TITLES: | USE AND USE REQUIREMENT: |
|---|---|
| Data Matrix Invert | Invert a range as a square matrix Specify the range of cells to invert |
| Data Matrix Multiply | Multiply cells in 2 ranges times one another using matrix multiplication to produce 3rd matrix of the products Specify multiplier and output ranges |

## APPLICATIONS

The DATA MATRIX commands are useful when performing matrix multiplication calculations. A complete discussion of the uses of matrix mathematics is beyond the scope of this book, but matrix techniques are used primarily to apply prescribed mathematical rules (as represented by a group [array] of numeric values) to another array of values. In matrix mathematics, the inverse of a square matrix is defined as a matrix that when multiplied by a square matrix results in what is known as an *identity* matrix. An identity matrix is characterized by number ones along the principal upper left to lower right diagonal and zeroes everywhere else.

## TYPICAL OPERATION

1. From the worksheet READY screen, enter the following values for cells A1 through B2.

| | | | |
|---|---|---|---|
| A1 | **1** | B1 | **2** |
| A2 | **2** | B2 | **2** |

2. Type **/DMI** to invert the matrix.

3. Mark cells A1 through B2 as the matrix range and then press **Return**.

> **NOTE**
> A range name can be used instead of cell locations.

4. Move the cell pointer to A4 and then press **Return**.

> **NOTE**
> Remember, when marking an output range, the location of the upper left-hand corner of the output range is all that is necessary.

Notice the following screen:

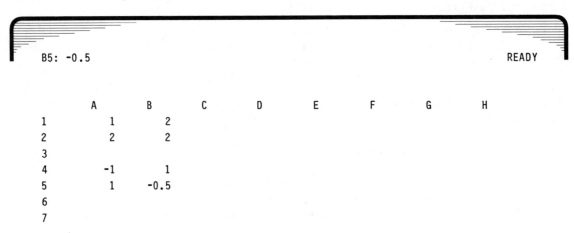

```
    B5: -0.5                                                    READY


            A        B        C      D       E       F       G       H
    1       1        2
    2       2        2
    3
    4      -1        1
    5       1      -0.5
    6
    7
```

To prove that the matrix generated using Lotus 1-2-3's Data Matrix Invert command is in fact the inverse of the square matrix in cells A1 through B2, perform the following steps to multiply the two matrices together:

5. Type **/DMM** to multiply the inverted matrix by the original matrix.

6. Mark cells A1 through B1 as the first matrix to multiply and then press **Return**.

7. Mark cells A4 through B5 as the second matrix to multiply and then press **Return**.

8. Move the cell pointer to C1 for the output range.

Notice the products display on the following screen starting at cell C1 and that they represent an identity matrix.

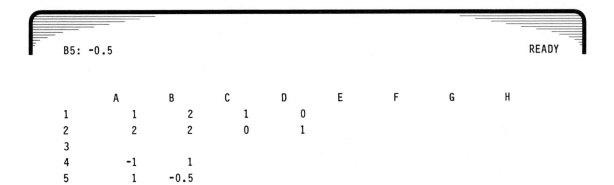

| | A | B | C | D | E | F | G | H |
|---|---|---|---|---|---|---|---|---|
| 1 | 1 | 2 | 1 | 0 | | | | |
| 2 | 2 | 2 | 0 | 1 | | | | |
| 3 | | | | | | | | |
| 4 | -1 | 1 | | | | | | |
| 5 | 1 | -0.5 | | | | | | |
| 6 | | | | | | | | |

9. Quit the worksheet.

10. Turn to Module 9 to continue the learning sequence.

# Module 8
## DATA PARSE

**DESCRIPTION**

Another significant addition to Lotus 1-2-3 with Release 2.01 is the ability it gives you to *parse* (split into worksheet usable columns) an imported ASCII text file. *Parsing* is the process of converting a long label into its component columns of shorter labels and/or numbers. The DATA PARSE commands format the imported file and break it into its component parts so that the information contained within it can be manipulated using the other Lotus 1-2-3 commands. The following table lists the format symbols used when parsing a text file:

| SYMBOL | PERFORMS: |
|--------|-----------|
| L | Denotes the first character in a label block. |
| V | Denotes the first character in a value block. |
| D | Denotes the first character in a date block. |
| T | Denotes the first character in a time block. |
| S | Indicates that the character below is to be skipped when parsing. |
| > | Denotes the continuation of the block. |
| * | Indicates a blank space immediately below the symbol is currently undefined, but could become a part of the block of information in the cell immediately following. |

The DATA PARSE commands are located and used from the worksheet READY screen by typing a / (slash) and then typing the first letters of the following menu titles:

```
MENU TITLES:            USE AND USE REQUIREMENT:

Data Parse              Split a column of labels into separate ranges
Data Parse
  Format-Line Create    Create a format line (Parse split) at the current cell
Data Parse
  Format-Line Edit      Edit the format line at the current cell
Data Parse
  Input-Column          Specify the range of labels to parse Specify range
```

```
Data Parse
  Output-Range            Specify the output range for the parsed labels Specify range
Data Parse Reset          Cancel all parse input and output ranges
Data Parse Go             Perform the parse
Data Parse Quit           Quit the parse menu
```

## APPLICATIONS

Use the DATA PARSE commands to create a new worksheet section that contains all the information from an imported text file, but that is broken into Lotus 1-2-3 command-usable columns. For example, the DATA PARSE command is useful when you have imported a text file containing numbers that you created using a word processing program, and you want to break down the imported text file into Lotus 1-2-3 usable columns of text and numbers. Being able to do this saves you the time it would take to type in all the information from the text file into a worksheet file.

## TYPICAL OPERATION

1. From the worksheet READY screen, type **/FIT** to import a text file.

2. Type **CANDYTXT** (the text file created in Module 16) as the text file to import and then press **Return**. Study the following screen:

```
┌─────────────────────────────────────────────────────────────────────────────
│ A1:                                                                    READY

        A         B         C         D         E         F         G         H
   1
   2
   3
   4
   5
   6        POPULAR CANDY SALES
   7        --------------------
   8                                              SQUARES OF
   9                                              DIFFERENCE
  10              CANDY NAME        UNITS SOLD  FROM MEAN    DOLLARS
  11              ----------        ----------  ----------   -------
  12        CHOCOLATE BARS               112       338.56    $140.00
  13        FRUIT GUMS                   200     11320.96    $156.00
  14        LICORICE                      28      4303.36     $50.12
  15        MINT PATTIES                  72       466.56     $64.08
  16        PEANUT BRITTLE                56      1413.76    $131.60
  17
  18        TOTAL                        468
  19
```

The spacing is exactly like the original CANDY worksheet but each row is continuous text inclusive of the numbers.

3. Move the cell pointer to A12 and type **/DP**.

4. Type **FC** to create a format line. Study the following screen:

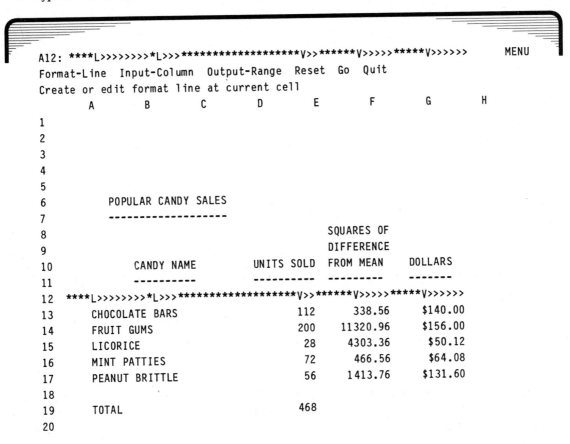

Lotus 1-2-3 makes a guess as to how each of the columns should be parsed. In this example, the candy types are text and the value columns are numbers.

5. Type **I** and then mark cells A12 through H19 as the columns to be parsed and press **Return**.

6. Type **O** and then mark cells A12 through H19 as the columns where the parsed information is to be output.

7.  Type **G** to parse the marked range. Notice the following screen:

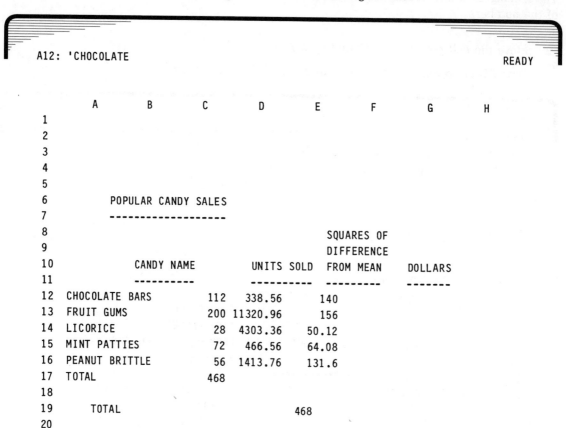

```
A12: 'CHOCOLATE                                                          READY


        A        B        C        D        E        F       G        H
   1
   2
   3
   4
   5
   6        POPULAR CANDY SALES
   7        --------------------
   8                                               SQUARES OF
   9                                               DIFFERENCE
  10                CANDY NAME         UNITS SOLD  FROM MEAN    DOLLARS
  11                ----------         ----------  ----------   -------
  12  CHOCOLATE BARS          112    338.56        140
  13  FRUIT GUMS             200  11320.96         156
  14  LICORICE                28   4303.36       50.12
  15  MINT PATTIES            72    466.56       64.08
  16  PEANUT BRITTLE          56   1413.76       131.6
  17  TOTAL                  468
  18
  19      TOTAL                            468
  20
```

The numeric information that was text is converted to numbers. Notice that the column widths are Lotus 1-2-3's default of nine characters. All of Lotus 1-2-3's worksheet features can now be used on the parsed range, for example, resetting the column widths.

8.  Quit the worksheet.

9.  Turn to Module 19 to continue the learning sequence.

# Module 9

## DATA QUERY

### DESCRIPTION

Use the DATA QUERY commands to search a worksheet range for selected database items, extract worksheet database items, remove worksheet database items, and copy database items selected from one area of a worksheet to another area of the worksheet.

The DATA QUERY commands are located and used from the worksheet READY screen by typing a / (slash) and then typing the first letters of the following menu titles:

```
MENU TITLES:              USE AND USE REQUIREMENT:

Data Query                Interrogate a range of worksheet values
Data Query Input          Specify range of data to query
Data Query Criterion      Specify the query parameters
Data Query Criterion
  Output                  Specify a range of cells for answers to query
Data Query Criterion
  Find                    Find a specific value in queried range
Data Query Criterion
  Extract                 Extract a specific value in queried range
Data Query Criterion
  Unique                  Find a unique value in queried range
Data Query Criterion
  Delete                  Delete a query range
Data Query Criterion
  Delete Cancel           Cancel deletion
Data Query Criterion
  Delete Delete           Delete settings
Data Query Reset          Clear all query settings
Data Query Quit           Quit query menu
```

### APPLICATIONS

The DATA QUERY commands are useful when using a Lotus 1-2-3 database worksheet. There are literally thousands of applications for these commands in the business world. For example, a typical business database might contain information about a company's customers such as customer account numbers, customer names, dates of last sales, units sold, and dollar amounts of sales. The DATA QUERY commands perform manipulations of this database information, for instance, creating a listing of all customers who have purchased more than $1,000 worth of products within the last 12 months by interrogating (querying) the database for such information.

## TYPICAL OPERATION

1. From the worksheet READY screen, create the following worksheet:

|   | A | B |
|---|---|---|
| 1 | FRUIT | POUNDS |
| 2 | PEARS | 75 |
| 3 | APPLES | 37 |
| 4 | LIMES | 10 |
| 5 | PEACHES | 48 |
| 6 | ORANGES | 25 |
| 7 | LEMONS | 12 |
| 8 | CHERRIES | 10 |

2. Type **/DQI** to mark the range within the worksheet that is used with the other Data Query commands.

3. Select cells A1 through B8 as the query range.

A query range is, in effect, the database from which information is extracted, or manipulated. Notice that the query range includes the names for each column.

4. Type **Q** and then copy cells A1 and B1 to cell A11 and B11.

5. Type **/DQC** and then mark cells A11 through B12 as the criterion range.

A criterion range is the range of cells that contain information that is the basis for an evaluation when using the other Data Query commands. Notice that the criterion range also contains the row headings.

6. Type **Q** and then copy cells A1 and B1 to cells C1 and D1.

7. Type **/DQO** and mark cells C1 through D8 as the range of cells to which the results of any queries are displayed.

8. Type **Q** and then move the cell pointer to B12; type **+B2>25** and press **Return**.

The following screen displays:

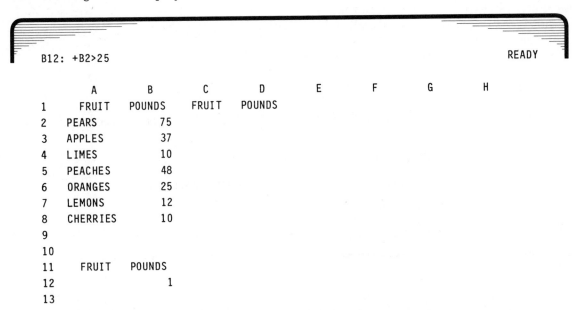

```
B12: +B2>25                                                      READY

            A         B        C        D        E        F        G        H
   1      FRUIT    POUNDS    FRUIT   POUNDS
   2      PEARS       75
   3      APPLES      37
   4      LIMES       10
   5      PEACHES     48
   6      ORANGES     25
   7      LEMONS      12
   8      CHERRIES    10
   9
  10
  11      FRUIT    POUNDS
  12                  1
  13
```

The contents of cell B12 is the test criterion to be used when querying the input range. All queries will test the information in cells B2 through B8 for values that exceed 25 pounds.

9.  Type **/DQF** to find the first value that exceeds the 25 pound limit in the criterion range.

Notice that the first pounds value for fruit (75) is highlighted. Seventy-five is greater than the test criterion of 25.

10.  Type **/DQE** to extract all values greater that 25 pounds.

Notice the following screen:

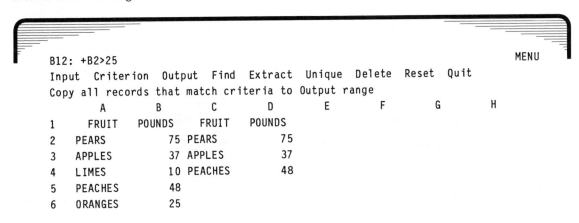

```
B12: +B2>25                                                       MENU
Input   Criterion   Output   Find   Extract   Unique   Delete   Reset   Quit
Copy all records that match criteria to Output range
            A         B         C         D       E       F       G       H
   1      FRUIT    POUNDS    FRUIT   POUNDS
   2      PEARS       75 PEARS       75
   3      APPLES      37 APPLES      37
   4      LIMES       10 PEACHES     48
   5      PEACHES     48
   6      ORANGES     25
```

```
 7    LEMONS        12
 8    CHERRIES      10
 9
10
11       FRUIT    POUNDS
12                     1
13
```

The extracted input range items that meet the criterion display in the cells marked as the output range.

11.    Type **D** to delete all items from the input range that meet the criterion.

Lotus 1-2-3 gives you the opportunity to cancel the deletion command.

12.    Select **D** to delete the criterion items.

Look at the following screen:

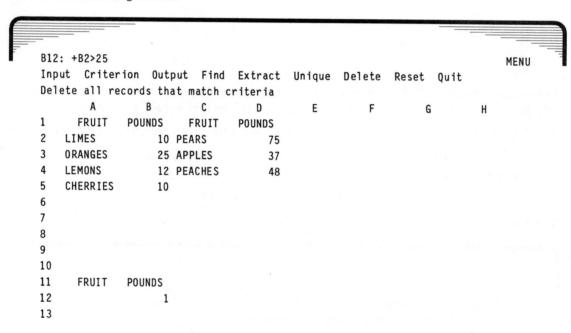

```
B12: +B2>25                                                    MENU
Input  Criterion  Output  Find  Extract  Unique  Delete  Reset  Quit
Delete all records that match criteria
          A         B         C         D      E      F      G      H
 1      FRUIT    POUNDS     FRUIT    POUNDS
 2    LIMES         10  PEARS         75
 3    ORANGES       25  APPLES        37
 4    LEMONS        12  PEACHES       48
 5    CHERRIES      10
 6
 7
 8
 9
10
11      FRUIT    POUNDS
12                   1
13
```

Lotus 1-2-3 automatically deletes the records that match the criterion.

13.    Type **R** to reset (clear) all input, output, and criterion range settings.

14.    Type **Q** to quit the Data Query menu.

15.    Quit the worksheet.

16.    The learning sequence continues with Module 10.

# Module 10

## DATA REGRESSION

### DESCRIPTION

The ability of Lotus 1-2-3, Release 2.01 to perform regression analysis on numeric information is a welcome addition to the power of the program. The *regression analysis* feature computes the various coefficient values for a formula that relates one or more independent variables to a range of dependent variables. These commands are commonly used to test prediction formulas, for example, using total market growth as a forecaster of increased sales levels.

The DATA REGRESSION commands must conform to the following limits:

- A maximum of 16 independent variables is allowed.
- The X and Y ranges must have the same number of rows.
- The output range for calculations performed by the regression analysis must be:
  - Nine rows longer than the number of independent variables.
  - At least two columns wider than the number of independent variables.
  - A minimum of four columns wide.

The DATA REGRESSION commands are located and used from the worksheet READY screen by typing a / (slash) and then typing the first letters of the following menu titles:

| MENU TITLES: | USE AND USE REQUIREMENT: |
|---|---|
| Data Regression | Perform regression analysis on a range of numerical information |
| Data Regression X-Range | Set the independent variable(s) of the X range Specify range |
| Data Regression Y-Range | Set the dependent variable for the Y range Specify range |
| Data Regression Output-Range | Set output range forthe results of regression analysis Specify range |
| Data Regression Intercept Compute | Compute the intercept |
| Data Regression Intercept Zero | Force intercept at origin |
| Data Regression Reset | Clear all regression ranges and the intercept option |
| Data Regression Go | Perform the regression analysis |
| Data Regression Quit | Quit the regression menu |

## APPLICATIONS

Use the DATA REGRESSION commands to analyze specific data and its relationship to other data based upon a hypothesis. Regression analysis is one of the most widely used business data analysis techniques. Most companies require periodic business forecasts for future planning. Forecast elements include items like budgets and sales forecasts for future periods. Regression analysis is applied to past financial performance to help determine relationships between various catagories of income and expense. These relationships (or *indices*) are used to predict future business. For example, analyzing the cost of raw materials in a manufacturing process might give results that support the hypothesis that for every dollar spent on raw materials, ten cents is spent on the energy to turn those raw materials into a salable product. While books have been written about the various aspects involved with regression analysis techniques, most companies find them useful to relate income or expense items to one another. This lets them make general statements about their operations such as "for every dollar of sales there is sixty cents of direct costs."

## TYPICAL OPERATION

1.  From the worksheet READY screen, create the following worksheet:

|    | A | B | C |
|----|---|---|---|
| 1  |   | SALES THROUGH | DIRECT MAIL |
| 2  |   | DIRECT MAIL | AD COSTS |
| 3  |   |   |   |
| 4  |   | $100,000 | $5,000 |
| 5  |   | $87,500 | $2,750 |
| 6  |   | $65,000 | $1,500 |
| 7  |   | $197,000 | $12,500 |
| 8  |   | $245,000 | $15,000 |
| 9  |   | $250,000 | $12,000 |
| 10 |   | $37,000 | $2,700 |
| 11 |   | $68,000 | $3,900 |
| 12 |   | $72,000 | $4,500 |
| 13 |   | $98,000 | $7,700 |
| 14 |   | $265,000 | $13,500 |
| 15 |   | $237,000 | $10,000 |

2.  Set column A to a 20-character width, columns B and C to a 15-character width, and then format the data in columns B and C to currency with no decimal point.

3.  Type **/DR** to perform a regression analysis on the information in the worksheet.

4.  Type **X** to select the X range (the independent variable).

5.  Mark cells C4 through C15 as the X range.

6.  Type **Y** to select the Y range (the dependent variable).

7.  Mark cells B4 through B15 as the Y range.

8. Type **IC** to select a computed intercept.

9. Type **O** to mark the output range.

10. Move the cell pointer to A17 and then press **Return**.

11. Type **G** to perform the regression analysis.

12. Move the cell pointer to A26. Study the following screen:

```
A26: [W20]                                              READY


           A              B            C           D        E
  7                    $197,000    $12,500
  8                    $245,000    $15,000
  9                    $250,000    $12,000
 10                     $37,000     $2,700
 11                     $68,000     $3,900
 12                     $72,000     $4,500
 13                     $98,000     $7,700
 14                    $265,000    $13,500
 15                    $237,000    $10,000
 16
 17                  Regression Output:
 18  Constant                                  14612.60
 19  Std Err of Y Est                          32129.61
 20  R Squared                                 0.876261
 21  No. of Observations                            12
 22  Degrees of Freedom                             10
 23
 24  X Coefficient(s)      16.981314886
 25  Std Err of Coef.       2.0179364472
 26
```

Lotus 1-2-3 displays the results of the regression analysis in cells A17 through D25. Remember, always reserve enough room for the results of an operation when marking cells for Lotus 1-2-3 outputs.

13. Quit the worksheet.

14. Turn to Module 12 to continue the learning sequence.

# Module 11

## DATA SORT

### DESCRIPTION

Lotus 1-2-3 allows you to sort worksheet information in alphabetical or numeric order. Use the DATA SORT commands to select the range to sort using up to two keys (criteria) as a basis. Before information is sorted, the cells in which the information is located are specified as a *Data-Range*; that is the total area of the worksheet that is affected by the sort. Once the Data-Range is specified, Lotus 1-2-3 allows you to select two sorting keys. These keys identify the worksheet cells that are actually sorted—primary first and then by secondary within the primary. Finally, you can reset, that is, clear all specified data ranges and keys using the DATA SORT RESET command.

The DATA SORT commands are located by typing a / (slash) and then typing the first letters of the following menu titles:

```
MENU TITLES:              USE AND USE REQUIREMENT:

Data Sort                 Sort worksheet data
Data Sort
   Data-Range             Specify range of all data to be sorted
Data Sort
   Primary-Key            Specify range of the first sorting key
Data Sort
   Secondary-Key          Specify the range of the second sorting key
Data Sort Reset           Erase all sorting parameters
Data Sort Go              Sort the worksheet
Data Sort Quit            Quit the sort menu
```

### APPLICATIONS

Use the DATA SORT command to sort information in a worksheet in *ascending* order (from the smallest value to the largest or from A to Z) or in *descending* order (the reverse order of ascending). An example of using the DATA SORT commands would be to sort a list of your friends by age as the primary key and then arrange them alphabetically as the secondary range. Also, the DATA SORT commands are useful when sorting numeric information because the resulting sorted information immediately reveals the high and low values for a set of numbers.

## TYPICAL OPERATION

1. Retrieve the CANDY worksheet saved in Module 18.

2. Move the cell pointer to A7.

3. Type **/D** and observe the following screen:

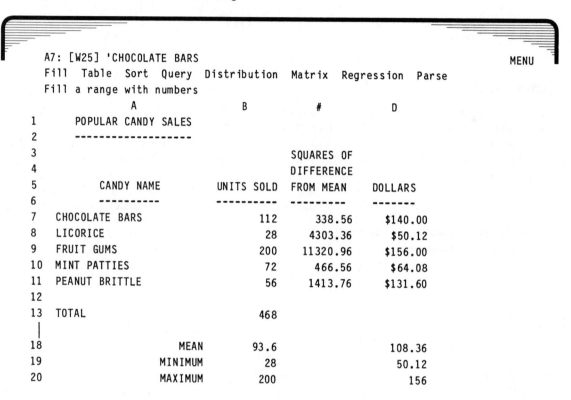

```
A7: [W25] 'CHOCOLATE BARS                                        MENU
Fill  Table  Sort  Query  Distribution  Matrix  Regression  Parse
Fill a range with numbers
                A              B           #           D
  1      POPULAR CANDY SALES
  2      --------------------
  3                                    SQUARES OF
  4                                    DIFFERENCE
  5         CANDY NAME       UNITS SOLD FROM MEAN    DOLLARS
  6         ----------       ---------- ----------   -------
  7    CHOCOLATE BARS            112       338.56    $140.00
  8    LICORICE                   28      4303.36     $50.12
  9    FRUIT GUMS                200     11320.96    $156.00
 10    MINT PATTIES               72       466.56     $64.08
 11    PEANUT BRITTLE             56      1413.76    $131.60
 12
 13    TOTAL                     468

 18                  MEAN         93.6                108.36
 19               MINIMUM           28                 50.12
 20               MAXIMUM          200                   156
```

This is Lotus 1-2-3's Data menu. The following table lists and describes each item on this menu.

| MENU ITEM | DESCRIPTION |
|---|---|
| FILL | FILLS A TABLE WITH INFORMATION. |
| TABLE | CREATES UP TO TWO TABLES FOR INFORMATION. |
| SORT | SORTS UP TO TWO LEVELS OF A RANGE OF INFORMATION IN EITHER ASCENDING OR DESCENDING ORDER. |
| QUERY | ALLOWS A RANGE OF INFORMATION TO BE INTERROGATED FOR ANSWERS TO A SPECIFIC QUESTION CRITERION. |

| | |
|---|---|
| DISTRIBUTION | GIVES THE DISTRIBUTION OF VALUES IN A RANGE OF INFORMATION. |
| MATRIX | MULTIPLIES AND INVERTS MATRICES OF ROW AND COLUMN CELL INFORMATION. |
| REGRESSION | PERFORMS STATISTICAL REGRESSION ANALYSIS ON A RANGE OF CELL INFORMATION. |
| PARSE | CONVERTS A COLUMN OF LONG LABELS INTO SEVERAL COLUMNS OF SHORTER LABELS AND/OR NUMBERS. |

*Lotus 1-2-3 Data Menu Choices*

See the specific modules on each of these menu choices for detailed information about how to use them.

4. Type **S** to select the Sort function and notice the following display:

```
  A7:[W25]  'CHOCOLATE BARS                                           MENU
  Data-Range  Primary-Key  Secondary-Key  Reset  Go  Quit
  Specify records to be sorted
                    A              B        C         D
  1     POPULAR CANDY SALES
  2     -------------------
  3                                        SQUARES OF
  4                                        DIFFERENCE
  5          CANDY NAME         UNITS SOLD  FROM MEAN   DOLLARS
  6          ----------        ----------  ---------   -------
  7     CHOCOLATE BARS                112     338.56   $140.00
  8     LICORICE                       28    4303.36    $50.12
  9     FRUIT GUMS                    200   11320.96   $156.00
 10     MINT PATTIES                   72     466.56    $64.08
 11     PEANUT BRITTLE                 56    1413.76   $131.60
 12
 13     TOTAL                         468
  |
 20                   MAXIMUM          200                 156
```

Notice that the data-range is not the range of cells which is actually sorted. For instance, when sorting the worksheet alphabetically, the data to be sorted would be the candy names (A7 through A11), but you would want the units sold and dollar values about each candy to match the candy

**47**

names in their newly sorted order. Therefore, the data-range must include all the cells between rows 7 and 11 in columns A through E.

5. Type **D**.

6. Highlight cells A7 through E11 as the data-range and then press **Return**.

7. Type **P** to select the primary sorting range.

8. Highlight cells B7 through B11 as the primary range to sort and then press **Return**.

Notice the following screen:

```
A7:[W25]  'CHOCOLATE BARS                                      EDIT
  Primary sort key address: B7..B11  Sort order (A or D): D


                  A              B          C          D
 1      POPULAR CANDY SALES
 2      -------------------
 3                                       SQUARES OF
 4                                       DIFFERENCE
 5          CANDY NAME        UNITS SOLD  FROM MEAN    DOLLARS
 6          ----------        ----------  ----------   -------
 7      CHOCOLATE BARS              112      338.56    $140.00
 8      LICORICE                    28      4303.36     $50.12
 9      FRUIT GUMS                 200     11320.96    $156.00
10      MINT PATTIES                72       466.56     $64.08
11      PEANUT BRITTLE              56      1413.76    $131.60
12
13      TOTAL                      468

18                    MEAN         93.6                 108.36
19                 MINIMUM          28                   50.12
20                 MAXIMUM         200                    156
```

9. Type **A** to select Lotus 1-2-3's ascending order choice and press **Return**.

10. Type **G** for Go and study the following display:

```
A7:[W25] 'LICORICE                                                    READY


                        A               B         C          D
    1      POPULAR CANDY SALES
    2      ═══════════════════
    3                                             SQUARES OF
    4                                             DIFFERENCE
    5           CANDY NAME          UNITS SOLD  FROM MEAN    DOLLARS
    6           ══════════         ══════════  ═════════    ═══════
    7      LICORICE                        28    4303.36     $50.12
    8      PEANUT BRITTLE                  56    1413.76    $131.60
    9      MINT PATTIES                    72     466.56     $64.08
   10      CHOCOLATE BARS                 112     338.56    $140.00
   11      FRUIT GUMS                     200   11320.96    $156.00
   12
   13      TOTAL                          468
   14
   15
   16
   17
   18                      MEAN           93.6              108.36
   19                   MINIMUM             28               50.12
   20                   MAXIMUM            200                 156
```

Lotus 1-2-3 automatically sorts all the candy-units-sold values and redisplays the worksheet in a newly sorted order.

Notice that the other values in the worksheet are sorted along with the units-sold values. The entire data range is sorted based upon the key range of units sold.

11. Save the newly sorted worksheet by replacing it for the name retrieved.

12. Turn to Module 65 to continue the learning sequence.

# Module 12

## DATA TABLE

### DESCRIPTION

Use the DATA TABLE commands to create tables that show the different values a formula calculates each time one or two variables are changed.

The DATA TABLE commands are located and used from the worksheet READY screen by typing a / (slash) and then typing the first letters of the following menu titles:

```
MENU TITLES:             USE AND USE REQUIREMENT:

Data Table               Create a data table
Data Table 1             Create data table 1 Specify range
Data Table 2             Create data table 2 Specify range
Data Table Rset          Erase all data table settings
```

### APPLICATIONS

The DATA TABLE commands are useful when performing sensitivity analysis on a calculated value in a worksheet. These commands perform multiple calculations based upon changes in variables affecting the calculation. A typical example is the business situation in which the expected net profits from sales varies with the volume of goods sold. Using the DATA TABLE commands allows you to easily see the profitability at different sales volumes.

### TYPICAL OPERATION

1.  From the worksheet READY screen, create the following worksheet:

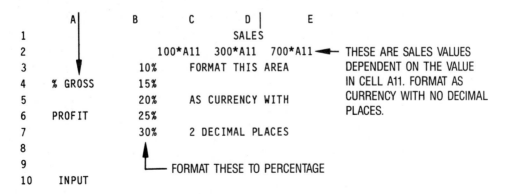

2. Move the cell pointer to A11 and enter **1**.

3. Type **/DT1** to create a data table.

4. Mark cells B2 through E7 as the table range.

This range includes the formulas and the variable percentage gross profit.

5. Select cell A11 as the input cell. The following screen displays:

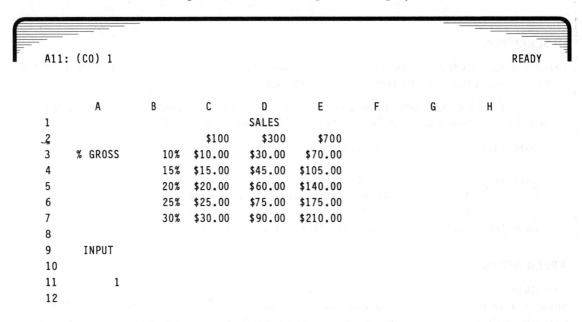

```
A11: (C0) 1                                                    READY


        A      B      C        D        E      F      G      H
 1                            SALES
 2                   $100     $300     $700
 3    % GROSS   10%  $10.00   $30.00   $70.00
 4              15%  $15.00   $45.00   $105.00
 5              20%  $20.00   $60.00   $140.00
 6              25%  $25.00   $75.00   $175.00
 7              30%  $30.00   $90.00   $210.00
 8
 9    INPUT
 10
 11         1
 12
```

Lotus 1-2-3 automatically replaces the input cell with each percentage value in the gross profit column, and then calculates the resulting dollar value and displays it in cells C3 through E7.

6. Quit the worksheet.

7. Turn to Module 32 to continue the learning sequence.

# Module 13

## FILE COMBINE

**DESCRIPTION**

Lotus 1-2-3 links separate worksheets in three different ways. Two Lotus 1-2-3 worksheets can be combined, information from one worksheet can be moved to another, or a text file can be imported into a worksheet.

You combine two worksheets by:

- Copying a range from a worksheet or the entire worksheet into another worksheet.
- Adding a range of numeric data or the entire numeric contents of one worksheet to another.
- Subtracting a range of numeric data or the entire numeric contents of one worksheet from another.

The FILE COMBINE commands are located and used from the worksheet READY screen by typing a / (slash) and then typing the first letters of the following menu titles.:

```
MENU TITLES:              USE AND USE REQUIREMENT:

File Combine              Combine one worksheet file with another
File Combine Copy         Copy one worksheet to another
File Combine Copy
  Entire File             Copy complete file Specify file name
File Combine Copy
  Named Range             Copy named range only Specify range name Specify file name
File Combine Add          Add numeric data or formulas from one worksheet to another
File Combine Add
  Entire File             Add numbers and formulas from entre file Specify file name
File Combine Add
  Named Range             Add #'s or formulas from named range Specify range and file name
File Combine Subtract     Subtract numeric data or formulas from one worksheet to another
File Combine Subtract
  Entire File             Subtract numbers or formulas from entire file Specify file name
File Combine Subtract
  Named Range             Subtract #'s or formulas from named range Specify range and file name
```

## APPLICATIONS

Use the FILE COMBINE commands to combine information from one worksheet with information from another. This command is very useful when you have created two or more worksheets that contain similar information or information that you would like to combine into another worksheet. Using the FILE COMBINE commands eliminates the need to retype information from one worksheet into another.

## TYPICAL OPERATION

1.  Type the word TEST into cell location A1 of a new worksheet and then save it using the worksheet name CANDYTST.

2.  Move the cell pointer to A10 and then type **/FC**. Look at the following display:

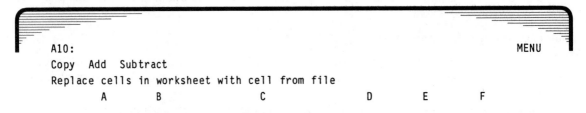

Use the Combine file function to copy, add, or subtract information from one worksheet to another.

3.  Type **C** to copy the worksheet and then notice the top of the following display:

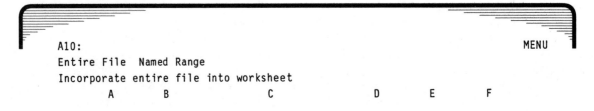

When copying a file, a range can be specified. This range must be named using Lotus 1-2-3's Range-Name-Create feature before it can be copied into another worksheet.

4.  Press **Return** to copy the entire file.

5. Select **CANDY** and then press **Return**. Study the following display:

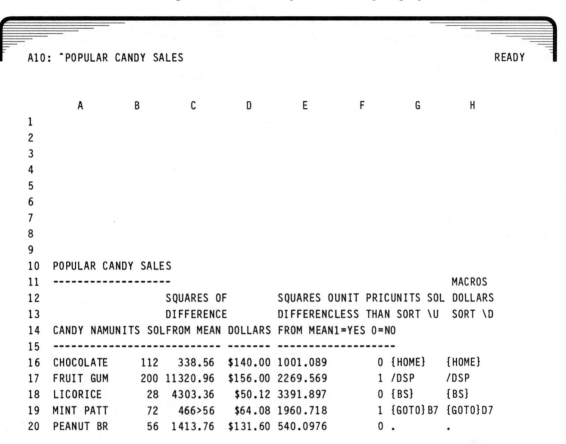

```
A10: ^POPULAR CANDY SALES                                          READY


        A       B        C        D        E        F      G        H
 1
 2
 3
 4
 5
 6
 7
 8
 9
10  POPULAR CANDY SALES
11  -------------------                                          MACROS
12                     SQUARES OF         SQUARES OUNIT PRICUNITS SOL DOLLARS
13                     DIFFERENCE         DIFFERENCLESS THAN SORT \U   SORT \D
14  CANDY NAMUNITS SOLFROM MEAN DOLLARS FROM MEAN1=YES 0=NO
15  -------------------------- ------- -------------------- ---
16  CHOCOLATE      112   338.56  $140.00 1001.089       0 {HOME}     {HOME}
17  FRUIT GUM      200 11320.96  $156.00 2269.569       1 /DSP       /DSP
18  LICORICE        28  4303.36   $50.12 3391.897       0 {BS}       {BS}
19  MINT PATT       72   466>56   $64.08 1960.718       1 {GOTO}B7   {GOTO}D7
20  PEANUT BR       56  1413.76  $131.60 540.0976       0 .          .
```

Notice that the CANDY worksheet format settings (column widths, etc.) did not copy over to the CANDYTST worksheet. Also, notice the cell references in the macro on the right-hand of the display. The copying process does not change these references. For the macro to work, it must be re-written inserting the new column and row coordinates for the cells to be evaluated by the macro.

6. Move the cell pointer to B35.

The formula in cell B35 has automatically adjusted itself to the location in the new worksheet. Lotus 1-2-3 automatically performs this when copying one worksheet to another.

**WARNING**

Lotus 1-2-3 changes the absolute cell references for formulas as well as the relative cell references by resetting the reference cell for absolute cell references to the upper-left-hand cell of the range to which the worksheet is copied. If you use the add or subtract feature of FILE COMBINE, be sure to check for absolute cell references which may be affected by this process.

7. Quit Lotus 1-2-3.

8. Turn to Module 16 to continue the learning sequence.

# Module 14

## FILE DIRECTORY

**DESCRIPTION**

Occasionally, the need arises to change the default directory in which Lotus 1-2-3 data files are listed and from which Lotus 1-2-3 retrieves files for use in the worksheet. Use the FILE DIRECTORY command to change the default data files directory.

The FILE DIRECTORY command is located and used from the worksheet READY screen by typing a / (slash) and then typing the first letters of the following menu titles:

```
MENU TITLES:           USE AND USE REQUIREMENT:

File Directory         Change file directory Specify new directory
```

**APPLICATIONS**

Use the FILE DIRECTORY command any time you want to set a new data files directory. For example, when you want to change the data files directory from the current directory setting on a hard disk drive C: to the diskette located in disk drive B: use the FILE DIRECTORY command.

**TYPICAL OPERATION**

1.  From the worksheet READY screen, type **/FD**. Notice the top of the following screen:

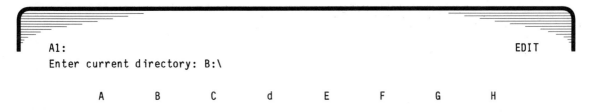

```
A1:                                                              EDIT
Enter current directory: B:\

         A        B        C        d        E        F        G        H
```

The current directory displays. Type a new directory over the old one to make a replacement.

**NOTE**

For hard disk drive users, the new directory can include a complete file path, for example, C:\LOTUS\WKSHEETS.

2. Press **Return** to accept the displayed directory.

3. Turn to Module 17 to continue the learning sequence.

# Module 15

## FILE ERASE

### DESCRIPTION

Use the FILE ERASE commands to delete one of the following types of disk files from the default directory:

- WORKSHEET      .WK? FILES
- PRINT      .PRN FILES
- GRAPH      .PIC FILES
- OTHER      OTHER TYPES OF FILES

The FILE ERASE commands are located and used from the worksheet READY screen by typing a / (slash) and then typing the first letters of the following menu titles:

```
MENU TITLES:            USE AND USE REQUIREMENT:

File Erase              Delete Lotus files
File Erase Worksheet    Delete a .WK? file Specify file name
File Erase Print        Delete a .PRN file Specify file name
File Erase Graph        Delete a .PIC file Specify file name
File Erase Other        Delete a file other than a .WK?, .PRN, or .PIC file
                        Specify file name
```

### APPLICATIONS

Use the FILE ERASE commands to delete files in the same manner as you would use the DOS system level command DELETE or ERASE. This command is useful when you want to erase a file from your data diskette, because there is not enough room to hold the current worksheet when it is saved. By being able to erase a selected file from within a worksheet, you are able to save your worksheet without trouble. This command is somewhat redundant, because with Lotus 1-2-3's new SYSTEM command, you can access the DOS operating system from within a worksheet and perform the same deletion function using the appropriate DOS command.

## TYPICAL OPERATION

1. From the worksheet READY screen, type **/FE** and notice the following screen:

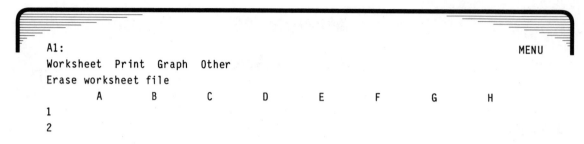

```
A1:                                                                    MENU
Worksheet  Print  Graph  Other
Erase worksheet file
          A         B         C         D         E         F         G         H
1
2
```

Choose the type of file you want to erase from this prompt.

2. Press **Return** to erase a worksheet and notice the following screen:

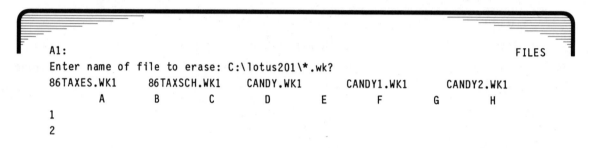

```
A1:                                                                    FILES
Enter name of file to erase: C:\lotus201\*.wk?
86TAXES.WK1      86TAXSCH.WK1      CANDY.WK1         CANDY1.WK1        CANDY2.WK1
          A         B         C         D         E         F         G         H
1
2
```

Notice the similarity between this prompt and the one displayed when retrieving a file. Use the cursor controls to move the highlighter to the file to delete or type the name of the file to delete.

3. Press **Return** to delete the highlighted worksheet. Notice the screen changes to the following:

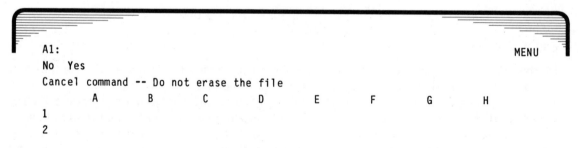

```
A1:                                                                    MENU
No   Yes
Cancel command -- Do not erase the file
          A         B         C         D         E         F         G         H
1
2
```

Lotus 1-2-3 allows you to cancel the ERASE process before actually erasing a file.

4. Type **N** to cancel the ERASE process.

5. Quit the worksheet.

6. Turn to Module 20 to continue the learning sequence.

# Module 16

## FILE IMPORT

### DESCRIPTION

Lotus 1-2-3 can copy information from a text file into a worksheet. Any text file can be copied, as long as there are no graphics characters. Importing information into a Lotus 1-2-3 worksheet is done in two ways:

- The imported information is treated as text only.
- The imported information is treated as numeric with named labels.

The FILE IMPORT commands are located and used from the worksheet READY screen by typing a / (slash) and then typing the first letters of the following menu titles:

```
MENU TITLES:            USE AND USE REQUIREMENT:

File Import             Copy a text file to a worksheet
File Import Text        Copy text only Specify file name
File Import Numbers     Copy text and numbers as numbers Specify file name
```

### APPLICATIONS

Use the FILE IMPORT commands to import a text file into a Lotus 1-2-3 worksheet. The text file can then be parsed into meaningful columns using the DATA PARSE commands. The FILE IMPORT commands perform the same function as the FILE COMBINE commands except that instead of a worksheet file, a text file can be combined with an existing worksheet. This command is extremely useful when you have created a file using a word processor and want to import into a worksheet the information contained in it.

### TYPICAL OPERATION

1. Retrieve the CANDY worksheet.

2. Type **/PPR** and mark the cell range A1 though D13.

3. Type **Q** and then type **/PF** and name the file **CANDYTXT**.

4. Press **Return** and then type **G**.

5. Type **Q** and then move the cell pointer to A30.

6. Type **/FI** and notice the following screen:

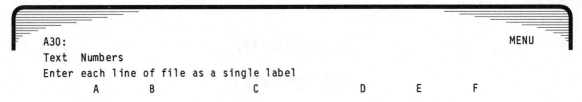

```
A30:                                                              MENU
Text   Numbers
Enter each line of file as a single label
         A         B              C            D       E       F
```

Lotus 1-2-3 treats the information contained in an imported text file as text or as numeric with text labels.

7. Type **T.**

Only files with a .PRN suffix display.

8. Type **CANDYTXT** as the text file to import and then press **Return.**

9. Move the cell pointer to A41 and study the following screen:

```
A41:[W25] '    CHOCOLATE BARS                112      338.56    $140.00    READY


                   A              B          C          D
22       VARIANCE                          3568.64
23       STANDARD DEVIATION          59.73809504
24
25    LOTUS @ CALCULATIONS
26       VARIANCE              3568.64                1832.67456
27       STANDARD DEVIATION  59.73809504              42.80974842
28
|
35          POPULAR CANDY SALES
36          ==================
37                                        SQUARES OF
38                                        DIFFERENCE
39              CANDY NAME     UNITS SOLD  FROM MEAN    DOLLARS
40              ==========     ==========  =========    =======
41    CHOCOLATE BARS              112      338.56       $140.00
```

The copied text file is imported into the worksheet as if it were text only and contained no numerical data. Notice that the spacing is exactly like the original CANDY worksheet but each row is considered continuous text, including the numbers.

10. Quit the worksheet.

11. Turn to Module 8 to continue the learning sequence.

# Module 17

## FILE LIST

### DESCRIPTION

When you are unsure of the names of particular files on the default directory, use the FILE LIST commands to display a listing on the computer screen. The types of files are listed by these commands:

- WORKSHEET    .WK? FILES
- PRINT        .PRN FILES
- GRAPH        .PIC FILES
- OTHER        OTHER FILES

The FILE LIST commands are located and used from the worksheet READY screen by typing a / (slash) and then typing the first letters of the following menu titles:

```
MENU TITLES:              USE AND USE REQUIREMENT:

File List                 List all files on current directory diskette
File List Worksheet       List .WKS files
File List Print           List .PRN files
File List Graph           List .PIC files
File List Other
```

### APPLICATIONS

Use the FILE LIST commands any time a listing of available Lotus 1-2-3 files or other files on the default directory is required. Typically, you would use this command to search for files on directories specified using the FILE DIRECTORY command.

## TYPICAL OPERATION

1.  From the worksheet READY screen, type **/FLW** to list the worksheet (.WK1) files on the default directory and notice the following screen:

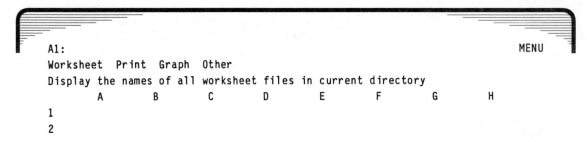

```
A1:                                                              MENU
Worksheet   Print   Graph   Other
Display the names of all worksheet files in current directory
            A        B        C        D        E        F        G        H
1
2
```

Lotus 1-2-3 can display the three types of Lotus 1-2-3 files as well as other types of files.

2.  Press **Return** to display worksheet files and notice the following screen:

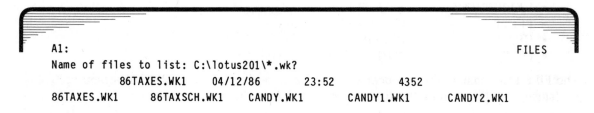

```
A1:                                                              FILES
Name of files to list: C:\lotus201\*.wk?
               86TAXES.WK1     04/12/86        23:52           4352
86TAXES.WK1        86TAXSCH.WK1     CANDY.WK1          CANDY1.WK1       CANDY2.WK1
```

All the worksheet (.WK1) files display. Use this same command to display other types of Lotus 1-2-3 files. Also notice that the date, time, and file size in kilobytes displays for the highlighted file. Use the arrow keys to move from one file to another.

3.  Quit the worksheet.

4.  Turn to Module 15 to continue the learning sequence.

# Module 18
## FILE SAVE, RETRIEVE

**DESCRIPTION**

Use the FILE SAVE command to save a worksheet to a disk file and the FILE RETRIEVE command to retrieve a saved worksheet from a disk file.

The FILE SAVE or FILE RETRIEVE commands are located and used from the worksheet READY screen by typing a / (slash) and then typing the first letters of the following menu titles:

```
MENU TITLES:            USE AND USE REQUIREMENT:

File Retrieve           Load a .WKS file into the worksheet Specify file name
File Save               Save a .WKS file on diskette Specify file name
```

**APPLICATIONS**

These commands are used to save and retrieve Lotus 1-2-3 worksheet files. A thorough familiarity with these two commands is necessary to manipulate worksheet files.

**TYPICAL OPERATION**

Follow these procedures to save the worksheet you created in Module 21.

1.  From the worksheet READY screen, create the worksheet used in Module 21. Remember, the completed worksheet looks like this:

```
  D20: @MAX(D11..D7)                                                    READY
```

```
                   A                 B           C           D
  1      POPULAR CANDY SALES
  2      -------------------
  3                                             SQUARES OF
  4                                             DIFFERENCE
  5           CANDY NAME          UNITS SOLD   FROM MEAN    DOLLARS
  6           ----------          ----------   ---------    -------
  7      CHOCOLATE BARS                  112      338.56     $140.00
  8      LICORICE                         28     4303.36      $50.12
  9      FRUIT GUMS                      200    11320.96     $156.00
 10      MINT PATTIES                     72      466.56      $64.08
 11      PEANUT BRITTLE                   56     1413.76     $131.60
 12
 13      TOTAL                           468
 14
 15
 16
 17
 18                   MEAN             93.6                  108.36
 19                MINIMUM               28                   50.12
 20                MAXIMUM              200                     156
```

2.   Type **/FS**.

Lotus 1-2-3 asks you to provide a filename for your worksheet. Use standard DOS filename convention: up to eight characters for the filename and up to three characters for the optional file extension in the form *filename.ext*. Lotus 1-2-3 assigns the extension WK1 automatically. This designates a worksheet file and is necessary for Lotus 1-2-3 to retrieve worksheet files later. Should you want to number your worksheets, type the extension with WK first and then a sequential number to denote the number of the worksheet.

### WARNING

If you do not specify the disk drive onto which the file is saved, Lotus 1-2-3 automatically saves the file to the source disk drive—in most cases disk drive A. Since disk drive A contains the system diskette and this diskette has a *write-*

*protect tab* (a small, gummed piece of foiled paper that prevents the computer's disk drive from writing to the diskette), always specify disk drive B for worksheets (files) saved using Lotus 1-2-3.

3. Press **Esc** twice and then type **B:CANDY** and press **Return.**

Notice the flashing WAIT in the worksheet condition block while the worksheet is being saved. When finished, the worksheet returns to the READY mode. Although the worksheet has been saved, it is still displayed. You can perform further work.

It is always a good idea to save your worksheets periodically during a Lotus 1-2-3 session. If you have a power failure or computer malfunction, you can lose everything unless it was saved on disk.

Follow these steps to retrieve the CANDY.WK1 file from the data diskette in disk drive B. Once retrieved, it is displayed on the monitor in the READY mode.

Lotus 1-2-3 retrieves worksheet files from a data diskette in one of two ways. If the data diskette has been specified as the Lotus 1-2-3 source diskette, you don't have to specify the drive designation. If a file is on a data diskette that is not the specified source drive, the drive upon which the file is located must be specified.

1. Type **/FR.**

Notice that CANDY is displayed under the "Enter name of file to retrieve:" prompt. Lotus 1-2-3 always displays the names of all worksheet (.WK1) files on the selected source disk. These names are a part of the Retrieve Menu. They are selected in the same manner as any menu item. Just use the arrow keys to highlight your choice. Of course, you can always type the name of the file instead of using the highlighter.

2. Press **Return** to retrieve the CANDY.WK1 worksheet file.

Remember to use the disk drive designator when retrieving a file from a drive other than the selected source drive. Once you press the Return key, Lotus 1-2-3 searches for the named file on the named disk drive.

When found, the file is loaded into the computer's memory and then displayed in the worksheet, which is in the READY mode. If you don't use a drive designator, Lotus 1-2-3 searches for the named file on the specified source drive (the default drive). If Lotus 1-2-3 does not find it, the program displays an error message.

**NOTE**

When you retrieve a Lotus 1-2-3 worksheet file, you do not have to type the file extension. Lotus 1-2-3 assumes the extension WK1.

After a worksheet is retrieved to perform additional work, it can be saved again. Follow these steps to retrieve the worksheet and then save it again.

1. Type **/FS**.

2. Press **Return** to accept the displayed name and look at the following display.

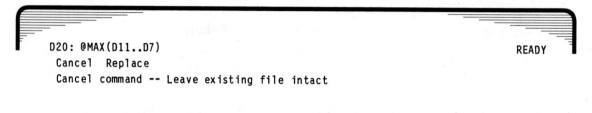

```
 D20: @MAX(D11..D7)                                          READY
  Cancel  Replace
  Cancel command -- Leave existing file intact


                     A              B         C          D
   1       POPULAR CANDY SALES
   2       -------------------
   3                                        SQUARES OF
   4                                        DIFFERENCE
   5            CANDY NAME        UNITS SOLD FROM MEAN    DOLLARS
   6            ----------        ---------- ----------   -------
   7       CHOCOLATE BARS            112       338.56    $140.00
   8       LICORICE                   28      4303.36     $50.12
   9       FRUIT GUMS                200     11320.96    $156.00
  10       MINT PATTIES               72       466.56     $64.08
  11       PEANUT BRITTLE             56      1413.76    $131.60
  12
  13       TOTAL                     468
  14
  15
  16
  17
  18                     MEAN        93.6                 108.36
  19                  MINIMUM          28                  50.12
  20                  MAXIMUM         200                    156
```

Lotus 1-2-3 gives you the opportunity to change your mind. You can cancel your decision to save the worksheet by pressing Return. Then follow the save procedure again and give the worksheet another name.

3. Select Replace and then press **Return**.

Lotus 1-2-3 replaces the old worksheet file with the one displayed on the screen and returns to the worksheet READY mode.

4. Quit the worksheet.

5. Turn to Module 70 to continue the learning sequence.

# Module 19

# FILE XTRACT

## DESCRIPTION

Lotus 1-2-3 extracts information from a worksheet in a manner similar to the way it combines information. However, it is different from information combinations in that extraction includes all formats, column-widths, print setting, and other attributes used by the worksheet from which the information is extracted. There are several critical conditions you must always remember before extracting information from a worksheet. They are:

- Use file extraction to convert a range of formulas to numbers.
- Store the range of formulas as "values only" if you want them to transfer to the new worksheet as numbers.
- Take care that the extracted formulas do not reference cells outside of the range being extracted.

The FILE XTRACT commands are located and used from the worksheet READY screen by typing a / (slash) and then typing the first letters of the following menu titles:

```
MENU TITLES:            USE AND USE REQUIREMENT:

File Xtract             Extract information from the current worksheet to a worksheet
File Xtract Formulas    Extract formulas Specify "extract to" file name Specify range
File Xtract Values      Extract formula values Specify "extract to" file name Specify range
```

## APPLICATIONS

Use the FILE XTRACT commands to extract the values only from the currently dispayed worksheet into another worksheet or to extract formulas only from the currently displayed worksheet into another worksheet. For example, if you are working with a worksheet whose calculations directly effect the information contained in another worksheet, use the FILE XTRACT commands to transfer the calculations. You also use the FILE COMBINE commands to combine the information, but to do so, you must save the currently displayed worksheet and retrieve the worksheet into which the calculations are to be combined.

## TYPICAL OPERATION

1.  Retrieve the CANDY worksheet.

2.  Press **Home**.

3.  Type **/FX**.

The Xtract choice allows you to extract the numeric values for formulas or the formulas themselves.

4.  Type **F**.

5.  Select the CANDYTST worksheet and then press **Return**.

6.  Move the cell pointer to D17 and then press **Return**.

Lotus 1-2-3 allows you to abort this procedure.

### WARNING

> This procedure extracts the information contained within the boundaries for cells A1 through D17 and inserts it into CANDYTST. This process erases the contents of those cells in the target worksheet.

7.  Type **R** and retrieve the CANDYTST worksheet.

Notice that the information specified in CANDY has been extracted and overwritten into cells A1 through D17 of CANDYTST.

8.  Quit the worksheet.

9.  Turn to Module 56 to continue the learning sequence.

# Module 20

## FORMULAS - ADVANCED

### DESCRIPTION

Lotus 1-2-3 allows you to write formulas which perform conditional transfers. A *conditional transfer statement* is defined as an instruction that is executed when a specified condition or set of conditions exist. If the conditions do not exist, the conditional transfer statement is skipped or another instruction is performed. A simple way to understand this type of statement is to imagine a wall with two doors in it; one five feet tall and the other seven feet tall. The conditional transfer statement asks if you can walk through the door without stooping. If you answer the conditional transfer statement with a yes, you pass through the seven foot door. If you answer no, the other door is taken.

Lotus 1-2-3's conditional transfer statements always begin with the @ symbol. They follow the form:

| Operator | Description |
|---|---|
| @ | Lotus 1-2-3's powerful command prefix. |
| IF | Tells Lotus 1-2-3 that this formula is a conditional transfer statement. |
| (Conditions) | The conditions to be met before the THEN instruction is processed. |
| THEN | Tells Lotus 1-2-3 that the following instruction is to be performed if, and only if, the IF condition has been met. |
| (Do this instruction) | The THEN instruction. |
| ELSE | Tells Lotus 1-2-3 that the following instruction is to be performed if and only if the IF condition has *not* been met. |
| (Or do this instruction) | The ELSE instruction. |

As you learned earlier, Lotus 1-2-3's @ functions are powerful tools. They allow you to create sophisticated formulas without having to deal with the complexities of the underlying mathematical principles. The following table lists @ functions in addition to those listed in Module 21. Remember, to find more information about a specific function, simply press the F1 function key while using the function to display Lotus 1-2-3 Help screens.

| LOTUS 1-2-3 @ FUNCTION | | DESCRIPTION |
|---|---|---|
| **MATHEMATICAL FUNCTIONS** | | |
| @ABS(x) | | Absolute value |
| @INT(x) | | Integer part |
| @MOD(x,y) | | X mod Y |
| @PI | | Pi |
| @RAND | | Random number between 0 and 1 |
| @SQRT(x) | | Square root |
| @ROUND(x,digits) | | Rounded up or down number |
| @LOG(x) | | Log base 10 |
| @LN(x) | | Log base e |
| @EXP(x) | | Exponential |
| @SIN(x) | | Sine |
| @COS(x) | | Cosine |
| @TAN(x) | | Tangent |
| @ASIN(x) | | Arc sine |
| @ACOS(x) | | Arc cosine |
| @ATAN(x) | | 2-quadrant arc tangent |
| @ATAN2(x,y) | | 4-quadrant arc tangent |
| **SPECIAL FUNCTIONS** | | |
| @NA | | The value NA (not available) |
| @ERR | | The value ERR (error) |
| @CHOOSE(t,v0,v1,v2,. . .,vn) | | Select value from list: if t = 0, select v0, if t = 1, select v1, etc. |
| @HLOOKUP(x,table_range,row#) | | Table lookup with index row |
| @VLOOKUP(x,table_range,column#) | | Table lookup with index column |
| @@ (cell address) | (Rel.2.01 only) | The contents of the cell referenced by the cell address. |
| @CELL(attribute,range) | (Rel.2.01 only) | The code representing the attribute of the specified range. |
| @CELLPOINTER(attribute) | (Rel.2.01 only) | The code representing the attribute of the highlighted cell. |
| @COLS(range) | (Rel.2.01 only) | The number of columns in a range. |
| @INDEX(range,column,row) | (Rel.2.01 only) | The value of the cell located at the intersection of the specified column and row within the specified range. |
| @ROWS(range) | (Rel.2.01 only) | The number of rows in a range. |
| **FINANCIAL FUNCTIONS** | | |
| @NPV(x,range) | | Net present value |
| @IRR(guess,range) | | Internal rate of return |
| @PMT(prn,int,term) | | Payment |
| @FV(pmt,int,term) | | Future value |
| @PV(pmt,int,term) | | Present value |
| @CTER(int,fv,pv) | (Rel.2.01 only) | The number of compound interest periods for an investment of pv to reach a future value of fv at a rate of interest of int. |
| @DDB(cost,salvage,life,period) | (Rel.2.01 only) | Computes double declining balance depreciation. |
| @RATE(fv,pv,term) | (Rel.2.01 only) | The interest rate required for the present value pv to grow to the future value fv during the term. |
| @SLN(cost,salvage,life) | (Rel.2.01 only) | Computes straight line depreciation. |
| @SYD(cost,salvage,life,period) | (Rel.2.01 only) | Computes the sum-of-the-year's digits depreciation. |

*Lotus 1-2-3 @ Functions*

| LOTUS 1-2-3 @ FUNCTION | | DESCRIPTION |
|---|---|---|

**FINANCIAL FUNCTIONS (continued)**

| | | |
|---|---|---|
| @TERM(pmt,int,fv) | (Rel.2.01 only) | The number of payment periods required to pay the future value fv of an investment at a specified interest rate int with payment amounts pmt. |

**CONDITIONAL LOGIC FUNCTIONS**

| | | |
|---|---|---|
| @FALSE | | The value 0 (meaning FALSE) |
| @TRUE | | The value 1 (meaning TRUE) |
| @ISNA(x) | | The value 1 (TRUE) if x = NA; otherwise, the value 0 (FALSE). |
| @ISERR(x) | | The value 1 (TRUE) if x = ERR; otherwise, the value 0 (FALSE). |
| @IF(x,true_value,false_value) | | If-then-else statement: If x is non-0 (TRUE), the value "true-value." If x is 0 (FALSE), the value "false-value." |
| @ISSTRING(x) | (Rel.2.01 only) | The value 1 (TRUE) if x = a string value; otherwise, the value 0 (FALSE). |
| @ISNUMBER(x) | (Rel.2.01 only) | The value 1 (TRUE) if x = a numeric value; otherwise, the value 0 (FALSE). |

**STATISTICAL DATABASE FUNCTIONS**

| | |
|---|---|
| @DCOUNT(inp_rng,offset,crit_rng) | Field count |
| @DSUM(inp_rng,offset,crit_rng) | Field sum |
| @DAVG(inp_rng,offset,crit_rng) | Field average |
| @DMIN(inp_rng,offset,crit_rng) | Field minimum |
| @DMAX(inp_rng,offset,crit_rng) | Field maximum |
| @DSTD(inp_rng,offset,crit_rng) | Field standard deviation |
| @DVAR(inp_rng,offset,crit_rng) | Field variance |

**DATE AND TIME FUNCTIONS**

| | | |
|---|---|---|
| @DATE(yr,mnth,dy) | | Serial number of day (1 = 01-Jan-00...73049 = 31-Dec-2099). The arguments must be single values within these ranges: yr: 0-199, mnth: 1-12, dy: 1-31 days in month |
| @NOW | (Rel.2.01 only) | Replaces Rel.1A's @TODAY function. @DATE value of entry you made at Enter New Date prompt when you started the computer. |
| @DAY(x) | | The day (1-31), month (1-12), and year |
| @MONTH(x) | | (0-199) of the day whose serial number |
| @YEAR(x) | | is 'x'. The argument value must be between 1 and 73049 (01-Jan-1900 to 31-Dec-2099). |
| @DATEVALUE(date string) | (Rel.2.01 only) | The date number of the specified date string. |
| @TIME(hr,min,sec) | (Rel.2.01 only) | The time number of the specified hour hr, minute min, and second sec. |
| @TIMEVALUE(time string) | (Rel.2.01 only) | The time number of the specified time string. |
| @HOUR(time number) | (Rel.2.01 only) | The hour number of the time number. |
| @MIN(time number) | (Rel.2.01 only) | The minute number of the time number. |
| @SEC(time number) | (Rel.2.01 only) | The second number of the time number. |

**STRING FUNCTIONS   (ALL RELEASE 2.01 ONLY)**

| | |
|---|---|
| @CHAR(x) | The ASCII character that corresponds to the number x. |
| @CODE(x) | The ASCII number that corresponds to the character x. |

*Lotus 1-2-3 @ Functions*

| LOTUS 1-2-3 @ FUNCTION | DESCRIPTION |
|---|---|
| STRING FUNCTIONS   (ALL RELEASE 2.01 ONLY)-CONTINUED | |
| @EXACT(string1,string2) | The value 1 (TRUE) if string1 = string2; otherwise, the value 0 (FALSE). |
| @FIND(search string,string,start number) | The position at which the first occurrence of search string begins in string. |
| @LEFT(string,n) | The first n characters in string. |
| @RIGHT(string,n) | The last n characters in string. |
| @LENGTH(string) | The number of characters in string. |
| @LOWER(string) | Sets all characters in string to lower case. |
| @UPPER(string) | Sets all characters in string to upper case. |
| @MID(string,start number,n) | Extract n characters from the string beginning with the start number. |
| @N(range) | The numeric value of the upper left-hand corner of the specified range. |
| @PROPER(string) | Sets all words in a string with the first letter in upper case and all the remaining letters in lower case. |
| @REPEAT(string,n) | Duplicate string n number of times. |
| @REPLACE(original string,start number,n,new,string) | Removes n characters from original string beginning at the start number, and then inserts the new string. |
| @S(range) | The string value of the upper left-hand corner of the specified range. |
| @STRING(x,n) | Sets the numeric value of x to string value with n decimal places. |
| @TRIM(string) | Strips all leading, trailing, and consecutive spaces from a string. |
| @VALUE(string) | Sets a string number to a true numeric value. |

*Lotus 1-2-3 @ Functions*

## TYPICAL OPERATION

Follow these procedures to write a conditional transfer formula. This formula examines the dollars and units sold values in the worksheet and creates a new column of numbers which contains only those candy items that have a unit price less than $1.00.

1.  Retrieve the CANDY worksheet saved in Module 42 and notice the following screen:

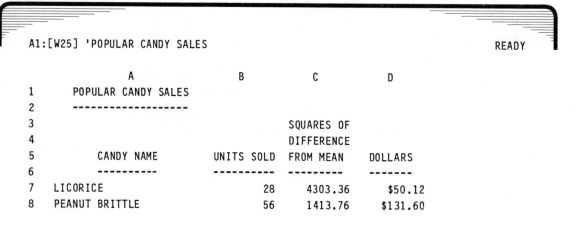

```
A1:[W25] 'POPULAR CANDY SALES                                    READY

                    A            B          C          D
  1      POPULAR CANDY SALES
  2      -------------------
  3                                      SQUARES OF
  4                                      DIFFERENCE
  5           CANDY NAME      UNITS SOLD FROM MEAN    DOLLARS
  6           ----------     ---------- ---------    -------
  7      LICORICE                    28   4303.36     $50.12
  8      PEANUT BRITTLE              56   1413.76    $131.60
```

| | | | | |
|---|---|---|---|---|
| 9 | MINT PATTIES | 72 | 466.56 | $64.08 |
| 10 | CHOCOLATE BARS | 112 | 338.56 | $140.00 |
| 11 | FRUIT GUMS | 200 | 11320.96 | $156.00 |
| 12 | | | | |
| 13 | TOTAL | 468 | | |
| 14 | | | | |
| 15 | | | | |
| 16 | | | | |
| 17 | | | | |
| 18 | MEAN | 93.6 | | 108.36 |
| 19 | MINIMUM | 28 | | 50.12 |
| 20 | MAXIMUM | 200 | | 156 |

2. Move the cell pointer to F3 and set the column width to 12 characters.

3. Type the following heading starting at F3, moving down one row at a time through F6.

**UNIT PRICE**
**LESS THAN $1**
**1=YES 0=NO**
_____

4. Move the cell pointer to F7 and type **@IF((**.

5. Move the cell pointer to D7 and type **/**.

6. Move the cell pointer to B7 and type **)<=**.

These mathematical symbols (< =) mean "smaller than or equal to." Lotus 1-2-3 uses the same conventions as algebra for the use of equality symbols and parentheses. If you can write an algebra formula, you will have no trouble with a Lotus 1-2-3 formula.

7. Type **1,**.

This is the condition to be met, that is, the unit cost must be less than or equal to $1.00.

8. Type **1,** for the THEN condition instruction.

9. Type **0** for the ELSE condition instruction.

10. Type **)** and then press **Return**.

Notice the following display:

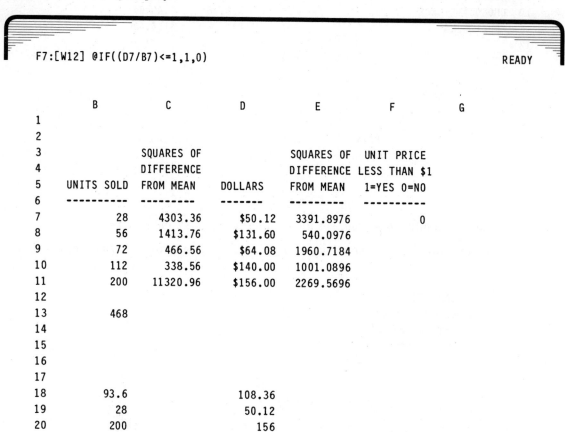

```
F7:[W12] @IF((D7/B7)<=1,1,0)                                    READY
```

|   | B | C | D | E | F | G |
|---|---|---|---|---|---|---|
| 1 | | | | | | |
| 2 | | | | | | |
| 3 | | SQUARES OF | | SQUARES OF | UNIT PRICE | |
| 4 | | DIFFERENCE | | DIFFERENCE | LESS THAN $1 | |
| 5 | UNITS SOLD | FROM MEAN | DOLLARS | FROM MEAN | 1=YES 0=NO | |
| 6 | ---------- | ---------- | ------- | ---------- | ---------- | |
| 7 | 28 | 4303.36 | $50.12 | 3391.8976 | 0 | |
| 8 | 56 | 1413.76 | $131.60 | 540.0976 | | |
| 9 | 72 | 466.56 | $64.08 | 1960.7184 | | |
| 10 | 112 | 338.56 | $140.00 | 1001.0896 | | |
| 11 | 200 | 11320.96 | $156.00 | 2269.5696 | | |
| 12 | | | | | | |
| 13 | 468 | | | | | |
| 14 | | | | | | |
| 15 | | | | | | |
| 16 | | | | | | |
| 17 | | | | | | |
| 18 | 93.6 | | 108.36 | | | |
| 19 | 28 | | 50.12 | | | |
| 20 | 200 | | 156 | | | |

The conditional transfer formula examines the calculated unit price and compares it to the limit (less than or equal to 1). If the condition is met, Lotus 1-2-3 automatically inserts a 1 (for YES) in column F. If the condition is not met, a zero (for NO) is inserted.

11.  Copy the conditional transfer formula from cell F7 to cells F8 through F11.

12.  Sort the entire worksheet (A7 through F11) alphabetically by candy name.

Notice that the formulas still operate even after you have sorted the worksheet. Remember, Lotus 1-2-3 evaluates all formulas using relative cell references unless they are made absolute using the dollar sign ($).

Follow these steps to calculate the *variance* and the *standard deviation* for both sets of information about the candy worksheet using the statistical formulas and Lotus 1-2-3's special @ functions.

The term *variance* is defined as being the average of the squares (mean square) of the values calculated by subtracting the average (arithmetic mean) for the values in a set of numbers from each individual value in the set of numbers. For example, the variance for the units sold numbers (column B) is found by calculating the average of all the squared values in column D.

The square root of the variance is known as the *standard deviation*. Without getting too technical, an understanding of the standard deviation can be more easily grasped if you think of it as a more precise measure of the variability between each value than is the average. The closer the standard deviation is to the mean, the more uniform is the spread of values throughout the data being examined.

1. Move the cell pointer to A21 and type the following information starting at A21 and moving down one row at a time:

    | | |
    |---|---|
    | **A21** | **MANUAL CALCULATIONS** |
    | **A22** | **VARIANCE** |
    | **A23** | **STANDARD DEVIATION** |

2. Move the cell pointer to C22 and type @**SUM(**.

3. Move the cell pointer to C11 and type **.** (period).

4. Move the cell pointer to C7 and type **)/5** and then press **Return**.

5. Move the cell pointer to C23 and type @**SQRT(**.

6. Move the cell pointer to C22 and type **)** and then press **Return**. Notice the following screen:

```
C23:[W12] @SQRT(C22)                                          READY
```

| | A | B | C | D |
|---|---|---|---|---|
| 4 | | | DIFFERENCE | |
| 5 | CANDY NAME | UNITS SOLD | FROM MEAN | DOLLARS |
| 6 | ---------- | ---------- | --------- | ------- |
| 7 | CHOCOLATE BARS | 112 | 338.56 | $140.00 |
| 8 | FRUIT GUMS | 200 | 11320.96 | $156.00 |
| 9 | LICORICE | 28 | 4303.36 | $50.12 |
| 10 | MINT PATTIES | 72 | 466.56 | $64.08 |
| 11 | PEANUT BRITTLE | 56 | 1413.76 | $131.60 |
| 12 | | | | |
| 13 | TOTAL | 468 | | |
| 14 | | | | |
| 15 | | | | |
| 16 | | | | |
| 17 | | | | |
| 18 | MEAN | 93.6 | | 108.36 |
| 19 | MINIMUM | 28 | | 50.12 |
| 20 | MAXIMUM | 200 | | 156 |
| 21 | MANUAL CALCULATIONS | | | |
| 22 | VARIANCE | | 3568.64 | |
| 23 | STANDARD DEVIATION | | 59.73809504 | |

The statistical formulas calculate the variance and standard deviation based upon the information contained in cells C7 through C11 (the squares of the differences from the mean for the units sold values).

7. Copy the formulas in C22 and C23 to E22 and E23.

8. Move the cell pointer to A25 and type the following descriptive information starting at A25 and moving down one row at a time:

| | |
|---|---|
| A25 | LOTUS @ CALCULATIONS |
| A26 | VARIANCE |
| A27 | STANDARD DEVIATION |

9. Move the cell pointer to B26 and type @**VAR(**.

10. Move the cell pointer to B11 and type . (a period).

11. Move the cell pointer to B7, type **)** and then press **Return**.

12. Move the cell pointer to B27 and type @**STD(**.

13. Move the cell pointer to B11 and type a period .

14. Move the cell pointer to B7, type **)** and press **Return**. Look at the following display on the monitor:

```
B27:[W12] @STD(B11..B7)                                              READY


                   A              B          C          D
 8   FRUIT GUMS                  200     11320.96   $156.00
 9   LICORICE                     28      4303.36    $50.12
10   MINT PATTIES                 72       466.56    $64.08
11   PEANUT BRITTLE               56      1413.76   $131.60
12
13   TOTAL                       468
14
15
16
17
18                   MEAN        93.6                 108.36
19                MINIMUM          28                  50.12
20                MAXIMUM         200                    156
21   MANUAL CALCULATIONS
22      VARIANCE                         3568.64
23      STANDARD DEVIATION           59.73809504
24
25   LOTUS @ CALCULATIONS
26      VARIANCE             3568.64
27      STANDARD DEVIATION  59.73809504
```

Notice that Lotus 1-2-3's @ function calculations for the variance and the standard deviation result in exactly the same values as those calculated by the statistical formulas. But there is one important difference. The @ functions operate directly upon the relative units sold information without having to go through the intermediate step of calculating the squares of the differences from the mean. This ability to work directly upon what is known as *raw data* is one of the greatest powers of the @ functions, saving much time, effort, and worksheet space.

15. Copy the formulas in B26 and B27 to D26 and D27.

16. Save the worksheet replacing it over the CANDY.WK1 retrieved at the beginning of this module.

17. Turn to Module 53 to continue the learning sequence.

# Module 21

## FORMULAS - PRIMER

### DESCRIPTION

Most people find the greatest advantage of Lotus 1-2-3 is its ability to create simple worksheets quickly. In a matter of minutes you can design a worksheet containing both numbers and text and enter formulas to perform mathematical calculations on the numbers. Of course, Lotus 1-2-3 can do much more. But a simple column of numbers combined with descriptive text is the core of the Lotus 1-2-3 worksheet system. All the other capabilities of Lotus 1-2-3 are elaborations of this basic theme.

Lotus 1-2-3 lets you write basic addition, subtraction, division, and multiplication formulas using the mathematical operators plus ( + ), minus ( − ), divide (/), and times (*). In addition to these, the program also provides sophisticated formula writing capabilities with the power of Lotus 1-2-3's @ functions.

### APPLICATIONS

Lotus 1-2-3 is used by many people for a variety of "real world" applications. In fact, nearly one-third of all the users are from the scientific community. However, the largest user group is the business community. Lotus 1-2-3 has faithfully served the needs of the financial side of business since the program was developed. The program's ability to make accounting analysis worksheets of all types an easy task has earned it a reputation for usefulness which is the envy of many other software makers. The following tables describe the basic mathematical operators and some of the most frequently used Lotus 1-2-3 @ functions:

| OPERATOR | DESCRIPTION | TYPICAL FORM |
|:---:|:---|:---:|
| + | TO ADD TWO CELLS TOGETHER | + B8 + B25 |
| − | TO SUBTRACT ONE CELL FROM ANOTHER | + B8 − B25 |
| / | TO DIVIDE ONE CELL BY ANOTHER | + B8 / B25 |
| * | TO MULTIPLY ONE CELL BY ANOTHER | + B8 * B25 |

| @ FORM | THE LOTUS FORMULA: |
|---|---|
| @COUNT(list) | COUNTS THE NUMBER OF ARGUMENT VALUES |
| @SUM(list) | ADDS TOGETHER ALL THE ARGUMENT VALUES |
| @AVG(list) | AVERAGES THE NUMBER OF ARGUMENT VALUES |
| @MIN(list) | FINDS AND DISPLAYS THE MINIMUM ARGUMENT VALUE |
| @MAX(list) | FINDS AND DISPLAYS THE MAXIMUM ARGUMENT VALUE |
| @STD(list) | FINDS THE STANDARD DEVIATION OF ALL THE ARGUMENT VALUES |
| @VAR(list) | FINDS THE VARIANCE OF ALL THE ARGUMENT VALUES |

*Basic Lotus 1-2-3 Mathematical Operators*

Use the @ functions to create "short-form" Lotus 1-2-3 formulas that perform the same operations as the basic mathematical operators.

There are many other Lotus 1-2-3 @ "short-forms" available. This chart lists and describes the most common ones used to create statistical formulas. All these formulas use what are called *arguments*. This is a mathematical term defined as the independent variables upon whose value a function depends. For example, in the first @ form listed in the chart, @COUNT is the function whose value depends upon the arguments contained in the (list).

**TYPICAL OPERATION**

1.   From the worksheet READY screen create a worksheet using the following information:

The following worksheet information is for a chart of the five most commonly purchased items from a drugstore candy department.

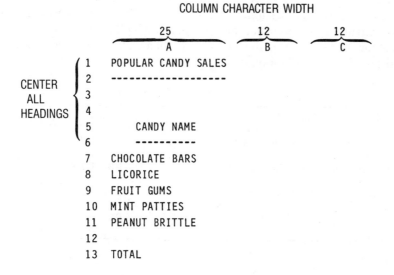

Lotus 1-2-3 interprets alphabetical characters, numbers, and punctuation marks as text when preceded by a single or double quote, circumflex, or backslash. Without one of these characters, Lotus 1-2-3 interprets numbers as values and the symbols +, –, *, and / as mathematical operators.

The worksheet now contains text and is ready for you to enter numerical information.

2. Move the cell pointer to B7 and type the following numbers. Move the cell pointer down one row at a time for each number. Press **Return** after you type each number.

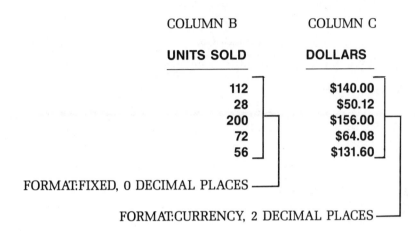

| COLUMN B | COLUMN C |
|----------|----------|
| **UNITS SOLD** | **DOLLARS** |
| 112 | $140.00 |
| 28 | $50.12 |
| 200 | $156.00 |
| 72 | $64.08 |
| 56 | $131.60 |

FORMAT:FIXED, 0 DECIMAL PLACES

FORMAT:CURRENCY, 2 DECIMAL PLACES

**NOTE**

Numbers and mathematical operators are interpreted correctly when not preceded with a quotation mark, backslash, or circumflex.

Notice that as you type the numbers, the worksheet condition block changes from READY to VALUE. Just as the LABEL display indicates that you are typing text, the VALUE display in the worksheet condition block indicates that you are typing numbers into the worksheet.

3. Move the cell pointer to A18 and type **MEAN** and then press **Return**.

"MEAN" is a mathematical term for the average of all numerical values.

4. Move the cell pointer to A19 and type **MINIMUM** and then press **Return**.

5. Move the cell pointer to A20 and type **MAXIMUM** and then press **Return**.

6. Move the cell pointer to A18 and type **/RL**.

7. Type **R** and then highlight cells A18 through A20 to move their contents over to the right margin of the column.

8. Move the cell pointer to C3, insert a blank column and then set that column's width to 12 characters.

9.  Type the following textual information into the referenced cells:

| Cell | Text |
|------|------|
| C3 | **SQUARES OF** |
| C4 | **DIFFERENCE** |
| C5 | **FROM MEAN** |
| C6 | ———————— |

10. Center the text in columns C3 through C6.

11. Move the cell pointer to E3 and set its column width to 12 characters.

Notice the following screen:

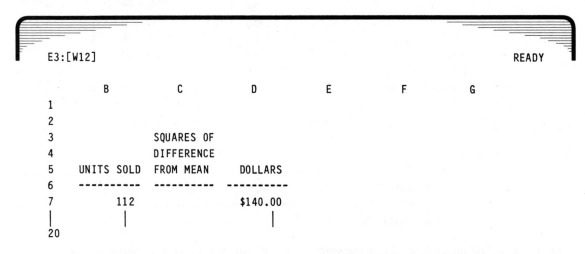

```
 E3:[W12]                                                        READY

             B           C           D          E        F       G
     1
     2
     3                SQUARES OF
     4                DIFFERENCE
     5    UNITS SOLD  FROM MEAN     DOLLARS
     6    ----------  ----------    ----------
     7       112                    $140.00
     |        |                        |
    20
```

When you move the cell pointer beyond the displayed right margin, the screen shifts to the left and redisplays the worksheet with column B at the left margin. This happens because Lotus 1-2-3 can only display an 80-character-wide screen at one time. When the cell pointer moves beyond this limit (either to the left or to the right), Lotus 1-2-3 automatically shifts the worksheet. The left margin starts at a column location which displays an 80-column screen, including the cell pointer location.

12. Copy the information contained in cells C3 through C6 to cells E3 through E6.

13. Move the cell pointer to cell B13 and type **+** (plus sign).

14. Move the cell pointer to cell B11 and type another **+** (plus sign).

Notice that the cell pointer returns to cell B13 automatically. Every time you type a mathematical operator into a worksheet formula, the cell pointer returns to the cell where the final result of the formula is to appear in the worksheet.

15. Move the cell pointer to cell B10 and type **+** (plus sign).

16. Continue moving the cell pointer up one row at a time (from cell B9 and B8) until all the cells have been typed into the formula. Be sure to type a plus sign ( + ) between each cell reference coordinate.

17. Move the cell pointer to the last cell to be included in the formula (cell B7). Since this is the final cell, do not type another plus sign.

18. Press **Return** to accept the formula.

Lotus 1-2-3 performs the calculation automatically and displays the result in the cell location of the formula.

The screen displays the following:

```
B13:(F0)[W12] +B11+B10+B9+B8+B7                              READY

                 A              B         C          D
  1    POPULAR CANDY SALES
  2    -------------------
  3                                   SQUARES OF
  4                                   DIFFERENCE
  5         CANDY NAME       UNITS SOLD FROM MEAN   DOLLARS
  6         ----------       ---------- ---------   -------
  7    CHOCOLATE BARS            112                $140.00
  8    LICORICE                   28                 $50.12
  9    FRUIT GUMS                200                $156.00
 10    MINT PATTIES               72                 $64.08
 11    PEANUT BRITTLE             56                $131.60
 12
 13    TOTAL                     468
 18                 MEAN
 19             MINIMUM
 20             MAXIMUM
```

The worksheet added all the units sold value for the candy and put the total into cell B13. Notice that the formula appears beside the cell reference block and that the worksheet returns to the READY mode once the total appears.

Writing formulas by typing a mathematical operator between each cell is like using long division when you have a calculator. The process of including every cell in the formula takes a long time when you have many cells to process. Fortunately, Lotus 1-2-3 can operate on numbers using a much shorter method.

Use the following short-cut formula to add the numbers in the column.

1.  Move the cell pointer to cell B13 and type @**SUM(**.

2.  Move the cell pointer to cell B11 and type . (a period).

Notice that Lotus 1-2-3 inserts two periods even though you typed only one.

3.  Move the cell pointer to cell B7.

Notice how Lotus 1-2-3 highlights all the cells in the addition formula. This visual aid helps you see which cells are included in the formula. It also eliminates the need to keep track of which cell references you have already typed into the formula.

4.  Type **)** (a close parentheses symbol) and then press **Return**.

The following screen displays:

```
 B13:(F0)[W12] @SUM(B11..B7)                                    READY


              A              B       C          D
   1      POPULAR CANDY SALES
   2      --------------------
   3                                 SQUARES OF
   4                                 DIFFERENCE
   5          CANDY NAME        UNITS SOLD FROM MEAN    DOLLARS
   6          ----------        ---------- ---------    -------
   7      CHOCOLATE BARS           112                  $140.00
   8      LICORICE                  28                   $50.12
   9      FRUIT GUMS               200                  $156.00
  10      MINT PATTIES              72                   $64.08
  11      PEANUT BRITTLE            56                  $131.60
  12
  13      TOTAL                    468
  |
  18                    MEAN
  19                MINIMUM
  20                MAXIMUM
```

Compare the ease of this method with the one-cell-at-a-time method. Lotus 1-2-3 has many more "short-cut" formula forms. These shorter forms use special code words and symbols to tell the program what to do.

The order in which you type these words and symbols is known as *syntax*. Mathematical syntax tells Lotus 1-2-3 how to process the highlighted cells.

The @ symbol formula form is a powerful Lotus 1-2-3 tool. However, you can also perform these functions using the basic four mathematical operators of addition, subtraction, multiplication, and division.

> **NOTE**
> The @ functions are used a great deal in the world of finance. The ease of setting up worksheets that automatically perform mathematical calculations that would require hours on an adding machine is one reason why Lotus 1-2-3 is so popular in the business world.

To write a formula to get the *mean* (the average) of the units sold, and dollar values perform the following steps:

1. Move the cell pointer to B18 and type **@SUM(**.

2. Move the cell pointer to B11 and type **.** (a period).

3. Move the cell pointer to B7 and type **)**.

4. Type **/**.

This is Lotus 1-2-3's symbol for division. The value you type after this symbol is the divisor. The sum of all values between cells B16 and B7 is divided by this value.

5. Type **5** and then press **Return**.

Look at the following screen:

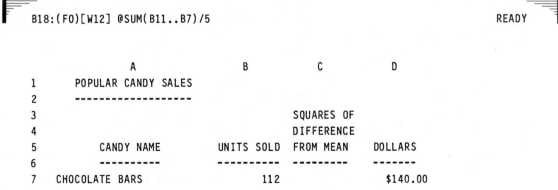

```
  B18:(F0)[W12] @SUM(B11..B7)/5                              READY


                    A              B          C          D
    1      POPULAR CANDY SALES
    2      ------------------
    3                                      SQUARES OF
    4                                      DIFFERENCE
    5           CANDY NAME        UNITS SOLD FROM MEAN    DOLLARS
    6           ----------       ---------- ---------    -------
    7    CHOCOLATE BARS               112              $140.00
```

| | | | |
|---|---|---:|---:|
| 8 | LICORICE | 28 | $50.12 |
| 9 | FRUIT GUMS | 200 | $156.00 |
| 10 | MINT PATTIES | 72 | $64.08 |
| 11 | PEANUT BRITTLE | 56 | $131.60 |
| 12 | | | |
| 13 | TOTAL | 468 | |

| | | | |
|---|---|---:|---:|
| 18 | MEAN | 93.6 | |
| 19 | MINIMUM | | |
| 20 | MAXIMUM | | |

Lotus 1-2-3 automatically adds all the values for the units sold values and divides the result by 5.

6. Copy the formula in B18 to cell D18.

Perform the following procedures to write a formula that subtracts the mean (average) of the units-sold values from each individual value and multiplies the result times itself (squares of the differences from the mean):

1. Move the cell pointer to C7 and type **(**.

2. Move the cell pointer to B7 and type **−** (a minus sign).

3. Move the cell pointer to B18, type **)** and then type **\***.

4. Type **(** and then move the cell pointer to B7.

5. Type **−** and then move the cell pointer to B18.

6. Type **)** and then press **Return**.

Notice the following on the monitor:

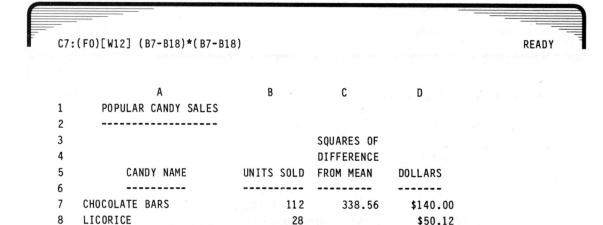

| 11 | PEANUT BRITTLE | | 56 | | $131.60 |
| 12 | | | | | |
| 13 | TOTAL | | 468 | | |
| | | | | | |
| 18 | | MEAN | 93.6 | | 108.36 |
| 19 | | MINIMUM | | | |
| 20 | | MAXIMUM | | | |

Lotus 1-2-3 performs what the formula asks it to do. The mean is subtracted from each individual units sold value and the result is multiplied times itself.

7.   Copy the formula in cell C7 to cells C8 through C11.

8.   Move the cell pointer to C8 and study the cell contents block on the display:

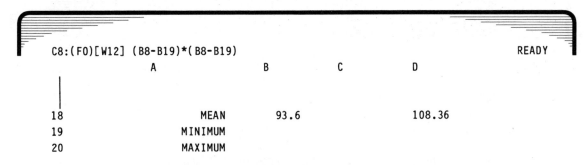

| | A | B | C | D |
|---|---|---|---|---|
| 18 | MEAN | 93.6 | | 108.36 |
| 19 | MINIMUM | | | |
| 20 | MAXIMUM | | | |

Top line: `C8:(F0)[W12] (B8-B19)*(B8-B19)`      READY

### CAUTION

Notice that the original formula has changed from (B7 – B18)*(B7 – B18) to (B8-B19)*(B8-B19). While the individual candy value is correct, the new formula subtracts the minimum value (B19) from it instead of the mean (B18). Remember, Lotus 1-2-3 uses relative cell coordinates to locate the cells upon which the mathematical operators work. When necessary, you must specify otherwise by freezing a location for a cell value.

To freeze the value for the mean (cell B18):

1.   Move the cell pointer to C7 and type **(**.

2.   Move the cell pointer to B7 and type **–** (a minus sign).

3.   Move the cell pointer to B18 and press **F4**.

Notice that Lotus 1-2-3 automatically inserts dollar signs ($) in front of the column and row number references. Pressing F4 saves you the time it takes to type the dollar signs on the keyboard. Remember, a dollar sign preceding a column and/or row number reference tells the Lotus 1-2-3 formula to use the value contained in the specified cell location only and no other.

4. Type **)** and then type **\***.

5. Type **(** and then move the cell pointer to B7.

6. Type **–** and then move the cell pointer to B18.

7. Press **F4** to insert the dollar signs.

8. Type **)** and then press **Return**.

9. Copy the formula in cell C7 to cells C8 through C11.

10. Move the cell pointer to C8.

Notice the following on the monitor:

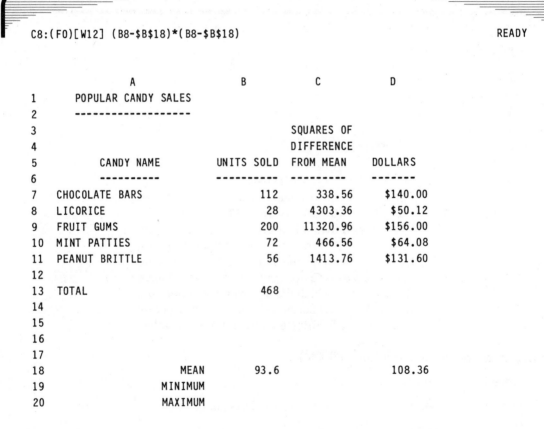

```
C8:(F0)[W12] (B8-$B$18)*(B8-$B$18)                              READY
```

|    | A | B | C | D |
|----|---|---|---|---|
| | | | SQUARES OF | |
| | | | DIFFERENCE | |
| | CANDY NAME | UNITS SOLD | FROM MEAN | DOLLARS |
| 1 | POPULAR CANDY SALES | | | |
| 2 | ------------------- | | | |
| 3 | | | SQUARES OF | |
| 4 | | | DIFFERENCE | |
| 5 | CANDY NAME | UNITS SOLD | FROM MEAN | DOLLARS |
| 6 | ---------- | ---------- | --------- | ------- |
| 7 | CHOCOLATE BARS | 112 | 338.56 | $140.00 |
| 8 | LICORICE | 28 | 4303.36 | $50.12 |
| 9 | FRUIT GUMS | 200 | 11320.96 | $156.00 |
| 10 | MINT PATTIES | 72 | 466.56 | $64.08 |
| 11 | PEANUT BRITTLE | 56 | 1413.76 | $131.60 |
| 12 | | | | |
| 13 | TOTAL | 468 | | |
| 14 | | | | |
| 15 | | | | |
| 16 | | | | |
| 17 | | | | |
| 18 | MEAN | 93.6 | | 108.36 |
| 19 | MINIMUM | | | |
| 20 | MAXIMUM | | | |

Lotus 1-2-3 now uses the individual units-sold values and correctly divides them by the mean for every formula in cells C7 through C11.

11.  Move the cell pointer to E7, type **(** and then move the cell pointer to D7 and type **–**.

12.  Move the cell pointer to D18, press **F4** and then type **)**.

13.  Type **^** .

**NOTE**

Since the value for the difference from the mean is multiplied by itself, *squaring* this value accomplishes the same thing. The caret ( ^ ) symbol, when used in a formula in any place other than at the beginning of the line, tells Lotus 1-2-3 to raise the previous value to the power indicated after the symbol.

14.  Type **2** and then press **Return**.

Lotus 1-2-3 performs the multiplication calculation just as if you had typed the formula the way you did for the units-sold values.

15.  Copy the formula in E7 to cells E8 through E11.

Notice that Lotus 1-2-3 uses the correct mean value for all copied formulas because pressing the F4 key inserted the dollar signs in front of the mean cell references.

Many formulas written using the four basic mathematical operators of addition, subtraction, multiplication, and division use the Lotus 1-2-3 @ formula short form.

1.  Move the cell pointer to B18 and type @**AVG(**.

2.  Move the cell pointer to B11 and type **.** (a period).

3.  Move the cell pointer to B7, type **)** and then press **Return**.

Compare this formula for finding the mean with the one you previously wrote (@SUM(B11. .B7)/5). Using the @AVG version saves several key strokes. You also do not need to know the number of units-sold values in the worksheet column.

4.  Copy the formula in B18 to cell D18.

Notice that the @AVG values for the mean change to two decimal places. This happens because any @ function uses two decimal places as a default value.

5.  Move the cell pointer to B19 and type @**MIN(**.

6.  Move the cell pointer to B11 and type **.** (a period).

7.  Move the cell pointer to B7 and type **)** then press **Return**.

8.  Move the cell pointer to B20 and type @**MAX(**.

9.  Move the cell pointer to B11 and type **.** (a period).

10. Move the cell pointer to B7 and type **)**.

11. Copy the mean, maximum, and minimum formulas from cells B18 through B20 to cells D18 through D20.

The screen displays the following:

```
  B18:(F0)[W12] @AVG(B11..B7)                                    READY


                    A              B        C          D
     1      POPULAR CANDY SALES
     2      -------------------
     3                                     SQUARES OF
     4                                     DIFFERENCE
     5           CANDY NAME        UNITS SOLD  FROM MEAN   DOLLARS
     6           ----------        ----------  ----------  -------
     7      CHOCOLATE BARS            112        338.56    $140.00
     8      LICORICE                   28       4303.36     $50.12
     9      FRUIT GUMS                200      11320.96    $156.00
    10      MINT PATTIES               72        466.56     $64.08
    11      PEANUT BRITTLE             56       1413.76    $131.60
    12
    13      TOTAL                     468
    14
    15
    16
    17
    18              MEAN             93.6                   108.36
    19           MINIMUM              28                     50.12
    20           MAXIMUM             200                       156
```

12. To eliminate the need to recreate this worksheet, you may want to save it using the steps outlined in Module 18, the next module in the recommended learning sequence.

# Module 22

## GRAPH OPTIONS B&W, COLOR

### DESCRIPTION

Use the GRAPH OPTIONS B&W, COLOR commands to select the type of display monitor used to view graphs.

The GRAPH OPTIONS B&W, COLOR commands are located and used from the worksheet READY screen by typing a / (slash) and then typing the first letters of the following menu titles:

```
MENU TITLES:              USE AND USE REQUIREMENT:

Graph Options Color       Display graph in color
Graph Options B&W         Display graph in black and white
```

### APPLICATIONS

When using a color or black and white monitor, use the GRAPH OPTIONS B&W, COLOR commands to select either monitor type.

### TYPICAL OPERATION

1. Retrieve the CANDY worksheet saved in Module 28.

2. Use the "CANDYG6" graph.

3. Type **/GV** and look at the following display:

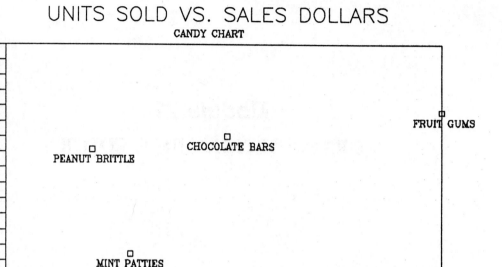

UNITS SOLD VS. SALES DOLLARS

4. Press **Esc** and then type **OBV**.

If you have a color monitor, notice that the graph is now displayed in monochrome.

5. Quit the worksheet.

6. Turn to Module 31 to continue the learning sequence.

# Module 23
## GRAPH NAME

**DESCRIPTION**

Once a graph type and the cell information used to plot the graph are marked, the graph must be named to save the specifications. Naming a graph IS NOT the same thing as saving a graph for printing using Lotus 1-2-3's Graph Program. All you save with "Name" are the parameters set in the worksheet (graph type, data ranges, etc.). You can have multiple named graphs with one worksheet. These parameters are recalled while you are in the worksheet to display the data as specified. Again, you cannot print a graph which has only been named and not saved.

The GRAPH NAME command is located and used from the worksheet READY screen by typing a / (slash) and then typing the first letters of the following menu titles:

```
MENU TITLES:              USE AND USE REQUIREMENT:

Graph Name                Create/use a name for a graph
Graph Name Use            Use the graph under specified name Specify name
Graph Name Create         Name the current graph in worksheet Specify name
Graph Name Delete         Delete a named graph  Specify name
Graph Name Reset          Delete all named graphs
```

**APPLICATIONS**

The GRAPH NAME command is used to name a set of graph specifications. This command is very useful when creating a series of graphs that contain incremental information. For example, you may create a graph for sales dollars over a period of months. Further refining the graph, you might add expense dollars to the worksheet and create another graph that reflects this information in addition to the information contained in the first graph. By naming each graph, you perform two functions:

- The graph is permanently connected with the worksheet from which the information was used to create it.
- The graph can be recalled by name any time you want to view it, create a graph .PIC print file or modify the parameters used to create it.

**TYPICAL OPERATION**

1. Retrieve the CANDY worksheet saved in Module 20.

2. Type **/GT** to select the type of graph.

3. Type **X** to choose the XY form of graph.

4. Type **X** to set the X-axis information range.

5. Move the cell pointer to B7 and type . (a period).

6. Move the cell pointer to B11 and press **Return**.

7. Type **A** to set the Y-axis information range.

8. Move the cell pointer to D7 and type . (a period).

9. Move the cell pointer to D11, press **Return** and type **N**.

10. Move the highlighter to the Create menu choice.

Look at the following screen:

```
A1:[W25] 'POPULAR CANDY SALES                                    MENU
Use   Create   Delete   Reset
Save the current graph as a named graph


                A               B          C           D
    1    POPULAR CANDY SALES
    2    -------------------
    3                                    SQUARES OF
    4                                    DIFFERENCE
    5           CANDY NAME        UNITS SOLD  FROM MEAN   DOLLARS
    6           ----------       ----------  ---------   -------
    7    CHOCOLATE BARS               112       338.56    $140.00
    8    FRUIT GUMS                   200     11320.96    $156.00
    9    LICORICE                      28      4303.36     $50.12
   10    MINT PATTIES                  72       466.56     $64.08
   11    PEANUT BRITTLE                56      1413.76    $131.60
   12
   13    TOTAL                        468

   20              MAXIMUM           200                    156
```

Use the Lotus 1-2-3 Name function to name graphs, delete graphs, and retrieve previously named graphs.

11. Press **Return**.

12. Type **CANDYG1** for the graph name; then press **Return**.

13. Type **Q** to quit the graph function and save the worksheet using the replace option.

14. Turn to Module 33 to continue the learning sequence.

# Module 24

# GRAPH OPTIONS DATA-LABELS

## DESCRIPTION

In addition to legends, especially on an XY graph, creating a name for each data point conveys helpful information about the graph. Use the GRAPH OPTIONS DATA-LABELS commands to create identifiers for each point plotted on the graph.

The GRAPH OPTIONS DATA-LABELS commands are located and used from the worksheet READY screen by typing a / (slash) and then typing the first letters of the following menu titles:

```
MENU TITLES:              USE AND USE REQUIREMENT:


Graph Options
   Data-Labels           Create labels for data points
Graph Options
   Data-Labels A         Create label for A data points Type label
Graph Options
   Data-Labels B         Create label for B data points Type label
Graph Options
   Data-Labels C         Create label for C data points Type label
Graph Options
   Data-Labels D         Create label for D data points Type label
Graph Options
   Data-Labels E         Create label for E data points Type label
Graph Options
   Data-Labels F         Create label for F data points Type label
Graph Options
   Data-Labels Quit      Quit data-label menu
Graph Options Quit       Quit Options menu
```

## APPLICATIONS

Use the GRAPH OPTIONS DATA-LABELS commands to add a descriptive name to each data point plotted on a graph. These commands are typically used when plotting data points that use the same units of measure, such as plotting different types of business expenses (all expressed in dollars). Each individual data point for expenses (data types A through F) could be labeled with a different name to denote the type of expense, such as RENT, UTILITIES, INSURANCE, LABOR. They are helpful in differentiating data points on line graphs.

**TYPICAL OPERATION**

1.  Retrieve the CANDY worksheet saved in Module 27.

2.  Use the CANDYG3 graph.

3.  Type **OD**. Study the following display:

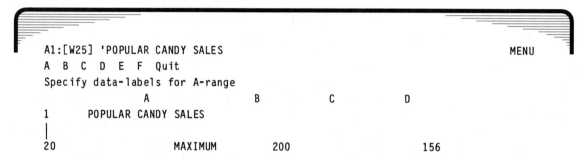

```
A1:[W25] 'POPULAR CANDY SALES                                          MENU
A  B  C  D  E  F  Quit
Specify data-labels for A-range
                    A              B          C          D
1        POPULAR CANDY SALES
|
20                   MAXIMUM        200                  156
```

Just as with legends, data labels must be specified for each data range in the graph.

4.  Press **Return** to select the A range.

5.  Move the cell pointer to A7 and type **.** (a period).

Data labels are ranges of information tied to each numerical data point—in this case, the candy names.

6.  Move the cell pointer to A11 and press **Return**. Look at the following screen:

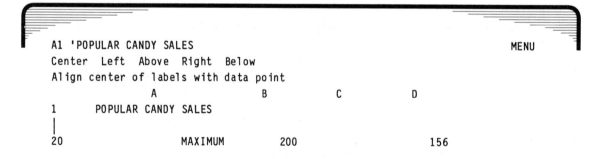

```
A1  'POPULAR CANDY SALES                                               MENU
Center  Left  Above  Right  Below
Align center of labels with data point
                    A              B          C          D
1        POPULAR CANDY SALES
|
20                   MAXIMUM        200                  156
```

Lotus 1-2-3 can position data-labels in five different areas around the data points.

7.  Type **R** to position the data-labels to the right of each data point.

8.  Type **Q** twice and then type **V**. Look at the graph displayed:

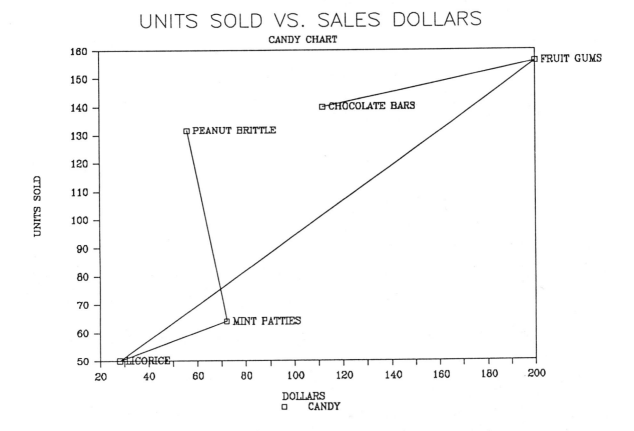

Notice that some of the candy names overwrite the data points or are too far to the right to be read. Good graph design includes the changing of detail information so that the final result is a graph that displays information in a readable form.

9.  Type **OD** and then type **A** and press **Return**.

10. Type **B** to position the data-labels below the data points.

11. Type **Q** twice and then press **V**. Notice the change in the following graph:

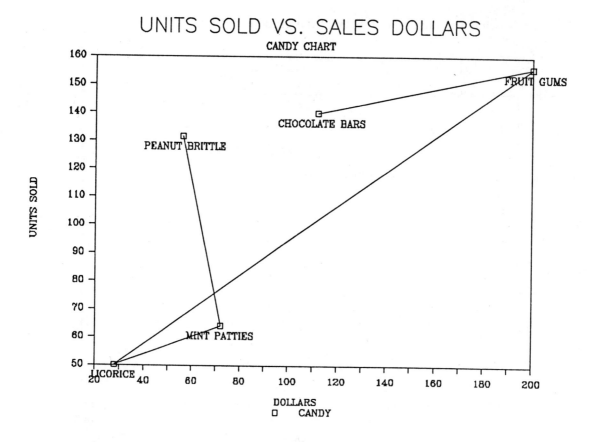

12. Press **Esc** and name the graph CANDYG4.

13. Type **Q** to quit the graph functions and then save the worksheet using the replace option.

14. The learning sequence continues with Module 25.

# Module 25
## GRAPH OPTIONS FORMAT

**DESCRIPTION**

Lotus 1-2-3 allows full formatting of graphic displays. Use the GRAPH OPTIONS FORMAT command to set the entire graph or selected data types to display the worksheet information with lines, symbols, or both lines and symbols.

The GRAPH OPTIONS FORMAT commands are located and used from the worksheet READY screen by typing / (slash) and then typing the first letters of the following menu titiles:

| MENU TITLES | USE AND USE REQUIREMENT: |
|---|---|
| Graph Options Format | Set display format for graphs |
| Graph Options Format Graph | Set display format for entire graph |
| Graph Options Format Graph Lines | Display lines connecting data points |
| Graph Options Format Graph Symbols | Display symbols for data points |
| Graph Options Format Graph Both | Display lines connecting and symbols for data points |
| Graph Options Format Graph Neither | Do not display lines connecting or symbols for data points |
| Graph Options Format A | Set display format for A range only |
| Graph Options Format A Lines | Display lines connecting data points |
| Graph Options Format A Symbols | Display symbols for data points |
| Graph Options Format A Both | Display lines connecting and symbols for data points |
| Graph Options Format A Neither | Do not display lines connecting or symbols for data points |
| Graph Options Format B | Set display format for B range only |
| Graph Options Format B Lines | Display lines connecting data points |

MENU TITLES:                    USE AND USE REQUIREMENT:

Graph Options Format B
  Symbols                       Display symbols for data points
Graph Options Format B
  Both                          Display lines connecting and symbols for data points
Graph Options Format B
  Neither                       Do not display lines connecting or symbols for data point:
Graph Options Format C         Set display format for C range only
Graph Options Format C
  Lines                         Display lines connecting data points
Graph Options Format C
  Symbols                       Display symbols for data points
Graph Options Format C
  Both                          Display lines connecting and symbols for data points
Graph Options Format C
  Neither                       Do not display lines connecting or symbols for data points
Graph Options Format D         Set display format for D range only
Graph Options Format D
  Lines                         Display lines connecting data points
Graph Options Format D
  Symbols                       Display symbols for data pints
Graph Options Format D
  Both                          Display lines connecting and symbols for data points
Graph Options Format D
  Neither                       Do not display lines connecting or symbols for data points
Graph Options Format E         Set display format for E range only
Graph Options Format E
  Lines                         Display lines connecting data points
Graph Options Format E
  Symbols                       Display symbols for data points
Graph Options Format E
  Both                          Display lines connecting and symbols for data points
Graph Options Format E
  Neither                       Do not display lines connecting or symbols for data points
Graph Options Format F         Set display format for F range only
Graph Options Format F
  Lines                         Display lines connecting data points
Graph Options Format F
  Symbols                       Display symbols for data points

```
MENU TITLES:              USE AND USE REQUIREMENT:

Graph Options Format F
  Both                    Display lines connecting and symbols for data points
Graph Options Format F
  Neither                 Do not display lines connecting or symbols for data points
Graph Options Format
  Quit                    Quit format menu
```

## APPLICATIONS

Use the GRAPH OPTIONS FORMAT commands to display XY and bar graphs with symbols, with lines, with lines and symbols, or without either lines or symbols. This command is used primarily to display graphs with formatting symbols to make reading the information they contain easier. If a graph is found to be more useful with symbols and/or lines, a .PIC graph printing file can be created and the graph printed with them.

## TYPICAL OPERATION

1.  Retrieve the CANDY worksheet saved in Module 24.

2.  Use the "CANDYG4" graph.

3.  Type **OF** and look at the following display:

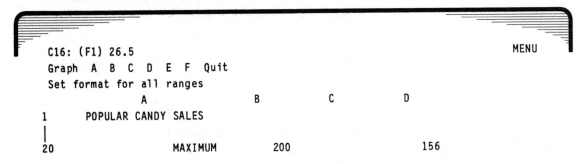

```
C16: (F1) 26.5                                              MENU
Graph  A  B  C  D  E  F  Quit
Set format for all ranges
                  A           B        C        D
1        POPULAR CANDY SALES
|
20                    MAXIMUM      200              156
```

The Format choice is used to set the graph so that it displays the worksheet information with lines, symbols, or both. Each display format can be set for all data ranges or for each one individually.

4.  Type **G** to set the graphic display for all ranges.

5.  Type **S** to set all ranges to symbols.

6.  Type **Q** twice to return to the main graph menu.

7. Type **V** and notice the following graph:

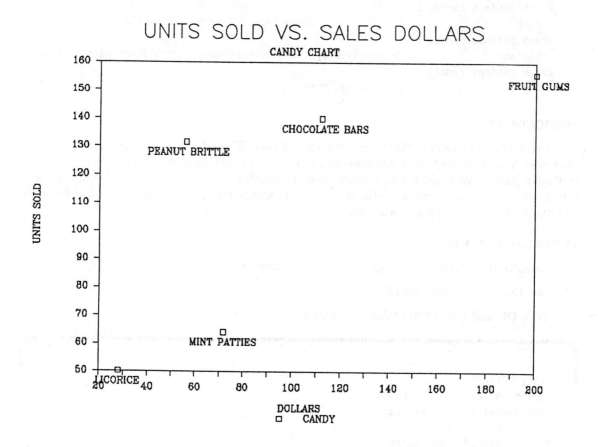

UNITS SOLD VS. SALES DOLLARS

CANDY CHART

Notice that the lines have disappeared. Each data point is much easier to see using symbols instead of lines.

8. Press **Esc** and name the graph CANDYG5.

9. Type **Q** to quit the graphs menu and then save the worksheet using the replace option.

10. The learning sequence continues with Module 26.

# Module 26

## GRAPH OPTIONS GRID

**DESCRIPTION**

Graphs can sometimes be difficult to read, especially if the data points are very close together. A grid can be set using the GRAPH OPTIONS GRID command that makes reference to the respective scales an easy task.

The GRAPH OPTIONS GRID commands are located and used from the worksheet READY screen by typing a / (slash) and then typing the first letters of the following menu titles:

```
MENU TITLES:              USE AND USE REQUIREMENT:


Graph Options Grid        Display grids on graph
Graph Options Grid
   Horizontal             Set horizontal grid
Graph Options Grid
   Vertical               Set vertical grid
Graph Options Grid
   Both                   Set both vertical and horizontal grids
Graph Options Grid
   Clear                  Erase grid display
```

**APPLICATIONS**

Use the GRAPH OPTIONS GRID commands to display XY and bar graphs with a horizontal grid, vertical grid, or both horizontal and vertical grids. As with the GRAPH OPTIONS FORMAT commands, these commands are used to display a graph with grids, making information on the graphs easier to read.

**TYPICAL OPERATION**

1. Retrieve the CANDY worksheet saved in Module 25.

2. Use the "CANDYG5" graph.

3. Type **OG** and look at the following display:

Module 26

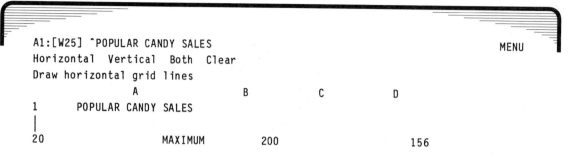

A1:[W25] ^POPULAR CANDY SALES                                        MENU
Horizontal   Vertical   Both   Clear
Draw horizontal grid lines
                    A              B         C         D
1        POPULAR CANDY SALES
|
20                  MAXIMUM        200                 156

4.  Type **B** to set both horizontal and vertical grids for the graphic display.

5.  Type **Q** twice to return to the main graph menu.

6.  Type **V** and notice the following graph:

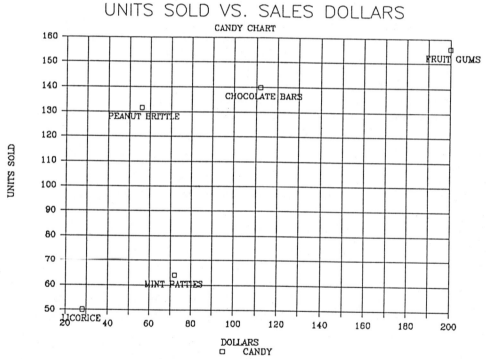

Notice that vertical and horizontal lines appear on the display. Referencing each data point to the X and Y scale is much easier.

7.  Press **Esc** and then type **OGC** to clear the grids from the graph.

8.  Type **Q** to quit the graphs menu and then save the worksheet using the replace option.

9.  Turn to Module 28 to continue the learning sequence.

# Module 27

## GRAPH OPTIONS LEGEND

### DESCRIPTION

A legend is a descriptive comment that explains what the data points on a graph represent. Use the GRAPH OPTIONS LEGEND commands to create legends for one or more of the data types plotted on the graph.

The GRAPH OPTIONS LEGEND commands are located and used from the worksheet READY screen by typing a / (slash) and then typing the first letters of the following menu titles:

```
MENU TITLES:              USE AND USE REQUIREMENT:

Graph Options
  Legend                  Create data legends
Graph Options
  Legend A                Create legend for A range data (Type legend)
Graph Options
  Legend B                Create legend for B range data (Type legend)
Graph Options
  Legend C                Create legend for C range data (Type legend)
Graph Options
  Legend D                Create legend for D range data (Type legend)
Graph Options
  Legend E                Create legend for E range data (Type legend)
Graph Options
  Legend F                Create legend for F range data (Type legend)
```

### APPLICATIONS

Use the GRAPH OPTIONS LEGEND commands to add a descriptive name to the information plotted on a graph. Legends are different from data labels. A legend denotes the category of data being plotted on the graph. For example, a typical business graph might have sales, cost of sales, and operating expenses plotted on a bar graph. These three items are all expressed in dollars and by assigning data legends to each category of the information the user can differentiate between the categories of dollars being represented on the graph.

**TYPICAL OPERATION**

1.  Retrieve the CANDY worksheet saved in Module 29.

2.  Type **/GNU**.

3.  Move the highlighter to CANDYG2 and press **Return**.

4.  Type **OL** and look at the following screen:

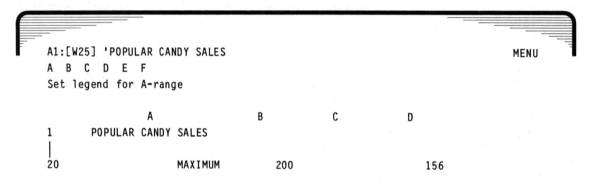

```
A1:[W25] 'POPULAR CANDY SALES                                       MENU
A  B  C  D  E  F
Set legend for A-range


                A                 B          C          D
1          POPULAR CANDY SALES
|
20                   MAXIMUM        200              156
```

You set legends for each type of information in a graph. Since the CANDYG2 graph is an XY graph, each data point is actually the combined coordinate location of the X and A (A being the Y axis) data ranges. Therefore, creating a legend for the A range creates the same legend for the X range.

5.  Press **Return** to create the A range legend.

6.  Type **CANDY** and then press **Return**.

7.  Type **Q** and then type **V**.

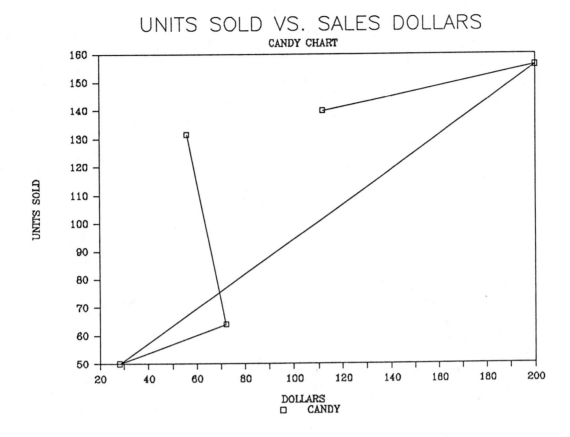

UNITS SOLD VS. SALES DOLLARS

Notice that the range legend appears with the symbol used to denote each type of candy's location on the graph.

8.  Press **Esc.**

9.  Name this graph CANDYG3 and quit the graphs menu.

10.  Save the worksheet using the replace option.

11.  Turn to Module 22 to continue the learning sequence.

# Module 28

## GRAPH OPTIONS SCALE

**DESCRIPTION**

One of the nicest features of the graph capabilities of Lotus 1-2-3 is the ability to reset the scale for a graph to make it much more clear and understandable. Graphs can sometimes be difficult to read if scales are not detailed enough to delineate the various data points. Use the GRAPH OPTIONS SCALE commands to manually set the scale and the skip interval between scale values for both the X and Y axis of a graph.

The GRAPH OPTIONS SCALE commands are located and used from the worksheet READY screen by typing a / (slash) and then typing the first letters of the following menu titles:

```
MENU TITLES:              USE AND USE REQUIREMENT:

Graph Options Scale       Set scale for X-axis and Y-axis on graph
Graph Options Scale Y
  Scale                   Set Y-axis scale
Graph Options Scale Y
  Scale Automatic         Let Lotus automatically scale based upon Y-axis values
Graph Options Scale Y
  Scale Manual            Manually scale Y-axis
Graph Options Scale Y
  Scale Lower             Set lower limit of Y-axis values
Graph Options Scale Y
  Scale Upper             Set upper limit of Y-axis values
Graph Options Scale Y
  Scale Format            Set display format for Y-axis scale numbers
Graph Options Scale Y
  Scale Format Fixed      # decimal places
Graph Options Scale Y
  Scale Format
  Scientific              Scientific notation
Graph Options Scale Y
  Scale Format Currency   # decimal places for $'s
Graph Options Scale Y
  Scale Format General    Default toggle
```

| MENU TITLES: | USE AND USE REQUIREMENT: |
|---|---|
| Graph Options Scale Y<br>Scale Format +/- | +/- graph |
| Graph Options Scale Y<br>Scale Format Percent | # decimal places for % |
| Graph Options Scale Y<br>Scale Format Date | Set date display |
| Graph Options Scale Y<br>Scale Format Date 1<br>(DD-MM-YY) | Display date as noted |
| Graph Options Scale Y<br>Scale Format Date 2<br>(DD-MM) | Display date as noted |
| Graph Options Scale Y<br>Scale Format Date 3<br>(MM-YY) | Display date as noted |
| Graph Options Scale Y<br>Scale Format Date 4<br>(Long Int'l) | Display date as noted |
| Graph Options Scale Y<br>Scale Format Date 5<br>(Short Int'l) | Display date as noted |
| Graph Options Scale Y<br>Scale Format Time 1<br>(HH:MM:SS AM/PM) | Display time as noted |
| Graph Options Scale Y<br>Scale Format Time 2<br>(HH:MM AM/PM) | Display time as noted |
| Graph Options Scale Y<br>Scale Format Time 3<br>(Long Int'l) | Display time as noted |
| Graph Options Scale Y<br>Scale Format Time 4<br>(Short Int'l) | Display time as noted |
| Graph Options Scale Y<br>Scale Format Text | Display formulas instead of values |
| Graph Options Scale Y<br>Scale Quit | Quit the Y-axis menu |
| Graph Options Scale X<br>Scale | Set X-axis scale |
| Graph Options Scale X<br>Scale Automatic | Let Lotus automatically scale based upon X-axis values |

MENU TITLES:              USE AND USE REQUIREMENT:

Graph Options Scale X
  Scale Manual            Manually scale X-axis
Graph Options Scale X
  Scale Lower             Set lower limit of X-axis values
Graph Options Scale X
  Scale Upper             Set upper limit of X-axis values
Graph Options Scale X
  Scale Format            Set display format for X-axis scale numbers
Graph Options Scale X
  Scale Format Fixed      # decimal places
Graph Options Scale X
  Scale Format
  Scientific              Scientific notation
Graph Options Scale X
  Scale Format
  Currency                # decimal places for $'s
Graph Options Scale X
  Scale Format General    Default toggle
Graph Options Scale X
  Scale Format +/-        +/- graph
Graph Options Scale X
Scale Format Percent      # decimal places for %
Graph Options Scale X
  Scale Format Date       Set date display
Graph Options Scale X
  Scale Format Date 1
  (DD-MM-YY)              Display date as noted
Graph Options Scale X
  Scale Format Date 2
  (DD-MM)                 Display date as noted
Graph Options Scale X
  Scale Format Date 3
  (MM-YY)                 Display date as noted
Graph Options Scale X
  Scale Format Date 4
  (Long Int'l)            Display date as noted
Graph Options Scale X
  Scale Format Date 5
  (Short Int'l)           Display date as noted
Graph Options Scale X
  Scale Format Time 1
  (HH:MM:SS AM/PM)        Display time as noted

```
MENU TITLES:                USE AND USE REQUIREMENT:

Graph Options Scale X
  Scale Format Time 2
  (HH:MM AM/PM)             Display time as noted
Graph Options Scale X
  Scale Format Time 3
  (Long Int'l)              Display time as noted
Graph Options Scale X
  Scale Format Time 4
  (Short Int'l)             Display time as noted
Graph Options Scale X
  Scale Format Text         Display formulas instead of values
Graph Options Scale X
  Scale Quit                Quit the X-axis menu
Graph Options Scale
  Skip                      Set skip factor for X-axis Specify skip #
```

## APPLICATIONS

Use the GRAPH OPTIONS SCALE commands to display graphs with a scale that is manually set and formatted for either the Y axis, the X axis, or both the Y and X axis. Typically, these commands are used when refining the display of information contained in a graph. For example, in an XY that plots the temperature of the Earth's surface over time, the scale for the time axis could be set to display in fifteen minute increments (the skip factor) and be formatted using short international time (military 24 hour clock time). Setting the time scale this way would prevent the graph form being cluttered with temperature variations that might occur every few seconds. These commands are quite useful when "cleaning up" a graph to make it neater in appearance.

## TYPICAL OPERATION

1. Retrieve the CANDY worksheet saved in Module 25.

2. Type **/GNU** and select the CANDYG5 graph and press **Return**.

3. Type **OS** and look at the following display:

```
A1:[W25] ^POPULAR CANDY SALES                                    MENU
Y Scale  X Scale  Skip
Set Y-axis scaling
              A              B          C          D
1        POPULAR CANDY SALES
|
20                 MAXIMUM       200              156
```

4.  Type **Y** to set the Y axis scale and look at the following screen:

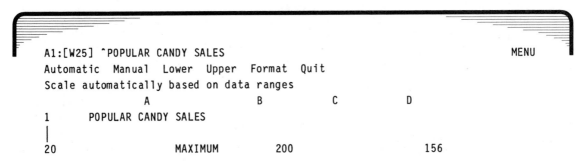

```
A1:[W25] ^POPULAR CANDY SALES                              MENU
Automatic  Manual  Lower  Upper  Format  Quit
Scale automatically based on data ranges
              A              B         C         D
1         POPULAR CANDY SALES
|
20                    MAXIMUM       200              156
```

Before an axis scale is set, the intention to do so must be declared by letting the Lotus 1-2-3 system know that you are going to set the graph scale manually.

5.  Type **M** to indicate a manual setting for the Y axis scale.

6.  Type **L** for the lower limit of the manually set scale. The screen displays the following:

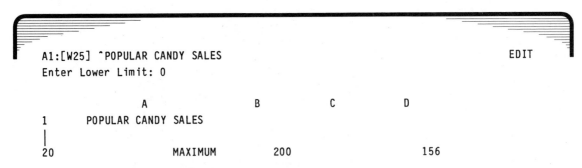

```
A1:[W25] ^POPULAR CANDY SALES                              EDIT
Enter Lower Limit: 0

              A              B         C         D
1         POPULAR CANDY SALES
|
20                    MAXIMUM       200              156
```

Since the Y axis is in dollars and the high dollar value does not exceed $200.00, a good scale would be from 0 to 200.

7.  Type **0** and then press **Return**.

8.  Type **U** to set the upper limit, type **200** and then press **Return**.

9.  Type **Q** twice to return to the main graph menu and then type **V**. Notice the following graph:

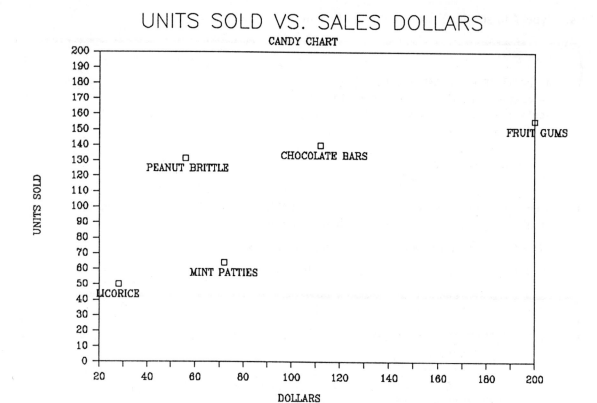

UNITS SOLD VS. SALES DOLLARS
CANDY CHART

Notice that the new scale brings all the data labels within the quadrant of the graph, making it much more neat in appearance.

10. Press **Esc** and name the graph CANDYG6.

11. Save the graph and then type **Q** to quit the graphs menu.

12. Save the worksheet using the replace option.

13. Turn to Module 30 to continue the learning sequence.

# Module 29

## GRAPH OPTIONS TITLES

**DESCRIPTION**

Often a graph needs a title and descriptions for the X and Y axes to explain the graphic display. Use the GRAPH OPTIONS TITLES commands to create a title for the graph and to create titles for the X and Y axes of the graph. Lotus 1-2-3 allows two lines of text for the graph title and one line of text each for the X and Y axes. Each line can be up to 39 characters in length.

The GRAPH OPTIONS TITLES commands are located and used from the worksheet READY screen by typing a / (slash) and then typing the first letters of the following menu titles:

```
MENU TITLES:                USE AND USE REQUIREMENT:

Graph Options Titles        Create graph titles
Graph Options Titles
    First                   Create first line of graph titles type text
Graph Options Titles
    Second                  Create second line of graph titles type text
Graph Options Titles
    X-Axis                  Create description for X-axis on graph type text
Graph Options Titles
    Y-Axis                  Create description for Y-axis on graph type text
```

**APPLICATIONS**

Use the GRAPH OPTIONS TITLES commands to add a name to a graph and to create identification information for the X and Y axes of the graph. Titles describe the type of graph being presented, for instance, a typical graph title might note what information is being plotted over what units of measure. An example would be a graph title such as TELEPHONE CALLS PER EMPLOYEE FOR THE MONTH OF JUNE. Titles are also used to define the units of measure used for the X axis and Y axis. In the telephone calls graph example, one axis could be titled NO. OF CALLS and the other axis titled EMPLOYEES.

## TYPICAL OPERATION

1. Retrieve the CANDY worksheet saved in Module 23.

2. Type **/GO** and then type **T** and notice the following display:

```
A1:[W25] 'POPULAR CANDY SALES                                    MENU
First  Second  X-Axis  Y-Axis
Specify first graph title line


                A              B          C          D
 1    POPULAR CANDY SALES
 2    -------------------
 3                                   SQUARES OF
 4                                   DIFFERENCE
 5       CANDY NAME         UNITS SOLD  FROM MEAN    DOLLARS
 6       ----------         ----------  ---------    -------
 7    CHOCOLATE BARS            112       338.56     $140.00
 8    FRUIT GUMS               200     11320.96     $156.00
 9    LICORICE                  28      4303.36      $50.12
10    MINT PATTIES              72       466.56      $64.08
11    PEANUT BRITTLE            56      1413.76     $131.60
12
13    TOTAL                    468

20               MAXIMUM       200                    156
```

3. Type **F** to select the first title line.

4. Type **UNITS SOLD VS. SALES DOLLARS** as the first line of the graph title and then press **Return**.

Notice that the screen returns to the Options menu with the highlighter on the Titles choice.

5. Press **Return** and then type **S**.

6. Type **CANDY CHART** and press **Return**.

To create descriptions for the X and Y axes:

7. Press **Return** and then type **X**.

8. Type **DOLLARS** and then press **Return** twice.

9. Type **Y**.

10. Type **UNITS SOLD** and press **Return**.

11. Type **Q** and then type **V**. Notice the following graphic display on the monitor:

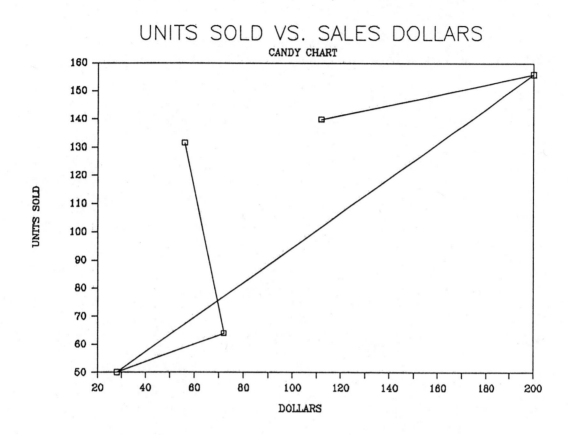

The title is automatically centered at the top of the graph and the descriptions for the X and Y axes are centered below and to the left of each respective axis.

12. Press **Esc**.

13. Name this graph CANDYG2 and then save the worksheet using the replace option.

14. Turn to Module 27 to continue the learning sequence.

# Module 30
## GRAPH RESET

**DESCRIPTION**

Sometimes it is less time consuming to reset all the information specified for a graph rather than trying to clear each item individually. Use the GRAPH RESET commands to clear all graph specifications for the entire graph or all graph specifications for specific data ranges.

The GRAPH RESET commands are located and used from the worksheet READY screen by typing a / (slash) and then typing the first letters of the following titles:

```
MENU TITLES:              USE AND USE REQUIREMENT:


Graph Reset               Delete data ranges
Graph Reset Graph         All data ranges
Graph Reset X             X data range only
Graph Reset A             A data range only
Graph Reset B             B data range only
Graph Reset C             C data range only
Graph Reset D             D data range only
Graph Reset E             E data range only
Graph Reset F             F data range only
Graph Reset Quit          Quit reset menu
```

**APPLICATIONS**

Use the GRAPH RESET commands to clear graph specifications previously set using the other menu items on the main graph menu. These commands are particularly useful when you need to reset all the graph settings for one or more of the graphs associated with a worksheet because the data from which they were created is no longer continued in the same locations in the worksheet that it had been previously.

**TYPICAL OPERATION**

1. Retrieve the CANDY worksheet saved in Module 28.

2. Use the CANDYG6 graph.

3. Type **R** and look at the following display:

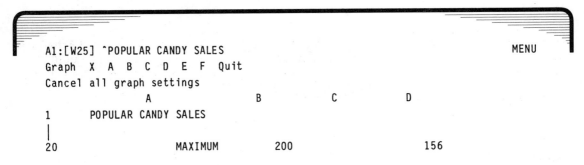

```
A1:[W25] ^POPULAR CANDY SALES                              MENU
Graph  X  A  B  C  D  E  F  Quit
Cancel all graph settings
                A                B        C        D
1         POPULAR CANDY SALES
|
20                    MAXIMUM       200              156
```

4. Type **G** to clear all graph settings and then type **V**.

Notice the screen blanks and a beep sounds. All the graph specifications for the CANDYG6 graph have been cleared.

5. Press **Esc** and then type **Q** to quit the graphs menu.

6. Quit the worksheet.

### NOTE

Do not save the worksheet. If you save the worksheet after this module, the graph information for the CANDYG6 graph will be lost.

7. Turn to Module 44 to continue the learning sequence.

# Module 31
## GRAPH SAVE

### DESCRIPTION

Once a graph is named, it can be saved or not saved as required. Many times a series of named graphs are created within a worksheet. Each separate graph is used to build upon the next until the right combination of parameters displays the data in an acceptable form. The final form is the graph usually saved for printing. Use the GRAPH SAVE command to save a graph to a disk file (.PIC file) that is later printed using the Lotus 1-2-3 PrintGraph program.

Saving a graph IS NOT the same thing as naming it. The save procedure creates a diskette file which is used to print the graph on a graphic printing device. Saving does not automatically name a graph. If the worksheet file is saved before naming the graph designed using its data, the parameters cannot be retrieved from the saved graph file. Think of the .PIC diskette file as simply a picture which does not contain the worksheet data upon which it was drawn.

The GRAPH SAVE command is located and used from the worksheet READY screen by typing a / (slash) and then typing the first letters of the following menu titles:

```
MENU TITLES:          USE AND USE REQUIREMENT:

Graph Save            Save .PIC file on diskette Specify name
```

### APPLICATIONS

Use the GRAPH SAVE command to save a graph for printing using Lotus 1-2-3's PrintGraph feature. You must save a graph to a .PIC file before you can print it.

### TYPICAL OPERATION

1. Retrieve the CANDY worksheet saved in Module 23.
2. Type **/GS**.
3. Type **CANDYG1** and then press **Return**.
4. Type **Q** and then display the directory of the default drive.

Notice that Lotus 1-2-3 saves the graph, attaching the file name suffix .PIC.

5. Turn to Module 34 to continue the learning sequence.

# Module 32

## GRAPH TYPE

**DESCRIPTION**

Lotus 1-2-3 can create five different types of graphs—line, XY, bar, stacked bar, and pie. The following chart describes these five types:

| GRAPH TYPE | DESCRIPTION | ILLUSTRATION |
|---|---|---|
| LINE | This is Lotus 1-2-3's default graph type. A line graph is one in which all data points (information values) are plotted along the Y axis. Lotus 1-2-3 allows up to six data point ranges. | 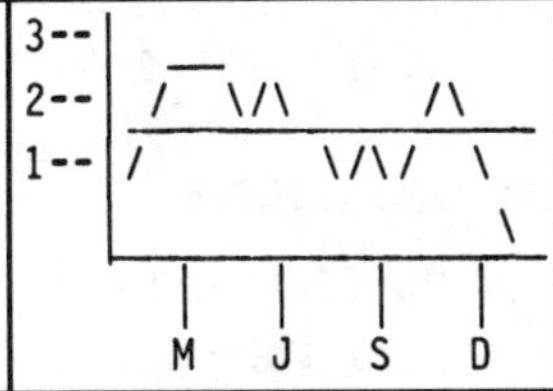 |
| XY | An XY graph is one in which the X axis range is equal to one set of data points and the Y axis is equal to one through six data point ranges | 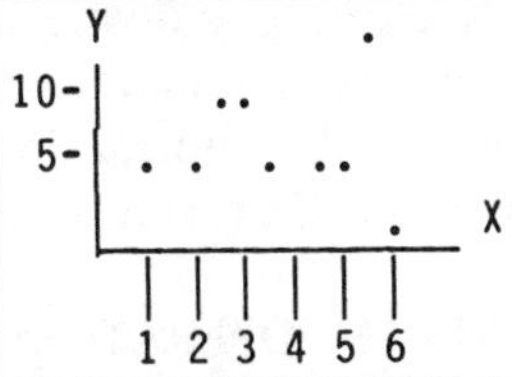 |
| BAR | Data point ranges are the same as for a line graph. The display is in bar form rather than line. | 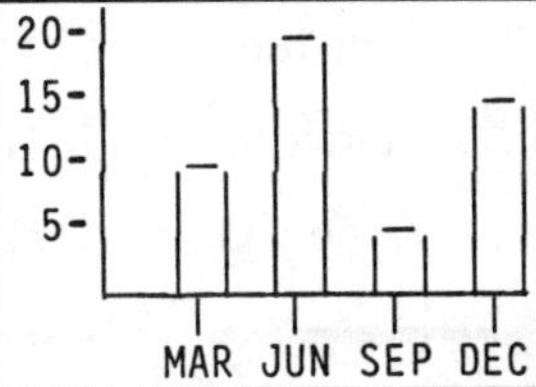 |
| STACKED BAR | Data point ranges are the same as for a line graph. The display is in bar form with each data point range stacked one on top of another (1st range through 6th). | 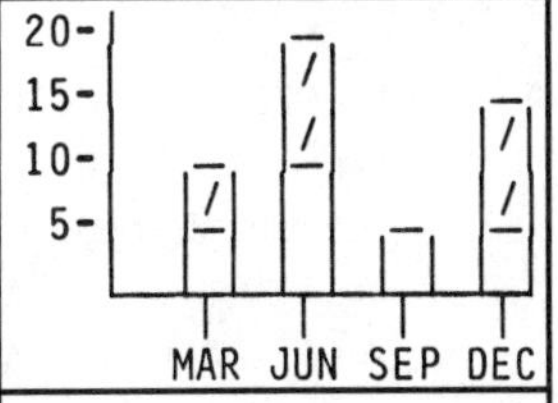 |
| PIE | Pie charts are circular and require only one data point range. All other ranges are ignored. | 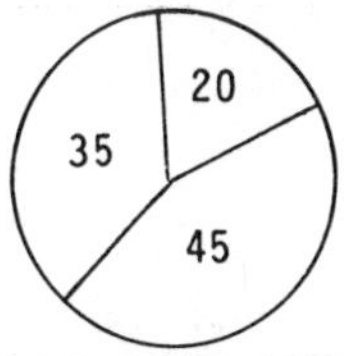 |

*Lotus 1-2-3 Graph Types*

Use the GRAPH TYPE commands to specify the style of graph that is to be created using worksheet information.

The GRAPH TYPE commands are located and used from the worksheet READY screen by typing a / (slash) and then typing the first letters of the following menu titles:

```
MENU TITLES:              USE AND USE REQUIREMENT:

Graph Type                Set the type of graph to create
Graph Type Line           Set line graph
Graph Type Bar            Set bar graph
Graph Type XY             Set XY graph
Graph Type Stacked-Bar    Set stacked-bar graph
Graph Type Pie            Set pie graph
```

## APPLICATIONS

Use the GRAPH TYPE command to specify the graph type before any features of the graph are specified. This command is necessary before any worksheet information is specified for the graph. After you have designated the information that the graph uses, the GRAPH TYPE command can be used again to alternate between display types to see which type gives a more understandable view of the information. For example, after setting up a bar graph, the type can be changed to line and then viewed using the GRAPH VIEW command.

## TYPICAL OPERATION

To select the type of graph, follow these instructions:

1. Retrieve the CANDY worksheet saved in Module 20.

2. Type **/G** and look at the following display:

```
A1:[W25] 'POPULAR CANDY SALES                                    MENU
   Type X A B C D E F Reset View Save Options Name Quit
   Set graph type
                A            B          C           D
1       POPULAR CANDY SALES
2       --------------------
3                                    SQUARES OF
4                                    DIFFERENCE
5           CANDY NAME       UNITS SOLD  FROM MEAN   DOLLARS
6           ----------       ----------  ---------   -------
7    CHOCOLATE BARS              112       338.56    $140.00
8    FRUIT GUMS                  200     11320.96    $156.00
```

| 9 | LICORICE | | 28 | 4303.36 | $50.12 |
| 10 | MINT PATTIES | | 72 | 466.56 | $64.08 |
| 11 | PEANUT BRITTLE | | 56 | 1413.76 | $131.60 |
| 12 | | | | | |
| 13 | TOTAL | | 468 | | |
| | | | | | |
| 20 | | MAXIMUM | 200 | | 156 |

This is Lotus 1-2-3's main graph menu. Use it every time you design a graph. However, you do not print a graph from this screen. Lotus 1-2-3's PrintGraph Program does that. This menu is only used to tell the Graph Program where to get the worksheet information in order to produce the graph and to save the graph to a disk file.

3. Type **T** to select the type of graph.

Notice that the screen displays the five forms of graphs Lotus 1-2-3 produces.

4. Type **X** to choose the XY form of graph.

The monitor returns to the main graph menu.

5. Type **Q** to quit the graph menu and then quit the worksheet.

6. Turn to Module 35 to continue the learning sequence.

# Module 33
## GRAPH VIEW

**DESCRIPTION**

Once a graph type has been selected and the cell information which Lotus 1-2-3 uses to plot the graph is marked, the graph can be viewed on the screen. Use the GRAPH VIEW command to display a graph on the monitor while a Lotus 1-2-3 worksheet is loaded.

The GRAPH VIEW command is located and used from the worksheet READY screen by typing a / (slash) and then typing the first letters of the following menu titles:

```
MENU TITLES:          USE AND USE REQUIREMENT:

Graph View            Display graph on monitor
```

**APPLICATIONS**

Use the GRAPH VIEW command to periodically view graphs on the monitor while still within the worksheet. This command is extremely useful when refining graph information, formats, and types. By periodically viewing a graph, any required adjustments can be easily seen on the screen and the appropriate changes made to the worksheet and/or graph options.

**TYPICAL OPERATION**

1.  Retrieve the CANDY worksheet saved in Module 23.

2.  Type **/GNU** and select CANDYG1 to use and press **Return**.

3. Type **V** to view the graph. The following graph displays:

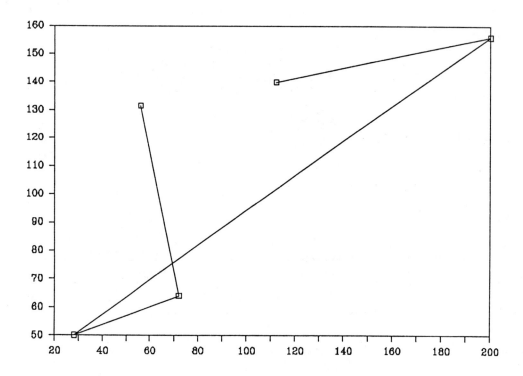

Lotus 1-2-3 plots the units sold and dollar values for each candy and connects each location with lines. Notice the scales for the X and Y axis. Lotus 1-2-3 automatically scales each axis based upon the data range specified.

4. Press **Esc** and then type **Q** to quit the graphs menu.

5. Quit the worksheet.

6. Turn to Module 29 to continue the learning sequence.

# Module 34
## GRAPH QUIT

**DESCRIPTION**

Use the GRAPH QUIT command to leave the main graph menu in a worksheet.

The GRAPH QUIT command is located and used from the worksheet READY screen by typing a / (slash) and then typing the first letters of the following menu titles:

```
MENU TITLES:              USE AND USE REQUIREMENT:

Graph Quit                Quit the graph menu
```

**APPLICATIONS**

Use the GRAPH QUIT command to leave the graph menu once you are finished setting the various parameters for a graph.

**TYPICAL OPERATION**

1.  Retrieve the CANDY worksheet saved in Module 23.
2.  Use CANDYG1 as the graph and then type **V** to view the graph.
3.  Press **Esc** and then type **Q** to quit the graph menu.
4.  Quit the worksheet.
5.  Turn to Module 24 to continue the learning sequence.

# Module 35
## GRAPH X, A, B, C, D, E, F

### DESCRIPTION

Once a graph type has been selected, it is necessary to mark the cell information which Lotus 1-2-3 uses to plot the graph. Lotus 1-2-3 can define six different graphs for each type. Use the GRAPH command to specify range for each range of graph information.

The GRAPH command is located and used from the worksheet READY screen by typing a / (slash) and then typing the first letters of the following menu titles:

```
MENU TITLES:            USE AND USE REQUIREMENT:

Graph X                 Specify data range for X data
Graph A                 Specify data range for A data
Graph B                 Specify data range for B data
Graph C                 Specify data range for C data
Graph D                 Specify data range for D data
Graph E                 Specify data range for E data
Graph F                 Specify data range for F data
```

### APPLICATIONS

The GRAPH commands are used to specify cell ranges that contain the data that the graph uses to plot the type of graph selected. Typically, these commands are used to specify a data range for the X and one of the A through F data types. You must take care that if more than one data type in the A through F categories is chosen, the units of measure are the same. For example, in a graph that plots sales dollars by the category of product over the months in the year, data types A through F might be different product types. You would want to plot all the sales in dollars and not mix unit sales values on the same graph. To do so would mix unlike units of measure (dollars and unit sales) and make the graph meaningless.

### TYPICAL OPERATION

Follow these procedures to select the graph data ranges:

1. Retrieve the CANDY worksheet saved in Module 20.

2. Type **/GX** to set the X axis information range.

Notice that the monitor displays the familiar range setting screen.

3.  Move the cell pointer to B7 and type . (a period).

4.  Move the cell pointer to B11 and press **Return**.

5.  Type **A** to set the Y axis information range.

Remember, Lotus 1-2-3 can accept up to six different Y axis information ranges (ranges A through F).

6.  Move the cell pointer to D7 and type . (a period).

7.  Move the cell pointer to D11 and press **Return**.

For more data ranges, this process is continued for each range letter (A, B, . . . F).

8.  Type **Q** to quit the graphs menu and then quit the worksheet.

9.  Turn to Module 23 to continue the learning sequence.

# Module 36
## MACROS

## DESCRIPTION

A Lotus 1-2-3 *macro* is a miniature computer program written into the worksheet that, upon execution, automatically performs a series of Lotus 1-2-3 steps in a previously specified order. An example would be the steps necessary to copy the values in one row to another row. In a macro, these steps are written into a program that is executed with a single keystroke.

Because macros are true computer programs, they depend upon a set of instruction symbols that, although brief in form, contain a great amount of power. The following table lists the primary set of Lotus 1-2-3 macro symbols:

| MACRO SYNTAX | ACTION PERFORMED |
|---|---|
| {(A specified function)} | Braces ({ }) are used to enclose function key names as well as editing and cell pointer movement commands. These include: |

| | |
|---|---|
| {Help} | F1: Displays Help screen |
| {Edit} | F2: Switches to/from Edit mode for current entry |
| {Name} | F3: (Point mode) Displays menu of range names |
| {Abs} | F4: (Point mode) Makes/Unmakes cell address "absolute" |
| {GoTo} | F5: Moves cell pointer to a particular cell |
| {Window} | F6: (split-screen only) Moves cell pointer to other window |
| {Query} | F7: Repeats most recent Data Query operation |
| {Table} | F8: Repeats most recent Data Table operation |
| {Calc} | F9: Ready mode: Recalculates all formulas—Value and Edit modes: Converts formula to its value |
| {Graph} | F10: Draws graph using current graph settings |

Cell Pointer Movement Keys

| | |
|---|---|
| {Home} | Moves to Home cell |
| {End}{Home} | Moves to last cell in worksheet |
| {Left} | Moves left one cell |
| {Right} | Moves right one cell |
| {Up} | Moves up one cell |
| {Down} | Moves down one cell |
| {PgUp} | Moves up one page on worksheet |
| {PgDn} | Moves down one page on worksheet |
| {BS} | Backspaces one character |
| {Del} | Backspaces one character and deletes it. |

| | Other | |
|---|---|---|
| | {?} | Pause in macro execution to accept input from the keyboard. |
| ~ | The tilde ( ~ ) performs the same function as pressing the Return key once. | |
| /(Worksheet key sequence) | Inserting the slash and any valid worksheet key sequence into a macro automatically executes that sequence just as if it were typed from the keyboard manually. | |

*Lotus Primary Macro Syntax Symbols*

In Module 20, you created a conditional statement formula using Lotus 1-2-3's @IF function. Unfortunately, the @IF function only operates on numerical information. Macros overcome this limitation. You can create a conditional statement macro instruction that operates on text as well as numbers. Conditional macros require the use of a set of macro instruction symbols called /X commands. You use these symbols in conjunction with the primary macro syntactical symbols described in the previous table. The following table describes the /X command symbols:

| MACRO SYNTAX | ACTION PERFORMED |
|---|---|
| /XGlocation ~ | Jumps to another cell location within the macro and continues reading the macro instructions located there. |
| /XClocation ~ | Jumps to another cell location within the macro and continues reading the macro instructions located there, but marks the place jumped from so that when a /XR command is encountered, you return to the place jumped from. |
| /XR | Returns from the /XC "subroutine" and continues reading the macro instructions starting with the instruction immediately following the one containing the /XC command. |
| /XIformula ~ . . . | The formula following the /XI is a conditional statement. If formula is TRUE (non-zero value), then continue reading the macro instructions on the same line (cell) as this one. If formula is false (zero value), then immediately jump to the next line (cell) and continue reading the macro instructions from that cell. |
| /XLmessage ~ location ~ | Displays "message" on the terminal. Pauses until the user types a label entry (text) and the "location" where the entry is to be placed. |
| /XNmessage ~ location ~ | Displays "message" on the terminal. Pauses until the user types a numeric entry and the "location" where the entry is to be placed. |
| /XMlocation ~ | PROCESS A "PROGRAMMER-DEFINED" MENU. Pauses until the user selects a menu item, then branches to another macro instruction based upon the menu choice. Uses the menu whose upper left-hand corner is at "location." |
| /XQ | Ends macro and returns control to the keyboard. |

*Lotus /X Command Macro Syntax Symbols*

Sorting the CANDY worksheet by its three types of information (candy names, units sold, and dollars) is accomplished by performing the worksheet-data-sort routine. This set of instructions can be programmed into a macro and executed with one keystroke. Follow these procedures to write this simple macro:

1.  Retrieve the CANDY worksheet saved in Module 28.

2.  Move the cell pointer to G7. Change the column width to 12 characters.

Before writing this macro, review the following steps. You would follow these procedures to sort the worksheet by typing the required letters and symbols directly on the keyboard.

| STEP | ACTION |
|------|--------|
| 1 | TYPE **/** TO DISPLAY THE MAIN WORKSHEET MENU. |
| 2 | TYPE **D** TO SELECT THE DATA CHOICE. |
| 3 | TYPE **S** TO SELECT THE SORT CHOICE. |
| 4 | TYPE **P** TO SET THE PRIMARY SORTING RANGE. |
| 5 | PRESS **BACKSPACE** TO FREE THE CELL POINTER. |
| 6 | MOVE THE CELL POINTER TO B7. |
| 7 | TYPE **.** (A PERIOD) TO MARK THE START OF RANGE. |
| 8 | MOVE THE CELL POINTER TO B11. |
| 9 | PRESS **RETURN** TO STORE THE SELECTED RANGE. |
| 10 | PRESS **RETURN** TO SELECT AN ASCENDING ORDER SORT. |
| 11 | TYPE **G** TO SORT THE WORKSHEET. |

Now, study the following table. It lists the corresponding macro program command for each keyboard stroke.

| STEP | ACTION | MACRO INSTRUCTION |
|------|--------|-------------------|
| 1 | TYPE **/** TO DISPLAY THE MAIN WORKSHEET MENU. | '/DSP |
| 2 | TYPE **D** TO SELECT THE DATA CHOICE. | |
| 3 | TYPE **S** TO SELECT THE SORT CHOICE. | |
| 4 | TYPE **P** TO SET THE PRIMARY SORTING RANGE. | |
| 5 | PRESS **BACKSPACE** TO FREE THE CELL POINTER. | {BS} |
| 6 | MOVE THE CELL POINTER TO B7. | {GOTO}B7 |
| 7 | TYPE **.** (A PERIOD) TO MARK THE START OF RANGE. | '. |
| 8 | MOVE THE CELL POINTER TO B11. | {GOTO}B11 ~ ~ |
| 9 | PRESS **RETURN** TO STORE THE SELECTED RANGE. | |
| 10 | PRESS **RETURN** TO SELECT AN ASCENDING ORDER SORT. | |
| 11 | TYPE **G** TO SORT THE WORKSHEET. | 'G |

3. Type **{HOME}** and then press **Return**.

It is always a good idea to start and end every macro program from the Home position on the worksheet.

4. Move the cell pointer to G8 and type **'/DSP** and then press **Return**.

Notice that you type a single close quotation mark ( ' ) before typing the worksheet keystroke letters. Typing the keystroke commands without the close quotation mark would invoke the selected menu items. As with ordinary labels (text) the close quotation mark is used within a macro to designate the following information as text to be included in the macro program and not to be executed until the macro is executed.

5. Move the cell pointer to G9 and type **{BS}** and then press **Return**.

This instruction tells Lotus 1-2-3 to press the Backspace key once.

6. Move the cell pointer to G10 and type **{GOTO}B7** and then press **Return**.

7. Move the cell pointer to G11 and type **'.** and then press **Return**.

This instruction marks the starting cell for the primary sort range.

8. Move the cell pointer to G12.

9. Type {**GOTO**}**B11** ~ ~ and then press **Return**.

Notice the two tildes ( ~ ) typed after the ending cell reference for the primary sorting range. The tilde is the macro equivalent of pressing the Return key. The first tilde stores the primary-sort cell range and the second selects ascending order (this is the default value on the sorting order screen).

10. Move the cell pointer to G13 and type '**G** and then press **Return**.

This tells Lotus 1-2-3 to "Go", that is, sort the worksheet as specified.

11. Move the cell pointer to G14 and type {**HOME**}. Press **Return**.

After sorting, this instruction moves the cell pointer back to the Home cell.

Notice the following display:

```
  G14:[W12] '{HOME}                                              READY


              D           E           F           G         H        I
      1
      2
      3                 SQUARES OF  UNIT PRICE
      4                 DIFFERENCE  LESS THAN $1
      5     DOLLARS     FROM MEAN   1=YES 0=NO
      6     -------     ---------   ----------
      7       $50.12    3391.8976           0  {HOME}
      8      $131.60     540.0976           0  /DSP
      9       $64.08    1960.7184           1  {BS}
     10      $140.00    1001.0896           0  {GOTO}B7
     11      $156.00    2269.5696           1  .
     12                                        {GOTO}B11~~
     13                                        G
     14                                        {HOME}
     15
     16
     17
     18      108.36
     19       50.12
     20         156
```

Notice that the macro flows from top to bottom. Lotus 1-2-3 executes macros by reading the top instruction first and then moves down one cell to read the next and so on until a blank cell is encountered. For Lotus 1-2-3 to do this, the range of cells which contain the macro must be specified.

Before a macro can be executed, the cells that contain the macro instructions must be specified. To name the macro which sorts the worksheet by the units sold values, perform the following steps:

1.   Type **/RN** and look at the following screen:

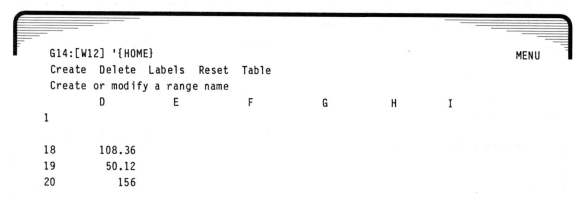

```
G14:[W12] '{HOME}                                                      MENU
Create  Delete  Labels  Reset  Table
Create or modify a range name
          D          E          F          G          H          I
  1

 18       108.36
 19        50.12
 20         156
```

Lotus 1-2-3 must have a name for the cells which contain the macro in order to locate them when the program is executed. Macro names are created by typing a backslash followed by a single letter.

2.   Press **Return**, type **\U** and then press **Return** again.

Notice that the name starts with a backslash ( ＼ ), not a slash (/). The U is a memory aid to help you remember that this macro sorts the worksheet by the Units sold values.

3.   Move the cell pointer to F7 and type . (a period), and then move the cell pointer to F14.

4.   Press **Return** and then type **Alt-U.**

Notice that the macro automatically performs all the instructions. The worksheet sorts by the units sold and then the cell pointer returns to the Home cell.

5.   Type **Alt-F2.**

Notice that STEP appears at the bottom of the worksheet. Lotus 1-2-3 is ready to execute the macro one step at a time.

6.   Type **Alt-U.**

The block appears at the bottom of the screen displaying SST. This stands for Single Step Test.

7.   Press **Return** 19 times, pausing a few seconds between each press.

As you press the Return key, the macro executes one step at a time. Each press of the Return key causes the program to perform one step and then stop for the next press of the Return key. This ability to step through a program is very useful when testing and modifying a new macro.

8. Type **Alt-F2** to turn off the single step feature.

Perform the following steps to copy the macro to columns G and H. Then modify them so that each sorts the worksheet by the candy names and the dollar values.

1.  Copy cells G7 through G14 to cells H7 through H14 and I7 through I14 after setting the column widths to 12.

2.  Move the cell pointer to H10 and type {**GOTO**}**D7** and then press **Return**.

3.  Move the cell pointer to H12 and type {**GOTO**}**D11** ~ ~ and then press **Return**.

4.  Move the cell pointer to I10 and type {**GOTO**}**A7** and then press **Return**.

5.  Move the cell pointer to I12 and type {**GOTO**}**A11** ~ ~ and then press **Return**.

6.  Name the dollars-sorting macro in column H **\D**.

This is the cell range H7 through H14.

7.  Name the name-sorting macro in column I by typing **\N**.

This is the cell range I7 through I14.

8.  Type the following headings for columns G, H, and I.

**COLUMN**

| ROW | G | H | I |
|---|---|---|---|
| 2 | | MACROS | |
| 3 | UNITS SOLD | DOLLARS | NAME |
| 4 | SORT \U | SORT \D | SORT \N |

Study the following display:

```
  I4:[W12] ^SORT \N                                              READY


         D          E          F          G          H          I
  1
  2                                                   MACROS
  3              SQUARES OF  UNIT PRICE  UNITS SOLD   DOLLARS     NAME
  4              DIFFERENCE  LESS THAN $1  SORT \U    SORT \D    SORT \N
  5    DOLLARS   FROM MEAN   1=YES 0=NO
  6    -------   ----------  ----------
  7    $50.12    3391.8976           0  {HOME}      {HOME}     {HOME}
  8   $131.60     540.0976           0  /DSP        /DSP       /DSP
  9    $64.08    1960.7184           1  {BS}        {BS}       {BS}
```

| | | | | | | |
|---|---|---|---|---|---|---|
| 10 | $140.00 | 1001.0896 | 0 | {GOTO}B7 | {GOTO}D7 | {GOTO}A7 |
| 11 | $156.00 | 2269.5696 | 1 | . | . | . |
| 12 | | | | {GOTO}B11¯¯ | {GOTO}D11¯¯ | {GOTO}A11¯¯ |
| 13 | | | | G | G | G |
| 14 | | | | {HOME} | {HOME} | {HOME} |
| 15 | | | | | | |
| 16 | | | | | | |
| 17 | | | | | | |
| 18 | 108.36 | | | | | |
| 19 | 50.12 | | | | | |
| 20 | 156 | | | | | |

### NOTE

Normally, when printing the worksheet, the macros would not be included in the print range. The headings are just a reminder that the macros are on the worksheet and of the name under which they are executed.

9. Type **Alt-D** to execute the dollars-sort macro.

10. Type **Alt-N** to execute the name-sort macro.

11. Save the worksheet using the replace option.

12. Turn to Module 13 to continue the learning sequence.

# Module 37
## MOVE

### DESCRIPTION

Use the MOVE command to move the information contained in one or more rows or columns from one location in a worksheet to another.

The MOVE command is located and used from the worksheet READY screen by typing a / (slash) and then typing the first letters of the following menu titles:

```
MENU TITLES:          USE AND USE REQUIREMENT:

Move                  Move a range of cells to a range of cells Specify from/to range
```

### APPLICATIONS

This command moves single cells and ranges of cells from one location in a worksheet to another location. As with the COPY command, the ability to move information saves time and effort and helps you prevent errors that occur when duplicating cell information manually. This command is typically used to remove information from one section of a worksheet and place it in another. You should pay particular attention to any cell relationships such as formulas and macros when moving cells. Unlike the COPY command, the column and row coordinates or the moved cells are left empty after using the MOVE command. If other cells in the worksheet depend on the information contained in the cell location that is moved to make calculations or to perform macro instructions, they will not work after the cell information is moved to another location.

### TYPICAL OPERATION

1.  From the worksheet READY screen, retrieve the worksheet used in Module 47.

2.  Move the cell pointer to B3 and type **/M**.

3.  Move the cell pointer to B5 and press **Return**.

4.  Move the cell pointer to C3 and type . (a period); then move the cell pointer to C5 and press **Return**.

Notice the following display on the monitor:

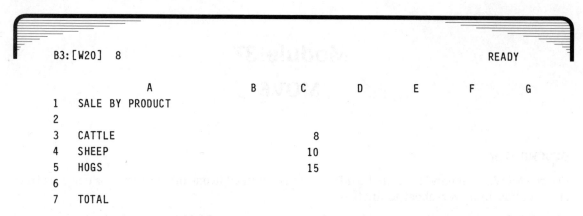

```
B3:[W20]  8                                                    READY

                  A              B    C       D       E       F       G
   1    SALE BY PRODUCT
   2
   3    CATTLE                        8
   4    SHEEP                         10
   5    HOGS                          15
   6
   7    TOTAL
```

Lotus 1-2-3 moved the information from column B to column C. Notice that the area is blank at the location in column B where the information had originally been. With the COPY command, you duplicate information at another location without affecting the original "copied-from" cells. With the MOVE command, you delete information from one location and transfer it to another.

5.  Quit the worksheet.

6.  Turn to Module 21 to continue the learning sequence.

# Module 38

## PRINT FILE

**DESCRIPTION**

Use the PRINT FILE command to print a worksheet to a disk text file instead of to a printer. All range and option commands are duplicated in the text file just as if they had been printed. With this feature, a diskette file (known in the Lotus 1-2-3 syntax as a .PRN file) is created and then can be used by a word processor. The information contained in the file can be manipulated using the word processor's features.

The PRINT FILE command is located and used from the worksheet READY screen by typing a / (slash) and then typing the first letters of the following menu titles:

```
MENU TITLES:              USE AND USE REQUIREMENT:

Print File               Print worksheet to a disk file Specify .PRN file name
```

**APPLICATIONS**

Use the PRINT FILE command to create a text file from a Lotus 1-2-3 worksheet that can be manipulated using a word processing program. This command is very useful when you want to merge a Lotus 1-2-3 worksheet into a text file. By printing the worksheet to a disk file, the resulting text format can be used just as if you had created it with a word processor.

The PRINT FILE command creates the text file based upon all the specifications you use with the PRINT PRINTER commands. Before printing a file to a text file, you should set up the worksheet for printing just as if you were going to print it to a printer.

**TYPICAL OPERATION**

1. Retrieve the CANDY worksheet saved in Module 42.

2. Move the cell pointer to A1, type **/PPR** and then mark the entire worksheet for printing.

3. Type **Q** and then type **/PF.**

Study the following display:

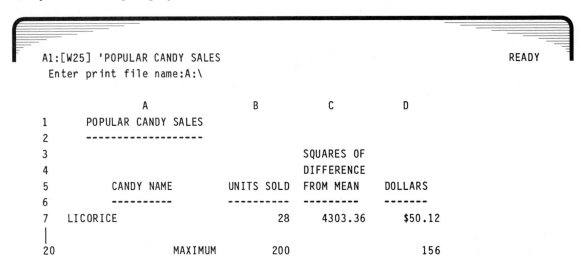

```
A1:[W25] 'POPULAR CANDY SALES                                    READY
  Enter print file name:A:\


                A            B         C          D
   1    POPULAR CANDY SALES
   2    -------------------
   3                                SQUARES OF
   4                                DIFFERENCE
   5        CANDY NAME       UNITS SOLD  FROM MEAN  DOLLARS
   6        ----------       ----------  ---------  -------
   7    LICORICE                    28    4303.36    $50.12
   |
  20                 MAXIMUM        200              156
```

Lotus 1-2-3 print file names are written the same way you name a worksheet file, that is, they follow the DOS filename conventions.

4.   Type **CANDYTXT** and then press **Return**.

5.   Type **G** to print the worksheet to a text file.

Do not type a three-letter suffix for the file name. Lotus 1-2-3 automatically attaches the .PRN to the file name.

### WARNING
Lotus 1-2-3 "prints" the worksheet to a .PRN file. This is not the same as saving a worksheet to a .WKS file. Lotus 1-2-3 interprets the .PRN suffix as a text file which cannot be processed by the program. Never print a worksheet to a file and assume that any changes made since retrieving the .WKS file have been saved.

6.   Type **Q** to quit the print menu and then quit the worksheet.

7.   Turn to Module 64 to continue the learning sequence.

# Module 39

## PRINT PRINTER ALIGN, LINE, PAGE

### DESCRIPTION

Use the PRINT PRINTER ALIGN, LINE, PAGE commands to cause the printer to align the page perforations on continuous form feed paper in the printer, or line feed one line, or page feed up to the next page.

The PRINT PRINTER ALIGN, LINE, PAGE commands are located and used from the worksheet READY screen by typing a / (slash) and then typing the first letters of the following menu titles:

```
MENU TITLES:            USE AND USE REQUIREMENT:

Print Printer Align     Align paper in printer
Print Printer Line      Advance one line on the printer
Print Printer Page      Advance one page on the printer
```

### APPLICATIONS

Use these commands to manipulate paper in the printer by sending a single line feed, a page feed, or by aligning the paper in the printer. An important aspect of these commands is that while Lotus 1-2-3 is printing, it takes control of the printer, that is, it supercedes the normal printer commands issued from your computer's operating system. For example, after a worksheet finishes printing, you should always make it a practice to use the PRINT PRINTER PAGE command to line feed the paper in your printer up to the next perforation. If you fail to do this, the printer's paper feed controls assume the top of the page is the position on the page where the worksheet stopped printing.

### TYPICAL OPERATION

1.  With the printer "on-line" and from the worksheet READY screen, type **/PPL**.

Notice that the paper moves up one line.

2.  Type **P**. Notice the paper move up to the start of the next page.

3.  Quit the worksheet.

4.  Turn to Module 43 to continue the learning sequence.

# Module 40
# PRINT PRINTER CLEAR

**DESCRIPTION**

Use the PRINT PRINTER CLEAR commands to clear all or selected printer settings.

The PRINT PRINTER CLEAR commands are located and used from the worksheet READY screen by typing a / (slash) and then typing the first letters of the following menu titles:

| MENU TITLES: | USE AND USE REQUIREMENT: |
|---|---|
| Print Printer Clear | Erase printer settings |
| Print Printer Clear<br>　All | Erase all printer settings |
| Print Printer Clear<br>　Range | Erase the range setting only |
| Print Printer Clear<br>　Borders | Erase the borders setting only |
| Print Printer Clear<br>　Format | Erase the format setting only |

**APPLICATIONS**

Use the PRINT PRINTER CLEAR commands to erase the range, borders, format, or all printer settings created using the PRINT PRINTER OPTIONS and PRINT PRINTER RANGE commands. These commands are useful when you have made so many changes to the printer options that it becomes easier to erase the existing specifications and start over with new ones. They also save time when selecting new ranges to print from a large worksheet.

**TYPICAL OPERATION**

1.  Retrieve the CANDY worksheet saved in Module 42.

2.  Type **/PPR**.

Notice the range set in Module 42 is still retained by the worksheet.

3.  Press **Return** and then type **C**.

4.  Type **R** and then type **/PPR**.

Notice that the range setting is cleared.

5.  Quit the worksheet.

6.  Turn to Module 38 to continue the learning sequence.

# Module 41
## PRINT PRINTER OPTIONS

**DESCRIPTION**

Use the PRINT PRINTER OPTIONS commands to create borders, headers, footers, and margins for a printed worksheet. Also use these commands to set print enhancement strings, specify printed worksheet page lengths, and change the way the information contained in the worksheet is printed. The following table lists the optional printer specifications and describes what each does:

| OPTION ITEM | DESCRIPTION |
| --- | --- |
| BORDERS | USED TO SELECT A ROW OR COLUMN OF INFORMATION FROM THE WORKSHEET AS A BORDER WHEN PRINTED. |
| HEADER | USED TO TYPE A HEADER THAT PRINTS ON EACH PAGE OF THE PRINTED WORKSHEET. |
| FOOTER | USED TO TYPE A FOOTER THAT PRINTS ON EACH PAGE OF THE PRINTED WORKSHEET. |
| MARGINS | THE NUMBER OF CHARACTERS FROM THE LEFT OR RIGHT OR TOP OR BOTTOM OF THE PAPER AT WHICH PRINTING OF THE WORKSHEET STARTS. |
| OTHER | PRINTS WORKSHEET AS A FORMATTED, UNFORMATTED, AS-DISPLAYED, OR CELL FORMULAS ONLY FORM. |
| SETUP | SETS A PRINT ENHANCEMENT CODE FOR THE WORKSHEET. |
| PG-LENGTH | SETS THE NUMBER OF LINES FOR THE WORKSHEET PAGE. |
| QUIT | QUITS THE PRINT PRINTER OPTIONS MENU. |

*Lotus 1-2-3 Print Printer Options*

The PRINT PRINTER OPTIONS commands are located and used from the worksheet READY screen by typing a / (slash) and then typing the first letters of the following menu titles:

| MENU TITLES: | USE AND USE REQUIREMENT: |
|---|---|
| Print Printer Options | Set printed worksheet options |
| Print Printer Options Borders | Set printed worksheet borders |
| Print Printer Options Borders Columns | Use column headings as borders |
| Print Printer Options Borders Rows | Use rows descriptions as borders |
| Print Printer Options Header | Create header for printed worksheet Type header |
| Print Printer Options Footer | Create footer for printed worksheet Type footer |
| Print Printer Options Margins | Set margins |
| Print Printer Options Margins Left | Set left margin Specify margin in # characters |
| Print Printer Options Margins Right | Set right margin Specify margin in # characters |
| Print Printer Options Margins Top | Set top margin Specify margin in # characters |
| Print Printer Options Margins Bottom | Set bottom margin Specify margin in # characters |
| Print Printer Options Other As-Displayed | Print worksheet as displayed on monitor |
| Print Printer Options Other Cell-Formulas | Print cell formulas |
| Print Printer Options Other Formatted | Print with all printer settings |
| Print Printer Options Other Unformted | Print ignoring printer settings |
| Print Printer Options Setup | Create setup string Specify string |
| Print Printer Options Page-Length | Set page length Specify length in # lines |
| Print Printer Options Other | Set miscellaneous print options |
| Print Printer Options Quit | Quit options menu |

## APPLICATIONS

When specialized printing enhancements are required for a worksheet, use the PRINT PRINTER OPTIONS commands. Typically, these commands are used to set the basic printing specifications for a worksheet such as the top and bottom margins, page length, left and right margins, and an alternate pitch string (compressed printing printer command) for your printer. When used in conjunction with the new Lotus 1-2-3 page numbering feature and the PRINT PRINTER RANGE command, you can set up the entire area of a large worksheet to automatically print without having to make adjustments after each page of the worksheet is printed. Also, many worksheet applications can be made more meaningful by creating a header or footer that prints at the top and bottom of each page.

## TYPICAL OPERATION

1. Retrieve the CANDY worksheet saved in Module 11.

2. Move the cell pointer to A1 and type **/PPR** and mark the entire worksheet for printing.

3. Type **/PPO**.

Study the following display:

```
A1:[W25] 'POPULAR CANDY SALES                                    MENU
   Header   Footer   Margins   Borders   Setup  Pg-Length  Other  Quit
                  A              B          C          D
  1       POPULAR CANDY SALES
  2       -------------------
  3                                     SQUARES OF
  4                                     DIFFERENCE
  5         CANDY NAME      UNITS SOLD  FROM MEAN   DOLLARS
  6         ----------      ----------  ---------   -------
  7    LICORICE                   28     4303.36     $50.12
  8    PEANUT BRITTLE             56     1413.76    $131.60
  9    MINT PATTIES               72      466.56     $64.08
 10    CHOCOLATE BARS            112      338.56    $140.00
 11    FRUIT GUMS               200    11320.96    $156.00
 12
 13    TOTAL                    468
```

Notice that the Options choice allows you to make certain printer setting changes which are also made using the /WGDP menu. Setting changes made using the /PPO screen are not permanently stored. The default setting changes are. This feature allows you to make temporary setting adjustments to meet the printing requirements of a specific worksheet without affecting the default values.

When printing multi-page worksheets (worksheets that exceed the specified lines per page), repetitive information at the top and bottom of each page is desirable to make the printed worksheet more understandable. The information at the top is known as a header, and the information at the bottom is known as a footer.

Make sure the printer is connected to the computer. Remember to connect it to the proper (parallel or serial) output port on the computer.

4. Type **H** to create a header. Look at the following display:

```
A1:[W25] 'POPULAR CANDY SALES                                    EDIT
  Enter Header Line:
                    A            B          C          D
  1         POPULAR CANDY SALES
  2         -------------------
  3                                      SQUARES OF
  4                                      DIFFERENCE
  5         CANDY NAME      UNITS SOLD  FROM MEAN    DOLLARS
  6         ----------      ----------  ----------   -------
  7  LICORICE                      28    4303.36     $50.12

 20                 MAXIMUM        200                 156
```

Lotus 1-2-3 accepts headers and footers that are up to 240 characters long. Any character that the printer can print is valid, but three characters serve special functions. The @ symbol tells Lotus 1-2-3 to insert the current date (the date typed in response to the DOS prompt when you loaded the program or from the clock if you have one installed in your computer). The # symbol inserts the page number and the | symbol is used to *delimit* (separate) left justified, centered, and right justified header and footer text.

5. Type |**THIS CHART WAS MADE BY:(Your Name)**| and then press **Return**.

6. Type **F** to create a footer.

7. Type #|**THIS CHART WAS MADE ON:**|@ and then press **Return**.

8. Press **Q** to quit this menu.

Make sure the printer is on line and set so the top of the print head is just below the perforation on the paper.

### NOTE
Make sure you have installed the correct Lotus
1-2-3 print driver for your computer system using
the installation procedures that come with the
Lotus 1-2-3 software package.

9. Type **G**.

Notice that the printer stops printing after line 20 of the worksheet (the last line) and that the footer did not print. This happens because Lotus 1-2-3 prints only the specified range on the worksheet. In this case, the range ends at line 20.

10. Type **P**. Notice the following printed worksheet:

```
               THIS CHART WAS MADE BY:(Your Name)


    POPULAR CANDY SALES
    -------------------
                               SQUARES OF              SQUARES OF
                               DIFFERENCE              DIFFERENCE
        CANDY NAME     UNITS SOLD FROM MEAN   DOLLARS   FROM MEAN
        ----------     ---------- ---------   -------   ----------
LICORICE                      28    4303.36    $50.12    3391.8976
PEANUT BRITTLE                56    1413.76   $131.60     540.0976
MINT PATTIES                  72     466.56    $64.08    1960.7184
CHOCOLATE BARS               112     338.56   $140.00    1001.0896
FRUIT GUMS                   200   11320.96   $156.00    2269.5696

TOTAL                        468




            MEAN       93.6                   108.36
         MINIMUM         28                    50.12
         MAXIMUM        200                   156

 1              THIS CHART WAS MADE ON:               05-Dec-86
```

Selecting Page from the Print menu causes Lotus 1-2-3 to automatically go to the end of the page. Once it reaches the end (the row just above the bottom margin) the footer prints. Notice that the header printed in the center of the page and that the footer printed the page number at the left margin, the text in the center, and today's date at the right margin.

11. Quit the worksheet.

12. Turn to Module 39 to continue the learning sequence.

# Module 42

## PRINT PRINTER RANGE

### DESCRIPTION

Use the PRINT PRINTER RANGE command to specify an area of a worksheet to print to a printer or to a disk file. The command sets the upper left hand cell reference and the lower right hand cell reference for the area to be printed.

The PRINT PRINTER RANGE command is located and used from the worksheet READY screen by typing a / (slash) and then typing the first letters of the following menu titles:

```
MENU TITLES:           USE AND USE REQUIREMENT:

Print Printer Range    Set the range of cells within the file to print Specify range
```

### APPLICATIONS

The PRINT PRINTER RANGE command is used to specify an area to print on a worksheet. A common problem encountered when using this command is that of setting the range for an area of the worksheet that exceeds the character-width or line-length limits of the printer. For example, if the PRINT PRINTER OPTIONS commands have been used to specify the page width as 80 characters and the page length as 66 lines, you would not want to specify a range for each printed page of the worksheet that is greater than 80 columns wide or more than 66 lines long (with no left, right, top or bottom margins) unless you have also set a compressed printing string for your printer. Also, note that the margin settings reduce the area of the worksheet that can be printed within the character-width and page-length limits.

### TYPICAL OPERATION

1.  Retrieve the CANDY worksheet saved in Module 11.

2.  Move the cell pointer to A1 and type **/PPR** to set the range of cells within the worksheet to be printed.

Notice the following screen:

```
A1:[W25] 'POPULAR CANDY SALES                                          POINT
Enter Print range: A1


                     A          B          C          D
    1        POPULAR CANDY SALES
    2        -------------------
    3                                  SQUARES OF
    4                                  DIFFERENCE
    5           CANDY NAME     UNITS SOLD FROM MEAN   DOLLARS
    6           ----------     ---------- ---------   -------
    7     LICORICE                   28    4303.36     $50.12
    8     PEANUT BRITTLE             56    1413.76    $131.60
    9     MINT PATTIES               72     466.56     $64.08
   10     CHOCOLATE BARS            112     338.56    $140.00
   11     FRUIT GUMS                200   11320.96    $156.00
   12
   13     TOTAL                     468
   14
   15
   16
   17
   18               MEAN          93.6                108.36
   19            MINIMUM            28                 50.12
   20            MAXIMUM           200                   156
```

Lotus 1-2-3 displays the familiar range setting screen. To specify the entire worksheet for printing:

3.   Type . (a period) and then move the cell pointer to E20.

Lotus 1-2-3 highlights the area of the worksheet to be printed. This allows you to specify only a selected area on the worksheet.

4.   Press **Return**. The complete worksheet is selected for printing.

5.   Type **Q** to quit the printer menu and then save the worksheet using the replace option.

**NOTE**
Once a worksheet is saved with a set print range, this range is stored along with all other information about the worksheet. Use the PRINT PRINTER RANGE command to change the saved setting to another setting.

6.   Turn to Module 41 to continue the learning sequence.

# Module 43

## PRINT PRINTER GO, QUIT

### DESCRIPTION

Once the area to be printed has been specified and any print options set, the worksheet is ready to print. Use the PRINT PRINTER GO command to print a worksheet on a printer. Use the PRINT PRINTER QUIT command to quit the PRINTER menu.

The PRINT PRINTER GO, QUIT commands are located and used from the worksheet READY screen by typing a / (slash) and then typing the first letters of the following menu titles:

```
MENU TITLES:            USE AND USE REQUIREMENT:

Print Printer Go        Print worksheet
Print Printer Quit      Quit printer menu
```

### APPLICATIONS

The PRINT PRINTER GO command is used to print a specified area on a worksheet to a printer. Once finished with all printing activities, use PRINT PRINTER QUIT to quit the PRINTER menu.

### TYPICAL OPERATION

1. Retrieve the CANDY worksheet saved in Module 42.

2. Ensure the printer is turned on and set on-line and that it is loaded with paper.

3. Type **/PPG** to print the CANDY worksheet.

The printed worksheet looks similar to the following illustration:

```
POPULAR CANDY SALES
-------------------

                                    SQUARES OF
                                    DIFFERENCE
            CANDY NAME    UNITS SOLD FROM MEAN    DOLLARS
            ----------    ---------- ----------   -------
LICORICE                         28    4303.36     $50.12
PEANUT BRITTLE                   56    1413.76    $131.60
MINT PATTIES                     72     466.56     $64.08
CHOCOLATE BARS                  112     338.56    $140.00
FRUIT GUMS                      200   11320.96    $156.00

TOTAL                           468


                MEAN            93.6              108.36
             MINIMUM              28               50.12
             MAXIMUM             200                 156
```

. . .THE SECOND PAGE

```
SQUARES OF
DIFFERENCE
FROM MEAN
---------
 3391.8976
  540.0976
 1960.7184
 1001.0896
 2269.5696
```

Notice that the specified worksheet area did not print on one page. This happened because the worksheet is wider than 80 characters. Eighty characters is the maximum width a letter-size printer can handle without first sending a special print-control code to the printer to compress the print. Lotus 1-2-3 printed what it could of the worksheet on the first page and then printed the remainder on a second sheet.

4. Type **/PPS**.

5. Type **/015** and then press **Return**.

This string prints the specified area of the worksheet using a compressed print mode for an Epson printer. Look in your printer's manual for the correct compressed-printing string for your printer.

6. Type **.G**. Look at the following compressed-printed worksheet:

```
POPULAR CANDY SALES
--------------------
                                SQUARES OF              SQUARES OF
                                DIFFERENCE              DIFFERENCE
          CANDY NAME   UNITS SOLD FROM MEAN  DOLLARS    FROM MEAN
          ----------   ---------- ---------  -------    ---------
LICORICE                      28   4303.36   $50.12     3391.8976
PEANUT BRITTLE                56   1413.76  $131.60      540.0976
MINT PATTIES                  72    466.56   $64.08     1960.7184
CHOCOLATE BARS               112    338.56  $140.00     1001.0896
FRUIT GUMS                   200  11320.96  $156.00     2269.5696

TOTAL                        468


                MEAN        93.6            108.36
             MINIMUM          28             50.12
             MAXIMUM         200               156
```

For different printers, the setup string used to print in a compressed mode would be different. Consult your printer's operating manual for the correct print-control codes to type into Lotus 1-2-3's setup string.

7. Quit the worksheet.

8. Turn to Module 40 to continue the learning sequence.

# Module 44

## PRINTGRAPH

**DESCRIPTION**

Before a graph is printed, Lotus 1-2-3's PrintGraph Program must be loaded into the computer's memory. Once loaded, use the PrintGraph Program to select the graph to print and to set the printing parameters for the size, grid, color, and fonts used to print the graph. You also select the type of printer used to print the graph and the way the printer is connected to the computer.

The following table lists the items on the PrintGraph Status screen and gives a brief definition of each.

| PRINTGRAPH STATUS ITEMS | DEFINITION |
|---|---|
| GRAPH IMAGES SELECTED | A listing of graphs selected for printing during this session only. |
| IMAGE OPTION RANGE COLORS | On color monitors, different colors are used for each data range specified. The listing notes each range and the color used to display the graph. |
| IMAGE OPTION FONT | PrintGraph can create graphs using many types of print styles known as fonts. This is the current font being used to print graphs. |
| IMAGE OPTION SIZE | The size and page orientation (rotation) of the graph. Not to be confused with page size, values are for the graph itself. |
| ACTION OPTIONS | Sets or disables automatic pausing and page feeding after each graph is printed. |
| HARDWARE SETUP | The disk drive location of the diskettes that have the font and graph files stored on them. |
| PRINTER TYPE | The printer type and computer connection type. |
| PRINTER PAPER | The size of paper that the printer uses—normally 8 ½ by 11 (letter) or 11 by 14 (legal). |

*Lotus 1-2-3 PrintGraph Status Items*

## TYPICAL OPERATION

1. From the Lotus 1-2-3 Access menu move the cell pointer to PrintGraph and press **Return**.

Lotus 1-2-3 displays a message that asks you to insert the PrintGraph program diskette into disk drive A.

2. Remove the Lotus 1-2-3 System diskette from disk drive A.

3. Insert Lotus 1-2-3's PrintGraph Program diskette into disk drive A and press **Return**.

Notice the following screen:

**NOTE**

The following screen may or may not contain the same status values as yours. This depends on your own hardware configuration, that is, printer type, computer, etc. Don't worry. You can always change the items on a status screen using PrintGraph.

```
Copyright 1986 Lotus Development Corp.  All Rights Reserved.  Release 2.01 MENU

Select graphs for printing
Image-Select  Settings  Go  Align  Page  Exit

   GRAPH       IMAGE OPTIONS                    HARDWARE SETUP
   IMAGES      Size                Range Colors    Graphs Directory:
   SELECTED    Top      .250       X Black           C:\lotus
               Left     .500       A Black        Fonts Directory:
               Width    6.852      B Black           A:\
               Height   9.445      C Black        Interface:
               Rotate  90.000      D Black           Parallel 1
                                   E Black        Printer Type:
               Font                F Black           Star High
               1  BLOCK1                         Paper Size
               2  BLOCK1                            Width      8.500
                                                    Length    11.000

                                                ACTION OPTIONS
                                                  Pause: Yes  Eject: No
```

This is PrintGraph's graph printing status screen. The information contained in this display tells you all about the status of the printer, fonts, page and graph printing sizes, range color, etc.

Selecting a particular graph to print is a procedure that must be performed each time you use PrintGraph. This listing is not permanently stored on the status screen. To select the CANDYG6 graph file to print, follow these steps to indicate that the graph file is on the diskette in disk drive B.

1.  Type **S** for the Settings item on the menu. Notice the following screen:

```
Copyright 1986 Lotus Development Corp.  All Rights Reserved.  Release 2.01 MENU


Specify colors, fonts and size
Image  Hardware  Action  Save  Reset  Quit


   GRAPH        IMAGE OPTIONS                   HARDWARE SETUP
   IMAGES       Size             Range Colors    Graphs Directory:
   SELECTED     Top        .250   X Black          C:\lotus
                Left       .500   A Black        Fonts Directory:
                Width     6.852   B Black          A:\
                Height    9.445   C Black        Interface:
                Rotate   90.000   D Black          Parallel 1
                                  E Black        Printer Type:
                Font              F Black          Star High
                1   BLOCK1                       Paper Size
                2   BLOCK1                         Width      8.500
                                                  Length    11.000

                                                ACTION OPTIONS
                                                Pause: Yes  Eject: No
```

You use Settings to specify most of the physical parameters on the status screen, including where files are located, the printer used and how it is connected to the computer, and the page size.

2.  Type **H**. Study the top of the following display:

```
Copyright 1986 Lotus Development Corp.  All Rights Reserved.  Release 2.01 MENU


Set directory containing graphs
Graphs-Directory  Fonts-Directory  Interface  Printer  Size-Paper  Quit


   GRAPH        IMAGE OPTIONS                   HARDWARE SETUP
```

PrintGraph must be told which disk drive to search for both the fonts used to print the graph and the graph files themselves.

3.  Type **G**. Remember, PrintGraph refers to graph files as .PIC files.

4.  Type **B:** for disk drive B and press **Return**.

Notice that the information for pictures under Directories changes to disk drive B. Since you are already here, set the fonts directory as follows:

5.  Type **F**; then type **A:** and press **Return**.

The PrintGraph font files are located on the PrintGraph Program diskette in drive A.

6.  Type **Q** twice. The screen returns to the main PrintGraph menu.

7.  Type **I** to select a graph to print. Study the following display:

```
 Copyright 1986 Lotus Development Corp.   All Rights Reserved.   Release 2.01 POINT

 Select graphs for output


    PICTURE      DATE     TIME      SIZE
                                            [SPACE] turns mark on and off
    CANDYG1    06-30-86  13:30       890     [RETURN] selects marked pictures
    CANDYG6    07-02-86  12:26      1280     [ESCAPE] exits, ignoring changes
                                            [HOME] goes to beginning of list
                                            [END] goes to end of list
                                            [UP] and [DOWN] move cursor
                                                List will scroll if cursor
                                                moved beyond top or bottom
                                            [GRAPH] displays selected picture



 Select graphs for output
```

PrintGraph searches the diskette in disk drive B and then displays all files which PrintGraph is capable of printing. Use this screen to select those graph files which PrintGraph prints.

8.  Read the information to the right of the file listing. The [Graph] function is usually F10 on most keyboards.

9.  Move the highlighter to CANDYG6 and press **F10**. Notice that the graph upon which the highlighter was placed is displayed on the monitor.

10. Press **Esc** and then press the **Spacebar** to mark CANDYG6 for printing.

Notice that the # symbol appears to the left of the graph file name. This symbol tags the graph filename for PrintGraph.

11. Press **Return**.

Before the selected graph can be printed, the type of printer and how it is connected to the computer (serial or parallel) must be specified for PrintGraph. Perform the following procedures to specify the printer and type of connection:

1.  Type **SHI**.

2.  Select 1 with the highlighter to specify a parallel connector and then press **Return**.

### NOTE

If you do not have a parallel printer connected to the computer or have more than one peripheral device connected to the computer, you may need to specify one of the following:

| | | |
|---|---|---|
| 2 | = | Serial 1 |
| 3 | = | Second Parallel |
| 4 | = | Second Serial |
| 5 | = | DOS Device LPT1 |
| 6 | = | DOS Device LPT2 |
| 7 | = | DOS Device LPT3 |
| 8 | = | DOS Device LPT4 |

3. Type **P** to select the type of printer. Study the following screen:

```
Copyright 1986 Lotus Development Corp.  All Rights Reserved.  Release 2.01 MENU

Select graph output device


                Type of Graphic Output
                                                    [SPACE] turns mark on and off
                                                    [RETURN] selects marked device
    StarzGemini 10X, 15XzLow Density                [ESCAPE] exits, ignoring changes
  # StarzGemini 10X, 15XzHigh Density               [HOME] goes to beginning of list
    Anadex 9620A Silent Scribe Printer              [END] goes to end of list
    Epson FX80 Printer, Single Density Mode         [UP] and [DOWN] move cursor
    Epson FX80 Printer, Double Density Mode             List will scroll if cursor
    Epson FX80 Printer, Triple Density Mode             moved beyond top or bottom
    Epson FX80 Printer, Quad Density Mode
    HP 7470A Plotter
    IBM Graphics Printer, Single Dens. Mode
    IBM Graphics Printer, Double Dens. Mode
    IBM Graphics Printer, Triple Dens. Mode
    IBM Graphics Printer, Quad Density Mode
    Epson MX80 or MX100, Single Dens. Mode
    Epson MX80 or MX100, Double Dens. Mode
    Epson MX80 or MX100, Triple Dens. Mode
    NEC 8023 Printer
    Okidata 82A or 83A Printer
```

This screen lists all the various types of printers and plotters which PrintGraph can use to print graphs. You make the selection the same way you do when choosing the graph files. You move the highlighter to the appropriate printer and press the Spacebar to mark it with a # symbol.

4. Move the highlighter to the "Epson FX80 Printer, Single Density Mode" choice and then press the **Spacebar**.

**NOTE**
This choice obviously presumes that you have an Epson printer connected to the computer. If you do not, mark the choice which matches the type of printer you have.

5. Press **Return** and type **Q**.

The final procedure before printing the selected graph is to set the printed graph size, the fonts to use, and the range colors. Follow these steps to do this:

1. Type **I**. Notice the top section of the following display:

```
Copyright 1986 Lotus Development Corp.  All Rights Reserved.  Release 2.01 MENU

Set size and orientation of graphs
Size   Font   Range-Colors   Quit

    GRAPH        IMAGE OPTIONS                   HARDWARE SETUP
    IMAGES       Size              Range Colors  Graphs Directory:
    SELECTED     Top         .250  X Black         C:\lotus
```

2. Type **R** for Range-Colors.

This choice sets the colors for the Range-Colors items on the graph status screen.

> **NOTE**
> PrintGraph displays a line of color choices if you
> are using a color monitor and have a graphics
> board installed in the computer. If not, the single
> menu item displayed is Black. This is the default
> value when no color has been previously
> specified or for monochrome monitors.

3. Type **B** and then type **Q**.

4. Type **F** to select the fonts PrintGraph uses to print the graph.

Two font style choices appear on the screen. PrintGraph can use one font style for graph headings and another for data labels.

5. Select 1 with the highlighter and then press **Return**.

6. Move the highlighter to Block1, press the **Spacebar** and then press **Return**.

PrintGraph automatically sets both font styles to the selection made for 1 unless 2 is changed to another style using this screen.

7. Type **S** to set the printed graph size.

Use this screen to set the size the graph prints. PrintGraph allows the automatic setting of full-sized and half-sized graph parameters as well as the ability to set all graph dimensions manually.

8. Type **H** to set the graph to print on a half page.

Notice that the Size section of the status screen automatically changes all the dimensions for the graph to conform to the Half menu selection.

9. Type **Q** twice.

Once all the PrintGraph specifications are made, they are saved to the program diskette file and the graph is printed. Perform the following procedures to save the PrintGraph specifications and print the CANDYG6 graph.

1.  Type **S.**

Examine the status screen very carefully. Once all settings are as shown, save it to a configuration file. Every time you load PrintGraph in the future, this configuration will be used to print selected graphs.

2.  Set the printer on-line and type **G** to print the graph shown below:

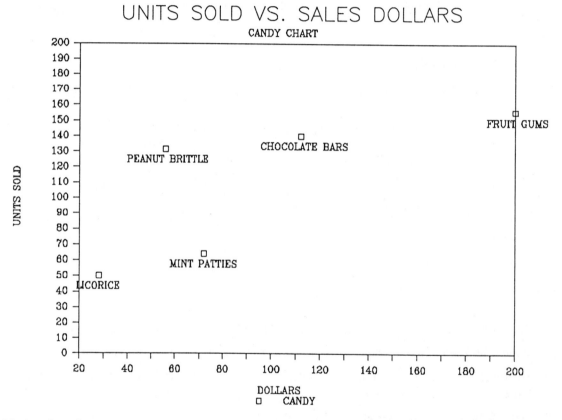

Notice that the printer stops immediately after printing the graph the same way it stops after printing a worksheet. PrintGraph has the same page feeding feature as the Lotus 1-2-3 worksheet program.

3.  Type **P.** The printer spaces up to the starting point on the next page.

4.  Type **EY** to exit the PrintGraph program.

5.  Turn to Module 36 to continue the learning sequence.

# Module 45
# QUIT

## DESCRIPTION

Use the QUIT command to terminate a Lotus 1-2-3 worksheet session. Once invoked, the QUIT command prompts you to either accept the command and terminate the session or reject the command and re-display the READY worksheet screen.

The QUIT command menu choice is located and used from the worksheet READY screen by typing a / (slash) and then typing the first letters of the following menu titles:

```
MENU TITLES:          USE AND USE REQUIREMENT:

Quit No               Do not quit the worksheet
Quit Yes              Do quit the worksheet
```

## APPLICATIONS

Use the QUIT command to leave the worksheet section of the Lotus 1-2-3 program and return to the Lotus 1-2-3 Access System menu.

### NOTE
The QUIT command *does not* automatically save the worksheet displayed on the monitor. Use the SAVE command to save a worksheet before ending a worksheet session.

## TYPICAL OPERATION

1.  From the worksheet READY screen, type **/Q**.

Notice the No    Yes display and description line. This screen gives you the opportunity to change your mind about quitting the Lotus 1-2-3 worksheet. Choosing No returns you to the READY worksheet screen.

2.  Type **Y**.

Notice that the Lotus 1-2-3 Access System menu is displayed. Once you quit the worksheet section of Lotus 1-2-3, you can end the program or select another section of the Lotus 1-2-3 program.

3.  Type **E**. The Lotus 1-2-3 program ends and the DOS prompt is displayed.

**CAUTION**

Do not open the floppy disk load lever when the red light is glowing. The red light indicates that the disk read/write head (a device similar to the needle on a phonograph player) is in motion. Opening the load lever while the red light is on can damage the diskette.

4.  Turn to Module 55 to continue the learning sequence.

# Module 46
## RANGE ERASE

### DESCRIPTION

Use the RANGE ERASE command to erase single cells or a range of cells. This command cannot erase cells that have been protected from accidental erasure or change. Once specific worksheet cells are erased, blank cells appear in their place for the entry of new information.

The RANGE ERASE command is located and used from the worksheet READY screen by typing a / (slash) and then typing the first letters of the following menu titles:

```
MENU TITLES:          USE AND USE REQUIREMENT:

Range Erase           Erase a range of cells
```

### APPLICATIONS

Use the RANGE ERASE command any time specific cells in a worksheet are to be erased. You should pay particular attention to any cells that may contain formulas that depend on the information contained in the cells you erase using this command. The formulas still use the referenced cells and will not calculate properly. Typically, the RANGE ERASE command is used to "wipe clean" a section of the worksheet that is no longer needed.

### TYPICAL OPERATION

1.  Retrieve the CANDY worksheet saved in Module 42.

2. Move the cell pointer to A13 and type **/RE**. Notice the following screen:

```
A13:[W25] 'TOTAL                                              POINT
Enter range to erase: A13..A13


           A              B          C          D
1    POPULAR CANDY SALES
2    -------------------
3                                 SQUARES OF
4                                 DIFFERENCE
5         CANDY NAME      UNITS SOLD FROM MEAN   DOLLARS
6    ----------          ----------  ----------  -------
7    LICORICE                    28    4303.36    $50.12
8    PEANUT BRITTLE              56    1413.76   $131.60
9    MINT PATTIES                72     466.56    $64.08
10   CHOCOLATE BARS             112     338.56   $140.00
11   FRUIT GUMS                 200   11320.96   $156.00
12
13   TOTAL                      468
14
15
16
17
18              MEAN          93.6               108.36
19           MINIMUM            28                50.12
20           MAXIMUM           200                  156
```

**WARNING**

Note that this is not the same Erase command as
the one reached by typing "/WE." The "/WE"
command is used to erase an entire worksheet.
The "/RE" command is used to erase selected
cells within a worksheet.

3. Press **Return**. Notice that Lotus 1-2-3 erases the word TOTAL from the worksheet.

4. Type **TOTAL** and then press **Return**.

5. Quit the worksheet.

6. Turn to Module 14 to continue the learning sequence.

# Module 47
# RANGE FORMAT

## DESCRIPTION

Use the RANGE FORMAT commands to display numbers and formulas in various formats. For example, you might display numbers as dollars and cents with a dollar sign and a decimal point.

Lotus 1-2-3 displays the value of a number or formula in many different ways. For example, using the RANGE FORMAT commands to format the number 5.125, it can be displayed in the following ways:

| | |
|---|---|
| FIXED | 5 |
| SCIENTIFIC | .5125E + 01 |
| CURRENCY | $5.12 |
| , | 5.125 |
| GENERAL | 5.125 |
| PERCENT | 512.5% |
| + / − | + + + + + |

### NOTE

With the fixed, scientific, currency, ",", general and percent formats, any number of decimal places between 0 and 15 can be selected. The + / − format displays a graph in which positive numbers use plus signs ( + ), negative numbers use minus signs ( − ), and a zero value uses a period (.).

In addition to numeric formatting, Lotus 1-2-3 contains several special RANGE FORMAT commands.

The five Lotus 1-2-3 RANGE FORMAT DATE commands display numbers as calendar dates. They are used in conjunction with the @DATE and @DATEVALUE functions to perform calendar date arithmetic. For example, the function @DATE(86,5,20) can be formatted as 20-May- 86, 20-May, May-86, 05/20/86, or 05/20.

The RANGE FORMAT DATE-TIME command can display time in three different ways. They are used in conjunction with the @TIME, @TIMEVALUE, and @NOW functions. The function @TIME(1,30,45) can be displayed as 01:30:45 AM, 01:30:45 PM, 01:30 AM, 01:30 PM, 01:30:45, or 13:30:45.

The RANGE FORMAT TEXT command displays the text of a formula within a worksheet instead of the numeric value of the formula.

The RANGE FORMAT HIDDEN command hides a range of cells, that is it suppresses the display of a range of cells.

The RANGE FORMAT RESET command cancels any special numeric formatting for a range of cells and resets the cell format to the global numeric display format currently in effect (Worksheet Global Format).

The RANGE FORMAT commands are located and used from the worksheet READY screen by typing a / (slash) and then typing the first letters of the following menu titles:

```
MENU TITLES:                 USE AND USE REQUIREMENT:

Range Format                 Set display form
Range Format Fixed           # decimal places Specify range
Range Format
  Scientific                 Scientific notation Specify range
Range Format
  Currency                   # decimal places for $'s Specify range
Range Format
  General                    Default toggle Specify range
Range Format +/-             +/- graph Specify range
Range Format Percent         # decimal places for % Specify range
Range Format Date            Set date display
Range Format Date 1
  (DD-MM-YY)                 Display date as noted
Range Format Date 2
  (DD-MM)                    Display date as noted
Range Format Date 3
  (MM-YY)                    Display date as noted
Range Format Date 4
  (Long Int'l)               Display date as noted
Range Format Date 5
  (Short Int'l)              Display date as noted
Range Format Time 1
  (HH:MM:SS AM/PM)           Display time as noted
Range Format Time 2
  (HH:MM AM/PM)              Display time as noted
Range Format Time 3
  (Long Int'l)               Display time as noted
```

```
Range Format Time 4
    (Short Int'l)        Display time as noted
Range Format Text        Display formulas instead of values
Range Format Hidden      Suppress the display of a range of cells Specify the cell range
Range Format Reset       Clear all format settings in entire worksheet
```

## APPLICATIONS

The RANGE FORMAT commands are some of the most widely used in Lotus 1-2-3 worksheets. Use them to "dress-up" the numbers in a worksheet or to hide columns, format date information used to perform calendar calculations, and to display worksheet formulas instead of values. The RANGE FORMAT commands can also be used to perform string function operations. For example, typing 1-2-3 into a worksheet results in the value $-4$, but you can use the RANGE FORMAT command to format the cell to display as text in the form 1-2-3.

## TYPICAL OPERATION

1. From the worksheet READY screen, type **/WCS25** and then press **Return** to set the column width to 25 characters.

2. Move the cell pointer down one row at a time from cell location A1 and type the following information:

|   | **A** |
|---|---|
| 1 | **SALE BY PRODUCT** |
| 2 | |
| 3 | **CATTLE** |
| 4 | **SHEEP** |
| 5 | **HOGS** |
| 6 | |
| 7 | **TOTAL** |

3. Move the cell pointer to B3 and type the following values for each type of product:

|   | **A** | **B** |
|---|---|---|
| 1 | **SALE BY PRODUCT** | |
| 2 | | |
| 3 | **CATTLE** | **8** |
| 4 | **SHEEP** | **10** |
| 5 | **HOGS** | **15** |
| 6 | | |
| 7 | **TOTAL** | |

177

4.  Move the cell pointer to B3 and type **/RF**. The screen displays the following:

```
B3:    8                                                          MENU
Fixed  Scientific  Currency  ,  General  +/-  Percent  Date  Text  Hidden  Reset
Fixed number of decimal places (x.xx)
                    A              B        C          D        E        F        G
1    SALE BY PRODUCT
2
3    CATTLE                8
4    SHEEP                10
5    HOGS                 15
6
7    TOTAL
```

The Format menu choice allows you to change the way numbers are displayed.

5.  Move the highlighter to +/− and read the descriptive information about this choice.

Lotus 1-2-3 can display numbers in a bar chart form. A bar chart is the visual presentation of numbers. Lotus 1-2-3 uses the plus sign ( + ) and the minus sign ( − ) to represent numbers. Each + or − is equal to one whole unit. For example, a value of seven in your worksheet would equal seven + 's ( + + + + + + + ) in a +/− display.

6.  Press **Return**.

Lotus 1-2-3 always asks you for the range of cells that you want displayed in the new format.

7.  Move the cell pointer to B5, press **Return** and study the following screen:

```
B3:    5                                                          MENU
Fixed  Scientific  Currency  ,  General  +/-  Percent  Date  Text  Hidden  Reset
Fixed number of decimal places (x.xx)
                    A              B        C          D        E        F        G
1    SALE BY PRODUCT
2
3    CATTLE                ++++++++
4    SHEEP                ********
5    HOGS                 ********
6
7    TOTAL
```

Notice that all the numbers in column B change to + symbols. Since each value in column B of the chart is positive, each number in the new display format is a +. The * (asterisks) indicate that column B is not wide enough to accept some of the numbers in the new format. When you see this symbol, you must change the column width to properly display the numbers (or bar chart display).

8. Type **/WCS20** and then press **Return**. The screen changes to the following display:

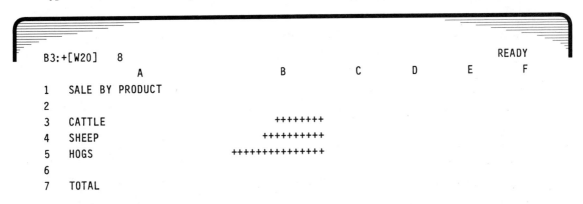

Lotus 1-2-3 changes the width of column B to 20 characters. Notice that the product numbers in the worksheet changed to the + graph format.

9. Type **/RFH**, move the cell pointer to B5, and press **Return**.

Notice that the graph in column B no longer displays.

10. Type **/RFR**, move the cell pointer to B5, and press **Return**.

The original number values for the products display.

**NOTE**

You may want to save this file. It is used to demonstrate the uses of the WORKSHEET GLOBAL FORMAT, WORKSHEET INSERT, WORKSHEET DELETE, COPY, and MOVE commands.

11. Save the worksheet.

12. Turn to Module 62 to continue the learning sequence.

# Module 48

## RANGE INPUT

### DESCRIPTION

Lotus 1-2-3 allows the marking of cell ranges for input only. Use the RANGE INPUT command to specify an input range that allows the cell pointer to move only within the marked cells.

The RANGE INPUT command is located and used from the worksheet READY screen by typing a / (slash) and then typing the first letters of the following menu titles:

```
MENU TITLES:            USE AND USE REQUIREMENT:

Range Input             Specify a range of cells for keyboard entry Specify range
```

### APPLICATIONS

The RANGE INPUT command is used to specify an area on a worksheet for input only and to prevent the cell pointer from moving to any other cells in the worksheet. This command is primarily used with Lotus 1-2-3 macros to prevent the user from accidentally changing information in the worksheet that would damage the worksheet's formulas or printing characteristics. Typically, after a worksheet has been fully developed, it requires updating from time to time. The RANGE INPUT command allows the developer to limit access to only those cells where changed information is entered. This allows anyone with minimal experience with Lotus 1-2-3 to perform the data entry without inadvertantly damaging the worksheet's cell relationships.

### TYPICAL OPERATION

1. Retrieve the CANDY worksheet saved in Module 20.

2. Move the cell pointer to B7 and type **/RI**.

3. Move the cell pointer to B11 and press **Return**.

Notice the following screen:

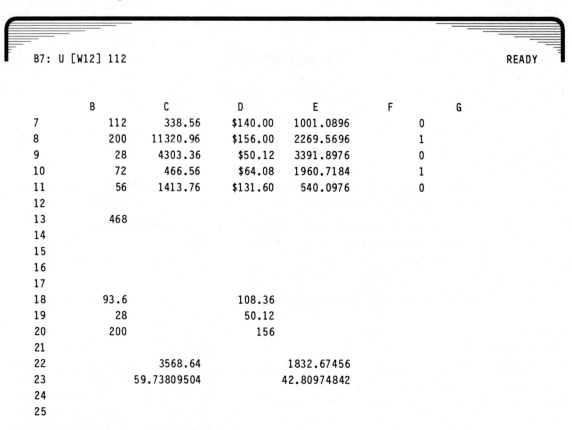

B7: U [W12] 112                                                        READY

|    | B        | C          | D        | E          | F | G |
|----|----------|------------|----------|------------|---|---|
| 7  | 112      | 338.56     | $140.00  | 1001.0896  | 0 |   |
| 8  | 200      | 11320.96   | $156.00  | 2269.5696  | 1 |   |
| 9  | 28       | 4303.36    | $50.12   | 3391.8976  | 0 |   |
| 10 | 72       | 466.56     | $64.08   | 1960.7184  | 1 |   |
| 11 | 56       | 1413.76    | $131.60  | 540.0976   | 0 |   |
| 12 |          |            |          |            |   |   |
| 13 | 468      |            |          |            |   |   |
| 14 |          |            |          |            |   |   |
| 15 |          |            |          |            |   |   |
| 16 |          |            |          |            |   |   |
| 17 |          |            |          |            |   |   |
| 18 | 93.6     |            | 108.36   |            |   |   |
| 19 | 28       |            | 50.12    |            |   |   |
| 20 | 200      |            | 156      |            |   |   |
| 21 |          |            |          |            |   |   |
| 22 |          | 3568.64    |          | 1832.67456 |   |   |
| 23 |          | 59.73809504 |         | 42.80974842 |  |   |
| 24 |          |            |          |            |   |   |
| 25 |          |            |          |            |   |   |

4. Try to move the cell pointer to C7.

Notice that the cell pointer is prevented from moving to C7. The marked range is the only area of the worksheet where the cell pointer is allowed to move.

5. Press **Esc** and quit the worksheet.

6. Turn to Module 51 to continue the learning sequence.

# Module 49

## RANGE JUSTIFY

### DESCRIPTION

Use the RANGE JUSTIFY command to reformat text so that all characters within one or more worksheet rows fill the available space in the worksheet column.

The RANGE JUSTIFY command is located and used from the worksheet READY screen by typing a / (slash) and then typing the first letters of the following menu titles:

```
MENU TITLES:          USE AND USE REQUIREMENT:

Range Justify         Set automatic margin justification for a range of cells Specify range
```

### APPLICATIONS

Typically, the RANGE JUSTIFY command is used to reformat text in a series of rows in the same manner that a word processing program reformats a paragraph. A good example is the business application where a column (or columns) of text describes the contents of cells to the right of the text. Using RANGE JUSTIFY allows you to reformat the text so that all the words fill the available space in the text columns.

### TYPICAL OPERATION

1.  From the worksheet READY screen, press **Home** and then type **/WCS25** and press **Return** to set the column width to 25 characters.

2.  Type **Now is the time for all** and then press **Return**.

3.  Move the cell pointer to A2, type **good men** and then press **Return**.

4.  Move the cell pointer to A3, type **to come to the aid of** and then press **Return**.

5. Move the cell pointer to A4, type **their country.** and then press **Return**. The following screen displays:

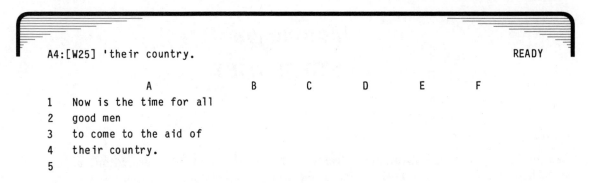

```
A4:[W25] 'their country.                                        READY

                  A           B         C         D         E         F
   1   Now is the time for all
   2   good men
   3   to come to the aid of
   4   their country.
   5
```

6. Type **/RJ**. The monitor displays the following screen:

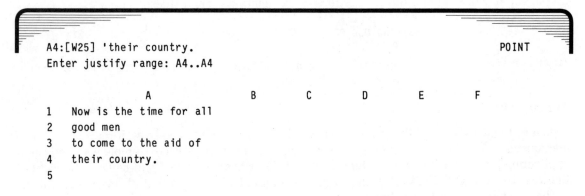

```
A4:[W25] 'their country.                                        POINT
Enter justify range: A4..A4

                  A           B         C         D         E         F
   1   Now is the time for all
   2   good men
   3   to come to the aid of
   4   their country.
   5
```

A single cell location or a range of cell locations can be marked for use with the RANGE JUSTIFY command.

7. Press **Esc** once and notice that the last cell in the displayed range disappears.

8. Move the cell pointer to A1. The first cell in the range changes to the cell where the cell pointer moves.

9. Type . (a period) and then move the cell pointer to A4.

As with all Lotus 1-2-3 range marking features, the marked cell range is highlighted.

10. Press **Return**. The screen changes to the following:

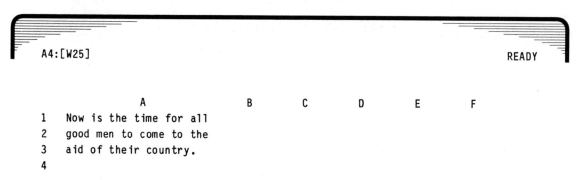

```
A4:[W25]                                               READY

                    A          B      C      D      E      F
   1    Now is the time for all
   2    good men to come to the
   3    aid of their country.
   4
```

The text in the worksheet is justified, that is, it moves so that all available character spaces are taken up with the text.

11. Quit the worksheet.

12. Turn to Module 63 to continue the learning sequence.

# Module 50
## RANGE LABEL

### DESCRIPTION

Use the RANGE LABEL commands to left-justify, right-justify, or center text in one or more worksheet columns or rows.

The RANGE LABEL commands are located and used from the worksheet READY screen by typing a / (slash) and then typing the first letters of the following menu titles:

```
MENU TITLES:              USE AND USE REQUIREMENT:

Range Label               Set justification of text
Range Label Left          Left justify Specify range
Range Label Right         Right justify Specify range
Range Label Center        Center text Specify range
```

### APPLICATIONS

Typically, the RANGE LABEL commands are used to center column headings and to left-justify or right-justify row descriptions. For example, a commonly used business worksheet is a cash flow projection that contains text in column A which describes the dollar values in one or more columns to the right of the text column. The RANGE LABEL commands can be used to center the major subject text and left-justify the indented text as shown in the following illustration:

```
    CASH FROM OPERATIONS ---Centered in column

Net Profits----------------Left-Justified in Column
Sale of Assets-------------Left-Justified in Column
```

### TYPICAL OPERATION

1. From the worksheet READY screen, press **Home** and then type **/WCS25** and press **Return** to set the column width to 25 characters.

2. Type **COLUMN A** and then press **Return.**

3. Move the cell pointer to A2, type **ROW 2** and then press **Return.**

The following screen displays:

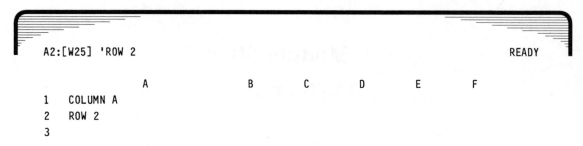

```
A2:[W25] 'ROW 2                                                    READY

                    A           B       C       D       E       F
1     COLUMN A
2     ROW 2
3
```

The text in rows 1 and 2 starts at the left-hand margin. The default location for text is left-justified.

4.  Type **/RLR** to right-justify. The monitor displays the following screen:

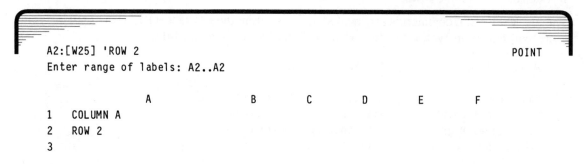

```
A2:[W25] 'ROW 2                                                    POINT
Enter range of labels: A2..A2

                    A           B       C       D       E       F
1     COLUMN A
2     ROW 2
3
```

A single cell location of a range of cell locations can be marked for use with all the RANGE LABEL commands.

5.  Move the cell pointer to A1. Notice that the marked cell range is highlighted.

6.  Press **Return**.

The text in the worksheet moves from the left-hand side of the column to the right-hand side.

7.  Move the cell pointer to A1, type **/RLC** and then press **Return**.

The screen changes to the following:

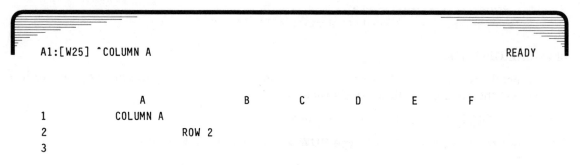

```
A1:[W25] ^COLUMN A                                                 READY


                    A           B       C       D       E       F
1                COLUMN A
2                            ROW 2
3
```

Notice the caret symbol ( ^ ) to the left of the text displayed in the cell contents block. The three justification commands can be performed directly from the keyboard without using the Lotus 1-2-3 menu. The following table lists the Lotus 1-2-3 text justification commands and the symbols required to use them.

| Operator | Result on Text |
|---|---|
| Single quote ( ' ) | Flush left |
| Double quote ( " ) | Flush right |
| Circumflex ( ^ or upper-case 6) | Centered |
| Backslash ( \ ) | Repeat next character across cell |

8.  Quit the worksheet.

9.  Turn to Module 49 to continue the learning sequence.

# Module 51
# RANGE NAME

**DESCRIPTION**

Lotus 1-2-3 allows the naming of cell ranges for use with the program's other features, to label information columns with the description columns adjacent to them, and to display a table of all range names and the cells they include. Use the RANGE NAME commands to mark and name a range of cells for use as labels or with other Lotus 1-2-3 commands and to list all ranges already named in the worksheet.

The RANGE NAME commands are located and used from the worksheet READY screen by typing a / (slash) and then typing the first letters of the following menu titles:

```
MENU TITLES:              USE AND USE REQUIREMENT:

Range Name                Name a range of cells Specify range
Range Name Create         Range name Specify range
Range Name Delete         Range name
Range Name Labels         Use labels to create names
Range Name Labels
  Right                   Specify range of cells to the right of labels
Range Name Labels
  Down                    Specify range of cells below the labels
Range Name Labels
  Left                    Specify range of cells to the left of labels
Range Name Labels
  Up                      Specify range of cells above the labels
Range Name Reset          Delete all names
Range Name Table          Create a table of all named range within the worksheet
```

**APPLICATIONS**

Use RANGE NAME commands to specify and name an area on a worksheet for use with macros, the translate feature, or as a list of labels that can be copied by specifying the range name rather than marking the range. Range naming is an easily learned skill, but one that is important, particularly with macros. A good example is using a named range in an automatic printing macro. Instead of marking each range to be printed, the range can be given a name. This saves macro steps as the PRINTER RANGE command can be answered with the range name (one step) rather than the beginning cell reference and the ending cell reference (two steps). Named ranges are also useful in conjunction with Lotus 1-2-3's many statistical @ functions, because range names are easier to use and more reliable than using beginning and ending cell coordinates.

**TYPICAL OPERATION**

1. Retrieve the CANDY worksheet saved in Module 20.

2. Move the cell pointer to B7 and type **/RNC**.

3. Type **UNITS** as the range name and press **Return**.

4. Move the cell pointer to B11 and press **Return**.

5. Move the cell pointer to A30, type **/RNT** and press **Return**.

Notice that the named range (UNITS) is listed in cell A30 and that the cell range referenced by that name displays in cell B30.

6. Quit the worksheet.

7. Turn to Module 5 to continue the learning sequence.

# Module 52

## RANGE PROTECT, UNPROTECT

### DESCRIPTION

After the worksheet protection feature is turned on (enabled), using the WORKSHEET PROTECTION command, use the RANGE PROTECT, UNPROTECT commands to specify those worksheet cells that you want safeguarded from accidental erasure, deletion, or change. The entire worksheet must be set so that the protective feature can be used before this command is effective.

The RANGE PROTECT, UNPROTECT commands are located and used from the worksheet READY screen by typing a / (slash) and then typing the first letters of the following menu titles:

```
MENU TITLES:              USE AND USE REQUIREMENT:

Range Protect             Protect from change a range of cells Specify range
Range Unprotect           Unprotect from change a range of cells Specify range
```

### APPLICATIONS

Use the RANGE PROTECT, UNPROTECT commands any time a range of cells is to be protected from accidental erasure or change. This command is typically used to "freeze" worksheet formulas and macros to prevent inexperienced Lotus 1-2-3 users from accidentally damaging a worksheet by changing or erasing information contained in it.

### TYPICAL OPERATION

1. Retrieve the CANDY worksheet saved in Module 42.

2. Type **/WGPE**.

3. Move the cell pointer to A1 and type **/RP**. Notice the following screen:

```
A1:[W25] 'POPULAR CANDY SALES                                    POINT
   Enter range to protect: A1..A1
                    A              B           C           D
    1       POPULAR CANDY SALES
    2       -------------------
    3                                       SQUARES OF
    4                                       DIFFERENCE
    5           CANDY NAME         UNITS SOLD FROM MEAN    DOLLARS
    6           ----------         ---------- ----------   -------
    7    LICORICE                      28     4303.36      $50.12
    8    PEANUT BRITTLE                56     1413.76     $131.60
    9    MINT PATTIES                  72      466.56      $64.08
   10    CHOCOLATE BARS               112      338.56     $140.00
   11    FRUIT GUMS                   200    11320.96     $156.00
   12
   13    TOTAL                        468
   14
   15
   16
   17
   18              MEAN             93.6                  108.36
   19           MINIMUM              28                   50.12
   20           MAXIMUM             200                     156
```

4. Move the cell pointer to A20.

The cells to be protected are highlighted. Lotus 1-2-3 protects all the cells within the highlighted area from selective erasure, deletion, and change.

5. Press **Return** to protect all the cells in the highlighted portion of the worksheet.

6. Move the cell pointer to A18 and type **/WDR** to delete row 18.

7. Press **Return**. Notice the following display:

```
D18:[W25] ' MEAN                                              ERROR
   Enter range of rows to delete: D18..D18
                    A            B          C          D
   1     POPULAR CANDY SALES
   2     -------------------
   3                                    SQUARES OF
   4                                    DIFFERENCE
   5          CANDY NAME       UNITS SOLD FROM MEAN   DOLLARS
   6          ----------       ---------- ---------   -------
   7     LICORICE                     28    4303.36    $50.12
   8     PEANUT BRITTLE               56    1413.76   $131.60
   9     MINT PATTIES                 72     466.56    $64.08
  10     CHOCOLATE BARS              112     338.56   $140.00
  11     FRUIT GUMS                  200   11320.96   $156.00
  12
  13     TOTAL                       468
  14
  15
  16
  17
  18                    MEAN        93.6              108.36
  19                 MINIMUM          28               50.12
  20                 MAXIMUM         200                 156
   Protected Cell
```

If your computer is equipped with audio capability, you heard a beep. Look at the message displayed in the lower left-hand corner of the screen. Lotus 1-2-3 cannot delete row 18 because it is protected. This same message always appears when you try to delete, erase, or change the information in protected cells.

8. Press **Esc** and move the cell pointer to A1 and then type **/RU**.

9. Move the cell pointer to A20 and press **Return** to unprotect the previously protected cells.

10. Quit the worksheet.

11. Turn to Module 46 to continue the learning sequence.

# Module 53

## RANGE TRANSPOSE

### DESCRIPTION

Lotus 1-2-3, Release 2.01 adds a command that has been long overdue. Many worksheet users have wished that information contained in a worksheet could be transposed, that is, rearranged from a columnar format to a row format or vice versa. Use the RANGE TRANSPOSE command to perform this function.

The RANGE TRANSPOSE command is located and used from the worksheet READY screen by typing a / (slash) and then typing the first letters of the following menu titles:

```
MENU TITLES:              USE AND USE REQUIREMENT:

Range Transpose           Copy cells from columns to rows & vice-versa
                          Specify copy "from/to" range
```

### APPLICATIONS

The RANGE TRANSPOSE command is used to specify an area on a worksheet in which the information is changed from a columnar format to a row format or from a row format to a columnar format. Many times a worksheet is far along in its development when the need arises to take a column or row of information and enter it as a row or column. With the Release 1A version of Lotus 1-2-3, the only way to do this was to retype the information. Lotus 1-2-3 Release 2.01 allows you to transpose columns or rows of information automatically, a time saving feature that has been long overdue.

### TYPICAL OPERATION

1. Retrieve the CANDY worksheet saved in Module 20.

2. Move the cell pointer to A7 and type **/RT**.

Notice the familiar range marking prompt.

3. Move the cell pointer to B11 and press **Return**.

4. Move the cell pointer to A15, type . (a period), and then move the cell pointer to E16.

5. Press **Return**. Notice the following screen:

```
  A7:[W25] 'CHOCOLATE BARS                                      READY


                 A               B          C          D
     1    POPULAR CANDY SALES
     2    -------------------
     3                                  SQUARES OF
     4                                  DIFFERENCE
     5        CANDY NAME          UNITS SOLD  FROM MEAN   DOLLARS
     6        ----------         ----------  ----------  -------
     7    CHOCOLATE BARS               112      338.56   $140.00
     8    FRUIT GUMS                   200    11320.96   $156.00
     9    LICORICE                      28     4303.36    $50.12
    10    MINT PATTIES                  72      466.56    $64.08
    11    PEANUT BRITTLE                56     1413.76   $131.60
    12
    13    TOTAL                        468
    14
    15    CHOCOLATE BARS         FRUIT GUMS  LICORICE  MINT PATTIES
    16                     112       200          28            72
    17
```

Lotus transposes the range so that the candy name and units sold information changes from the column format to the row format.

6. Quit the worksheet.

7. The learning sequence continues with Module 54.

# Module 54

## RANGE VALUE

**DESCRIPTION**

Lotus 1-2-3, Release 2.01 allows formula values to be copied from one location to another without the formula itself, that is only the value of the calculation performed by the formula is copied. Use the RANGE VALUE command to perform this function.

The RANGE VALUE command is located and used from the worksheet READY screen by typing a / (slash) and then typing the first letters of the following menu titles:

```
MENU TITLES:          USE AND USE REQUIREMENT:

Range Value           Copy cell values without the formulas Specify the copy "from/to" range
```

**APPLICATIONS**

The RANGE VALUE command is used to specify a worksheet area containing formulas in which only the calculated values for the formulas are copied to another worksheet area. For example, if the calculated values of a set of formulas is required in a section of another worksheet, use RANGE VALUE. If, on the other hand, you use formulas written with relative cell references, improperly calculated values would result.

**TYPICAL OPERATION**

1. Retrieve the CANDY worksheet saved in Module 20.

2. Move the cell pointer to B18.

Notice the formula @SUM(B11. .B7) displayed in the cell contents block.

3. Type **/RV**.

4. Press **Return** and move the cell pointer to C18 and then press **Return**.

5. Move the cell pointer to C18.

The value 93.6 copied but the formula did not. To copy a formula, use the COPY command.

6. Quit the worksheet.

7. Turn to Module 48 to continue the learning sequence.

# Module 55

## SYSTEM

**DESCRIPTION**

Use the SYSTEM command to go to the computer's DOS operating system from within a Lotus 1-2-3 worksheet. Once this "shell" command is invoked, all DOS internal and external commands, can be performed as they would normally. Typing EXIT and then pressing the Return key from the DOS system level returns you to the worksheet READY screen from which the command was used.

The SYSTEM command is located and used from the worksheet READY screen by typing a / (slash) and then typing the first letters of the following menu titles:

```
MENU TITLES:           USE AND USE REQUIREMENT:

System                 Exit to DOS
```

**APPLICATIONS**

Use the SYSTEM command to leave the worksheet displayed on the monitor and access the DOS operating system. This command is very useful to check file status, disk space, etc. without terminating the program. This command serves as a replacement for the Lotus 1-2-3 File-Manager and Disk-Manager utilities found in Lotus 1-2-3 Release 1A.

> **NOTE**
> The SYSTEM command *does not* terminate Lotus 1-2-3. The worksheet displayed on the monitor remains in the computer's memory until EXIT is typed at the DOS level and the Return key is pressed. Should the computer be turned off while using the SYSTEM command, the worksheet is lost.

**TYPICAL OPERATION**

1.  From the worksheet READY screen remove the Lotus 1-2-3 System diskette from drive A and replace it with the DOS diskette.

**NOTE**
This step is unnecessary with hard disk drive
systems.

2. Type **/S**. Notice that the system prompt appears.

3. Type **DIR** and press **Return**.

The DOS DIRECTORY command lists all the files on the diskette (or hard drive subdirectory).

4. Remove the DOS diskette and replace it with the Lotus 1-2-3 System diskette.

5. Type **EXIT** and press **Return**.

The Lotus 1-2-3 worksheet displays in the READY mode.

6. Quit the worksheet.

7. Turn to Module 57 to continue the learning sequence.

# Module 56

## TRANSLATE

### DESCRIPTION

The Lotus 1-2-3, Release 2.01 translate feature is greatly improved over the earlier version of the program. In addition to being able to convert a Lotus 1-2-3 worksheet file into a database file, the new release is capable of translating the following:

FROM ANY OF THESE:

1-2-3 release 1A
1-2-3 rel 2 or 2.01
dBase II
dBase III
DIF
Jazz
SYMPHONY 1.0
SYMPHONY 1.1 or 1.2
VISICALC

TO ANY OF THESE:

1-2-3 rel 2 or 2.01
dBase II
dBase III
DIF
SYMPHONY 1.0
SYMPHONY 1.1 or 1.2

### TYPICAL OPERATION

Translation of Lotus 1-2-3 worksheets into databases is a major use of the translate feature. A *database* is defined as a collection of files which contain information, abstracts, or references on a particular subject or subjects. A typical database might be an address book in which you keep the names, addresses, and telephone numbers of all your friends. Computer databases offer the user the ability to continuously update the information contained within them. Once translated, the database can be used just as you created it using the applicable database program.

1.  Retrieve the CANDY worksheet saved in Module 28.

Before translating the CANDY worksheet into a dBASE III file, a series of one line column headings must be created. Lotus 1-2-3 reads the first line in a range of information to be translated as the field names for the database.

### NOTE
The line of headings should not contain a column title more than eight characters in length. The database uses these headings as names for fields within the database records. Field names must contain valid characters.

2. Move the cell pointer to A7, type **/WIR** and press **Return** to insert one row.

3. Type the following headings in cells A7 and B7.

| **UNDER:** | **TYPE:** |
|---|---|
| **CANDY NAME** | **NAME** |
| **UNITS SOLD** | **UNITS** |

Notice the following screen:

```
B7:[W12] 'UNITS                                                    READY


                    A            B         C           D
      1     POPULAR CANDY SALES
      2     -------------------
      3                                 SQUARES OF
      4                                 DIFFERENCE
      5           CANDY NAME    UNITS SOLD FROM MEAN   DOLLARS
      6           ----------    ---------- ---------   -------
      7     NAME                UNITS
      8     CHOCOLATE BARS            112    338.56    $140.00
      9     FRUIT GUMS               200  11320.96    $156.00
     10     LICORICE                  28   4303.36     $50.12
     11     MINT PATTIES              72    466.56     $64.08
     12     PEANUT BRITTLE            56   1413.76    $131.60
     13
     14     TOTAL                    468
     15
     16
     17
     18
```

For Lotus 1-2-3 to translate the information contained between cells A7 through B12, this range must be named.

4. Move the cell pointer to A7 and type **/RNC**.

5. Type **DBRANGE** and press **Return**.

6. Move the cell pointer to B12 and press **Return**.

Once the range has been named, the Lotus 1-2-3 Translate function is used to create a .DBF file.

7. Save the worksheet using the replace option and quit the worksheet.

8. Select the Translate choice from the Lotus 1-2-3 Access menu.

9. Remove the Lotus 1-2-3 System diskette in response to the prompt and replace it with the Lotus 1-2-3 Utility diskette and press **Return**.

Look at the following display:

```
              Lotus  1-2-3  Release 2.01 Translate Utility
         Copyright 1986 Lotus Development Corporation  All Rights Reserved


    What do you want to translate FROM?

            1-2-3 release 1A
            1-2-3 rel 2 or 2.01                               •
            dBase II
            dBase III
            DIF
            Jazz
            SYMPHONY 1.0
            SYMPHONY 1.1 or 1.2
            VISICALC




           Move the menu pointer to your selection and press [RETURN].
              Press [ESCAPE] to leave the Translate Utility.
                  Press [HELP] for more information.
```

Select which type of source file Lotus 1-2-3 is to translate from this menu.

10.  Select 1-2-3, Release 2 or 2.01. The following screen displays:

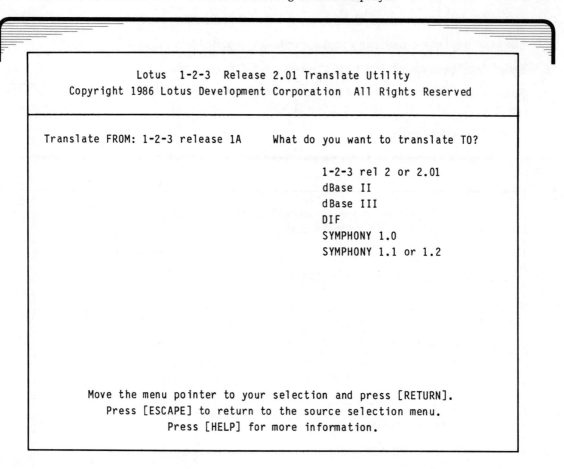

Specify the type of file the translation is to create from this menu.

11. Select dBase III. The following information screen appears:

```
          Lotus  1-2-3  Release 2.01 Translate Utility
    Copyright 1986 Lotus Development Corporation  All Rights Reserved


    The 1-2-3 file, or the range you have requested for translation,
    must meet the following criteria:

    1. The entire file or range must be a database.
    2. The first row of the file or range must consist of field names.
       These field names must be label cells beginning with a letter.
    3. The second row must be the first data record. Each field/cell
       in this row must contain data or be formatted.
    4. Columns must be wide enough to display the data or the data
       will be truncated.
    5. Scientific format should not be used because there is no equivalent
       format in dBASE-III.

    The database records may consist of 1-128 fields.  Each field
    has a field type (such as label or number).  Translate matches
    the field types in each dBASE-III record with the field types in
    the first data record of the worksheet/range.

                   Press [RETURN] for next page
                   Press [ESCAPE] to continue
```

12. Press **Return** to display the next information screen.

```
              Lotus  1-2-3  Release 2.01 Translate Utility
      Copyright 1986 Lotus Development Corporation  All Rights Reserved
```

The format found in each field of the first data record is used for the entire database, regardless of the content of the subsequent records.

Field names should conform to dBASE-III naming restrictions and numbers should be valid dBASE-III numbers. Numeric columns should not be wider than 19 characters.

Before translating the 1-2-3 file, Translate displays a menu with the options Worksheet and Range.

o "Worksheet" translates the entire 1-2-3 file.
o "Range" translates a named range of the 1-2-3 file. Cell
   coordinates may NOT be used in lieu of a named range.

ALL cells in the active worksheet or range will be translated, including blank cells.

```
              Press [BACKSPACE] for previous page
                   Press [ESCAPE] to continue
```

13. Press **Esc** and notice the following display:

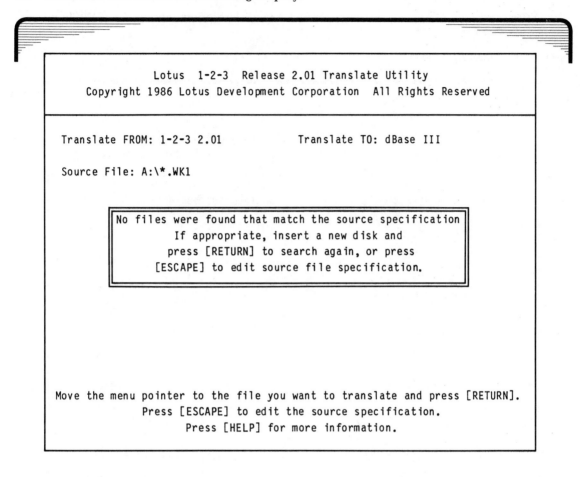

Lotus 1-2-3 looks for .WK1 files on the indicated disk drive. Most data files are kept on disk drive B.

14. Press **Esc** to edit the drive path.

15. Press **Backspace** to erase the displayed disk drive information and type **B:\ * .WK1** and then press **Return**.

Notice the following screen:

```
           Lotus  1-2-3  Release 2.01 Translate Utility
      Copyright 1986 Lotus Development Corporation  All Rights Reserved


  Translate FROM: 1-2-3 2.01            Translate TO: dBase III

  Source File: B:\*.wk1

   CANDY    WK1   1/01/80   2:41a      3900

         CANDY    WK1












  Move the menu pointer to the file you want to translate and press [RETURN].
            Press [ESCAPE] to edit the source specification.
                  Press [HELP] for more information.
```

16. Select CANDY and press **Return**. Notice that the filename appears beside the drive path.

17. Press **Return** to create the destination file on disk drive B.

Lotus 1-2-3 allows you to translate an entire worksheet or a range of cells within a worksheet. Since you marked a range within CANDY, this range must be named.

18. Type **R**. Notice that Enter Range Name: and a cursor appear.

19. Type **DBRANGE** and press **Return**.

You can abort this entire translation procedure from this screen.

20. Type **Y** to translate the worksheet into a dBase III file.

Lotus 1-2-3 works for a few seconds displaying the percentage of the file that is being translated. When finished a TRANSLATION SUCCESSFUL message appears on the screen.

21. Press **Esc** twice and type **Y** to leave the translate feature.

Lotus 1-2-3 translates the range from the CANDY worksheet file into CANDY.DBF. The translation does not effect the original worksheet file. The following illustration is a computer screen display of the database file contents and structure when loaded into dBase III.

```
                       . display structure
                       Structure for database : B:CANDY.DBF
The # of Candies-Number of data records :      5
                       Date of last update    : 07/02/86
The one line-----Field  Field name  Type      Width   Dec
headings are          1  NAME       Character   25
converted to          2  UNITS      Numeric     12      2
dBASE field        ** Total **                  38
names.
                       . display all
The units sold---Record#  NAME                    UNITS
data for each         1  CHOCOLATE BARS          112.00
candy type is         2  FRUIT GUMS              200.00
stored as             3  LICORICE                 28.00
individual            4  MINT PATTIES             72.00
dBASE records         5  PEANUT BRITTLE           56.00
```

This is the last module in the learning sequence.

# Module 57
## WORKSHEET COLUMN

**DESCRIPTION**

Use the WORKSHEET COLUMN commands to set the character width of a specific worksheet column or to reset the specific column width to the value created using the WORKSHEET GLOBAL COLUMN-WIDTH command. Also use the WORKSHEET COLUMN commands to hide or display one or more worksheet columns.

Use the four functions for the WORKSHEET COLUMN commands to perform the following:

- **Set Width** — Used to set the width of the column where the cell pointer is located. The width can be any number from 1 to 240 characters. Lotus 1-2-3, Release 1A is limited to a maximum column width of 72 characters.
- **Reset Width** — Used to set the width of the column that contains the cell pointer to the value created using the WORKSHEET GLOBAL COLUMN-WIDTH command.
- **Hide** — Used to hide (suppress) the display and printing of one or more columns.
- **Display** — Used to display columns hidden using the Hide function of the WORKSHEET COLUMN commands.

**NOTE**

The WORKSHEET COLUMN commands work independently within worksheet windows. Column functions within each window must be set separately.

The WORKSHEET COLUMN commands are located and used from the worksheet READY screen by typing a / (slash) and then typing the first letters of the following menu titles:

```
MENU TITLES:              USE AND USE REQUIREMENT:

Worksheet Column         Set width of column(s)
Worksheet Column
  Set Width              Set width of column in # characters Specify range
Worksheet Column
  Reset Width            Set width of all columns in # of characters for entire worksheet
Worksheet Column
  Hide                   Hide the information in a column of cells Specify column range
Worksheet Column
  Display                Display the information in a column of cells Specify column range
```

## APPLICATIONS

Use the four functions of the WORKSHEET COLUMN commands to set the width of specified columns so that they can properly display the information they contain, or to hide and display columns of information. The hide/display function is a new Lotus 1-2-3 feature that allows you to hide columns of information and then redisplay them. This is particularly useful when you have used one or more columns for the sole purpose of containing interim formula calculations. These columns are really not part of the worksheet that you want to present to the user, therefore, use the WORKSHEET COLUMN HIDE command to suppress their display.

## TYPICAL OPERATION

1. From the worksheet READY screen, type **/WC**. The following screen displays:

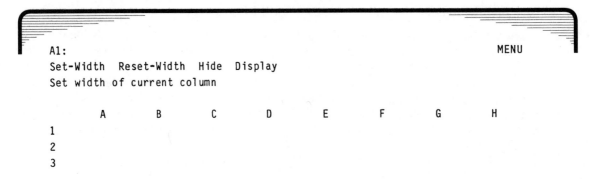

2. Type **S** to set the width of column A. Look at the following display:

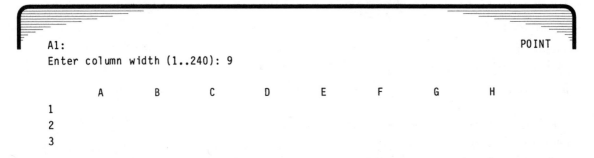

Lotus 1-2-3 automatically displays the number 9 for the column width. This is known as a *default setting.* Lotus 1-2-3 initially sets the width of all the columns in a worksheet to nine characters. Use the WORKSHEET GLOBAL COLUMN-WIDTH command to change the default setting.

Notice the numbers inside the parentheses (1. .240). Lotus 1-2-3 accepts a column width setting as small as one character and as large as 240 characters.

3. Type **25** for the new column width of column A.

Notice that Lotus 1-2-3 erases the 9 and displays the 25.

4. Press **Return**.

Lotus 1-2-3 changes the width of column A to 25 characters. Notice that the highlighter expands to fill the new width and the new column width displays in brackets ([ ]) beside the cell contents block.

5. Type **TEST** and press **Return**.

6. Type **/WCH** and press **Return**.

Notice that the display of column A is suppressed.

7. Type **/WCD**, type **A1** and press **Return**.

8. Press **Home**.

The display of the word "TEST" is turned-on again.

9. Quit the worksheet.

10. Turn to Module 59 to continue the learning sequence.

# Module 58

# WORKSHEET DELETE

**DESCRIPTION**

WORKSHEET DELETE commands delete one or more rows or columns from a worksheet.

The WORKSHEET DELETE commands are located and used from the worksheet READY screen by typing a / (slash) and then typing the first letters of the following menu titles:

```
MENU TITLES:              USE AND USE REQUIREMENT:

Worksheet Delete          Remove columns and rows
Worksheet Delete
  Column                  Remove column(s) Specify range
Worksheet Delete
  Row                     Remove row(s) Specify range
```

**APPLICATIONS**

When a worksheet is developed, there is often a need to remove rows or columns, for example, when you have consolidated worksheet information and eliminated the need for an existing column of information.

**TYPICAL OPERATION**

1. From the worksheet READY screen, retrieve the worksheet used in Module 47.

2. Move the cell pointer to B3 and type **/WI**.

3. Select "C" to insert a column and press **Return**.

Notice that this is the same worksheet as created in Module 66.

4.  Type **/WD** and then type **C**. The screen displays the following:

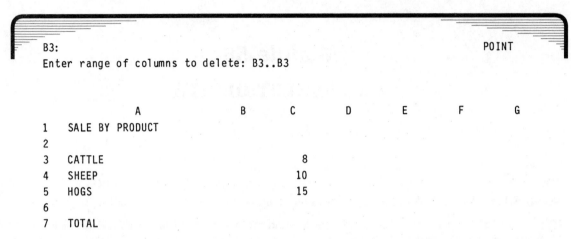

```
B3:                                                    POINT
Enter range of columns to delete: B3..B3


              A            B      C      D      E      F      G
1    SALE BY PRODUCT
2
3    CATTLE                       8
4    SHEEP                       10
5    HOGS                        15
6
7    TOTAL
```

Though the cell pointer is on row B3, Lotus 1-2-3 makes no distinction between it and any other row when deleting a column. It is the column letter that is important when deleting a column. The row number is important when deleting a row.

5.  Press **Return** to select column B for deletion. Notice the following screen:

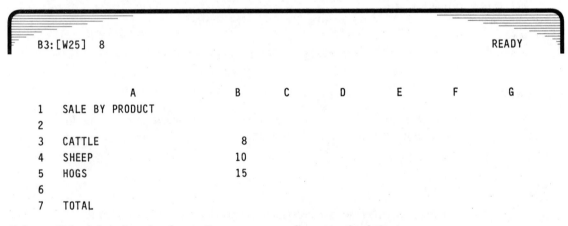

```
B3:[W25]   8                                           READY


              A            B      C      D      E      F      G
1    SALE BY PRODUCT
2
3    CATTLE                8
4    SHEEP                10
5    HOGS                 15
6
7    TOTAL
```

Column B is deleted and column C moves one column to the left.

### NOTE
Just as the Lotus 1-2-3 "Insert" command is used to insert columns and rows, the "Delete" command is used to delete rows as well as columns.

6.  Quit the worksheet.

7.  Turn to Module 4 to continue the learning sequence.

# Module 59
## WORKSHEET GLOBAL COLUMN-WIDTH

**DESCRIPTION**

Use the WORKSHEET GLOBAL COLUMN-WIDTH command to set the character width for all worksheet columns, that is to reset the worksheet column width to a value other than the default value of nine characters. The worksheet column width can be any number from 1 to 240 characters. Lotus 1-2-3, Release 1A is limited to a maximum of 72 characters. When windows are split, each side can have a different setting for the worksheet column width.

The WORKSHEET GLOBAL COLUMN-WIDTH command is located and used from the worksheet READY screen by typing a / (slash) and then typing the first letters of the following menu titles:

```
MENU TITLES:              USE AND USE REQUIREMENT:

Worksheet Global
  Column-Width           Set column width in # of characters
```

**APPLICATIONS**

Typically, the WORKSHEET GLOBAL COLUMN-WIDTH command is used to reset the default nine-character column width for all worksheet columns to a width that accommodates all information displayed in the worksheet. The WORKSHEET GLOBAL COLUMN-WIDTH command is exactly the same as the WORKSHEET COLUMN command except that the WORKSHEET COLUMN command is used to set the character widths of a specific range of columns in a worksheet. The WORKSHEET GLOBAL COLUMN-WIDTH is useful when first creating a worksheet to set column widths, etc. for the entire worksheet before entering information.

## TYPICAL OPERATION

1.  From the worksheet READY screen, type **/WGC**. The following screen displays:

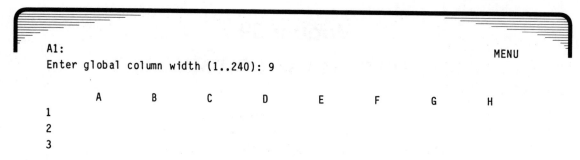

```
A1:                                                      MENU
Enter global column width (1..240): 9

            A       B       C       D       E       F       G       H
1
2
3
```

2.  Press the **Right-Arrow**.

Notice that the column width setting increases from the default of 9 characters. Each press of the arrow key moves the column width up one character and immediately displays the results on the worksheet.

3.  Type **25** to set the width of all columns in the worksheet to 25 characters and then press **Return**.

The columns in the worksheet increase to the new global setting.

4.  Quit the worksheet.

5.  Turn to Module 69 to continue the learning sequence.

# Module 60

## WORKSHEET ERASE

### DESCRIPTION

Even though cell protection always prevents the accidental erasure of individual cells, Lotus 1-2-3 allows you to erase the entire worksheet from the screen regardless of whether or not it contains protected cells. The WORKSHEET ERASE command erases an entire worksheet. Once the worksheet is erased, a blank worksheet is displayed in the READY mode. Erasure does not delete the .WK? file. This command erases only the screen (and any changes made to the worksheet since it was last saved on the data diskette).

The WORKSHEET ERASE command is located and used from the worksheet READY screen by typing a / (slash) and then typing the first letters of the following menu titles:

```
MENU TITLES:              USE AND USE REQUIREMENT:

Worksheet Erase           Erase entire worksheet
Worksheet Erase No        Do not erase entire worksheet
Worksheet Erase Yes       Do erase entire worksheet
```

### APPLICATIONS

Use this command any time an entire worksheet is to be erased. For example, when you want to erase the current worksheet and then create a new one.

### TYPICAL OPERATION

1.  Retrieve the CANDY worksheet saved in Module 42.

2. Type **/WE**. Notice the following screen:

```
A1:[W25] 'POPULAR CANDY SALES                                    MENU
  No  Yes
  Do not erase the worksheet; return to READY mode
              A                 B         C         D
   1    POPULAR CANDY SALES
   2    ------------------
   3                                   SQUARES OF
   4                                   DIFFERENCE
   5         CANDY NAME        UNITS SOLD FROM MEAN  DOLLARS
   6         ----------       ---------- ---------  -------
   7    LICORICE                   28      4303.36    $50.12
   8    PEANUT BRITTLE             56      1413.76   $131.60
   9    MINT PATTIES               72       466.56    $64.08
  10    CHOCOLATE BARS            112       338.56   $140.00
  11    FRUIT GUMS               200     11320.96   $156.00
  12
  13    TOTAL                    468
  14
  15
  16
  17
  18              MEAN          93.6               108.36
  19           MINIMUM           28                50.12
  20           MAXIMUM          200                  156
```

**WARNING**

Note that this is not the same Erase command as
the one reached by typing "/RE". "/WE" is used
to erase an entire worksheet. "/RE" is used to
erase selected cells within a worksheet.

3. Select "Yes" and press **Return**.

Notice that the screen is erased leaving a blank, READY mode worksheet.

4. Quit the worksheet.

5. Turn to Module 52 to continue the learning sequence.

# Module 61
## WORKSHEET GLOBAL DEFAULT

**DESCRIPTION**

Use the WORKSHEET GLOBAL DEFAULT commands to set default values for the printer used with Lotus 1-2-3. Also use this command to set the directory in which Lotus 1-2-3 files are saved, to check the status of the default values, and to update those values.

Before printing a Lotus 1-2-3 worksheet, you must review and select the values required in the printing operation section of the program. This includes setting the margin size, page length, line feed, page feed, and the way the printer is connected to the computer. The following table lists the WORKSHEET GLOBAL DEFAULT PRINTER settings and the information required to set them:

| DEFAULT ITEM | DESCRIPTION | |
|---|---|---|
| Printer | Interface: | Type of printer, serial or parallel |
| | Auto Line-Feed: | Yes if printer issues a line feed after each carriage return |
| | Left margin: | 0. .240 characters |
| | Right margin: | 0. .240 characters |
| | Top margin: | 0. .32 characters |
| | Bottom margin: | 0. .32 characters |
| | Page-Length: | 10. .100 lines |
| | Wait: | Yes if printer pauses at end of page |
| | Setup string: | String of characters that controls printer |
| | Name: | Text printer name |
| Directory | Drive/directory from which you started 1-2-3 | |
| Help access Method | Instant: | Press the F1 key for instant assistance The Help disk must stay in the drive |
| | Removable: | 1-2-3 prompts you to put in the disk that contains 123.HLP |

| Clock on Screen | Standard: | Sets standard date and time formats for screen display |
| | International: | Sets international date and time formats for screen display |
| | None: | Date and time do not display on screen |
| International | Punctuation: | A ., ,     E ., |
| | | B ,..     F ,. |
| | | C .;,     G .; |
| | | D ,;.     H ,; |
| | Point: | Punctuation character for decimal point |
| | Argument: | Punctuation character delimiting arguments |
| | Thousands: | Punctuation character delimiting 1000s |
| | Currency: | Currency character and location |
| | Date Format: | International date formats (D4 and D5) |
| | | A    MM/DD/YY     C    DD.MM.YY |
| | | B    DD/MM/YY     D    YY-MM-DD |
| | Time Format: | International time formats (D8 and D9) |
| | | A    HH:MM:SS     C    HH,MM,SS |
| | | B    HH.MM.SS     D    HHhMMmSSs |

*Lotus 1-2-3 Global Default Settings*

**NOTE**

Most personal computer printers are connected by a cable to a *parallel port* (a multiple pin connector) located at the back of the computer cabinet. Some printers must be connected to a serial port. Make sure the printer you use is connected properly to the computer before setting the default value.

The WORKSHEET GLOBAL DEFAULT commands are located and used from the worksheet READY screen by typing a / (slash) and then typing the first letters of the following menu titles:

```
MENU TITLES:            USE AND USE REQUIREMENT:


Worksheet Global
  Default               Set default settings
Worksheet Global
  Default Printer       Set default settings for printer
Worksheet Global
  Default Printer
  Interface             Set interface type
```

MENU TITLES:                    USE AND USE REQUIREMENT:

Worksheet Global
  Default Printer
    Interface 1              Parallel
Worksheet Global
  Default Printer
    Interface 2              Serial
Worksheet Global
  Default Printer
    Interface 3              Parallel
Worksheet Global
  Default Printer
    Interface 4              Serial
Worksheet Global
  Default Printer
    Auto-LF                 Set automatic line feeding
Worksheet Global
  Default Printer
    Auto-LF Yes             Automatic line feed
Worksheet Global
  Default Printer
    Auto-LF No              No automatic line feed
Worksheet Global
  Default Printer
    Left                    Set left margin in # of characters
Worksheet Global
  Default Printer
    Right                   Set right margin in # of characters
Worksheet Global
  Default Printer
    Top                     Set top margin in # of characters
Worksheet Global
  Default Printer
    Bottom                  Set bottom margin in # of characters
Worksheet Global
  Defult Printer
    Page-Length             Set page length in # of characters
Worksheet Global
  Default Printer
    Wait                    Set pause between pages feature
Worksheet Global
  Default Printer
    Wait No                 Do not pause between each page

```
MENU TITLES:            USE AND USE REQUIREMENT:

Worksheet Global
  Default Printer
    Wait Yes            Pause between each page
Worksheet Global
  Default Printer
    Setup               Set default setup string
Worksheet Global
  Default Printer
    Quit                Quit default printer settings menu
Worksheet Global
    Default Directory   Set program start-up directory Specify new directory
Worksheet Global
    Default Status      Display default settings
Worksheet Global
    Default Update      Save default settings to a configuration file
Worksheet Global
    Default Quit        Quit default menu
```

## APPLICATIONS

Use the WORKSHEET GLOBAL DEFAULT commands to set the default values for the printer connected to the computer and to set the directory in which the Lotus 1-2-3 worksheet files are saved and from which Lotus 1-2-3 files are retrieved.

## TYPICAL OPERATION

Perform the following steps to set printer settings:

1.  From the worksheet READY screen, type **/WGDS**. The following screen displays:

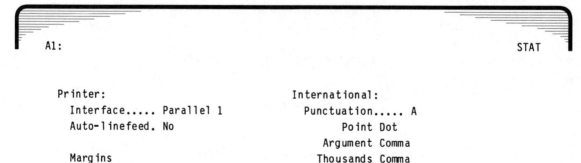

```
  A1:                                                      STAT


    Printer:                    International:
      Interface..... Parallel 1     Punctuation..... A
      Auto-linefeed. No                  Point Dot
                                      Argument Comma
      Margins                       Thousands Comma
        Left 4      Top 2
        Right 76  Bottom 2        Currency........ $ (Prefix)
                                  Date format D4.. A (MM/DD/YY)
```

```
     Page length... 66                    Time format D8.. A (HH:MM:SS)
     Wait.......... No
     Setup string..
     Name.......... Star Gemini 10X, 15X

   Directory at startup: a:

   Help access method: Removable

   Clock on screen: Standard




   02-Jan-88  01:57 AM
```

This is Lotus 1-2-3's printer status screen. The settings shown for each item are known as the *default values*. Each time you load Lotus 1-2-3 into the computer's memory, these default settings are automatically used to print all worksheets. The Lotus 1-2-3 pre-set default settings assume that you are using a printer with 8 ½-inch-by-11 ½-inch (letter-size) paper connected to the computer. Letter-size paper is 80 characters wide and 66 lines long. Remember these size limitations if you change the default settings or if you are using a printer that has a different size paper.

2.  Press any key to return to the worksheet global menu.

3.  Type **P.** Notice the following screen:

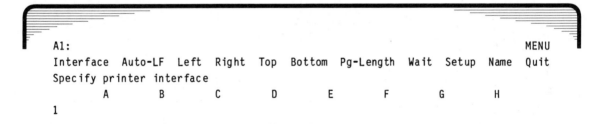

```
   A1:                                                              MENU
   Interface  Auto-LF  Left  Right  Top  Bottom  Pg-Length  Wait  Setup  Name  Quit
   Specify printer interface
             A        B       C      D     E       F          G     H
   1
```

Use the items on this menu to make changes to Lotus 1-2-3's default printer settings. Notice that each choice on the menu corresponds to an item on the printer status screen.

4.  Type **Q** to quit this menu once all printer setting changes are made.

5.  Type **D**. Notice the following screen:

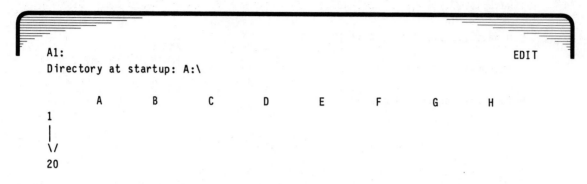

```
A1:                                                                    EDIT
Directory at startup: A:\

            A       B       C       D       E       F       G       H
   1
   |
   \/
   20
```

Lotus 1-2-3 uses the displayed directory as the default when looking for files.

6.  Press the **Backspace** key twice to erase the displayed directory, type **B:\** and press **Return**.

7.  Type **U** to save all changes to printer settings and the default directory.

8.  Type **Q** to quit the worksheet global default menu.

9.  Turn to Module 68 to continue the learning sequence.

# Module 62

## WORKSHEET GLOBAL FORMAT

**DESCRIPTION**

Use the WORKSHEET GLOBAL FORMAT commands to display numbers and formulas for the entire worksheet in various formats. These commands operate in the same manner as those used to display numbers and text for a range of worksheet cells. The WORKSHEET GLOBAL FORMAT commands have the effect of setting a default display format for the entire worksheet.

**NOTE**

Remember, a worksheet can be split into two windows and the display format set for each side independently.

The WORKSHEET GLOBAL FORMAT commands are located and used from the worksheet READY screen by typing a / (slash) and then typing the first letters of the following menu titles:

```
MENU TITLES:              USE AND USE REQUIREMENT:

Worksheet Global
 Format                   Set display forms
Worksheet Global
 Format Fixed             # decimal places
Worksheet Global
 Format Scientific        Scientific notation
Worksheet Global
 Format Currency          # decimal places for $'s
Worksheet Global
 Format General           Default toggle
Worksheet Global
 Format +/-               +/- graph
Worksheet Global
 Format Percent           # decimal places for %
Worksheet Global
 Format Date              Set date display
Worksheet Global
 Format Date 1
  (DD-MM-YY)              Display date as noted
```

```
MENU TITLES:              USE AND USE REQUIREMENT:

    Worksheet Global
     Format Date 2
      (DD-MM)              Display date as noted
    Worksheet Global
     Format Date 3
      (MM-YY)              Display date as noted
    Worksheet Global
     Format Date 4
      (Long Int'l)         Display date as noted
    Worksheet Global
     Format Date 5
      (Short Int'l)        Display date as noted
    Worksheet Global
     Format Time 1
      (HH:MM:SS AM/PM)     Display time as noted
    Worksheet Global
     Format Time 2
      (HH:MM AMPM)         Display time as noted
    Worksheet Global
     Format Time 3
      (Long Int'l)         Display time as noted
    Worksheet Global
     Format Time 4
      (Short Int'l)        Display time as noted
    Worksheet Global
     Format Text           Display formulas instead of values
    Worksheet Global
     Format Hidden         Hide text within a worksheet
```

## APPLICATIONS

Use the WORKSHEET GLOBAL FORMAT commands to set the default display format for all the columns and rows in a worksheet. With the fixed, scientific, currency, ",", general and percent formats, any number of decimal places between 0 and 15 can be selected. The +/− format displays a graph in which positive numbers use plus signs ( + ), negative numbers use minus signs ( − ), and a zero value uses a period (.).

In addition to numeric formatting, Lotus 1-2-3 contains the following special WORKSHEET GLOBAL FORMAT commands:

- The five Lotus 1-2-3 WORKSHEET GLOBAL FORMAT DATE commands display numbers as calendar dates. They are used in conjunction with the @DATE and @DATEVALUE functions to perform calendar date arithmetic. For example, the function @DATE(86,5,20) can be formatted as 20-May-86, 20-May, May-86, 05/20/86, or 05/20.
- The WORKSHEET GLOBAL FORMAT DATE-TIME command can display time in three different ways. They are used in conjunction with the @TIME, @TIMEVALUE, and @NOW functions. The function @TIME(1,30,45) can be displayed as 01:30:45 AM, 01:30:45 PM, 01:30 AM, 01:30 PM, 01:30:45, or 13:30:45.
- The WORKSHEET GLOBAL FORMAT TEXT command displays the text of a formula within a worksheet instead of the numeric value of the formula.
- The WORKSHEET GLOBAL FORMAT HIDDEN command hides all worksheet cells, that is, it suppresses the display of all cells.
- The WORKSHEET GLOBAL FORMAT RESET command cancels any special numeric formatting for the entire worksheet and resets the cell format to the Lotus 1-2-3 default global format.

## TYPICAL OPERATION

1. From the worksheet READY screen, retrieve the worksheet used in Module 47.

2. Move the cell pointer to B3 and type **/WGF**. The screen dispays the following:

```
B3:[W20]   8                                                          MENU
Fixed   Scientific   Currency  ,   General  +/-  Percent  Date  Text  Hidden  Reset
Fixed number of decimal places (x.xx)
                    A              B      C      D      E      F      G
1    SALE BY PRODUCT
2
3    CATTLE                        8
4    SHEEP                        10
5    HOGS                         15
6
7    TOTAL
```

The WORKSHEET GLOBAL FORMAT menu choice allows you to change the way numbers and formulas are displayed in the entire worksheet.

3. Type **C** for currency. The following screen displays:

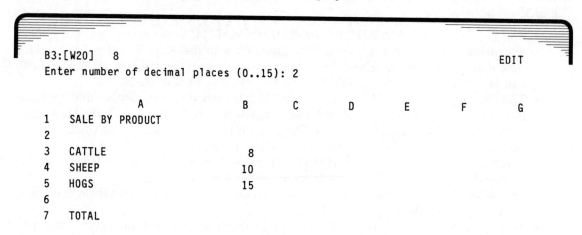

```
B3:[W20]   8                                              EDIT
Enter number of decimal places (0..15): 2

                  A              B       C       D       E       F       G
1    SALE BY PRODUCT
2
3    CATTLE                      8
4    SHEEP                      10
5    HOGS                       15
6
7    TOTAL
```

Remember, Lotus 1-2-3 accepts up to 15 decimal places for displayed numbers.

4. Type **3** and press **Return**. The screen changes to the following display.

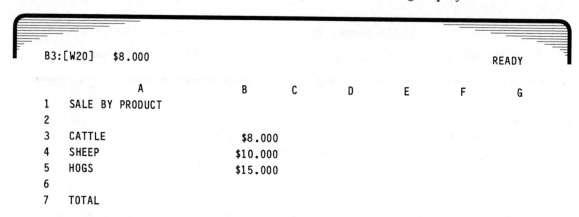

```
B3:[W20]   $8.000                                         READY

                  A              B       C       D       E       F       G
1    SALE BY PRODUCT
2
3    CATTLE                  $8.000
4    SHEEP                  $10.000
5    HOGS                   $15.000
6
7    TOTAL
```

Lotus 1-2-3 displays all numbers in the worksheet as dollar values with three decimal places to the right of the decimal point.

5. Quit the worksheet.

6. Turn to Module 66 to continue the learning sequence.

# Module 63

# WORKSHEET GLOBAL LABEL-PREFIX

### DESCRIPTION

Use the WORKSHEET GLOBAL LABEL-PREFIX commands to set the worksheet default status so that text is automatically left-justified, right-justified or centered when typed.

The WORKSHEET GLOBAL LABEL-PREFIX commands are located and used from the worksheet READY screen by typing a / (slash) and then typing the first letters of the following menu titles:

```
MENU TITLES:             USE AND USE REQUIREMENT:


Worksheet Global
   Label-Prefix          Set justification of text
Worksheet Global
   Label-Prefix Left     Left justify
Worksheet Global
   Label-Prefix Right    Right justify
Worksheet Global
   Label-Prefix Center   Center text
```

### APPLICATIONS

Typically, the WORKSHEET GLOBAL LABEL-PREFIX commands are used to center, left-justify, or right-justify all textual information subsequently typed within a worksheet. The WORKSHEET GLOBAL LABEL-PREFIX commands perform the same functions as the RANGE LABEL commands except that they justify information in the entire worksheet.

### NOTE
Lotus 1-2-3 does not treat numbers as text and the Label-Prefix commands do not operate on them.

### TYPICAL OPERATION

1.  From the worksheet READY screen, type **/WCS25** and press **Return** to set the column width to 25 characters.

2. Type **/WGL**. The following displays on the screen:

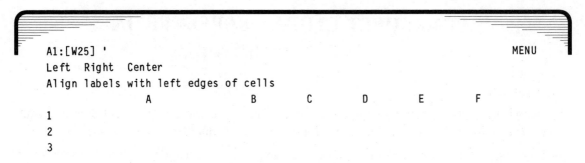

```
A1:[W25] '                                                    MENU
Left   Right   Center
Align labels with left edges of cells
                        A              B       C       D       E       F
1
2
3
```

3. Type **C** to set the default for the worksheet to center all text.

4. Type **COLUMN A** and press **Return**. Notice the text automatically centers.

5. Quit the worksheet.

6. Turn to Module 47 to continue the learning sequence.

# Module 64

## WORKSHEET GLOBAL PROTECTION

### DESCRIPTION

Safeguarding worksheet cells from accidental erasure or deletion is an important Lotus 1-2-3 function. It prevents you from making any unintentional changes to protected cells. Before individual cells are protected from erasure, deletion, or change, the entire worksheet must be set so that the protective feature can be used. Use the WORKSHEET GLOBAL PROTECTION commands to enable or disable cell protection.

The WORKSHEET GLOBAL PROTECTION commands are located and used from the worksheet READY screen by typing a / (slash) and then typing the first letters of the following menu titles:

```
MENU TITLES:              USE AND USE REQUIREMENT:


Worksheet Global
   Protection             Set protected cells feature
Worksheet Global
   Protection Enable      Can protect cells
Worksheet Global
   Protection Disable     Cannot protect cells
```

### APPLICATIONS

Use the WORKSHEET GLOBAL PROTECTION command any time a range of cells is to be protected from accidental erasure or change. This command is typically used to "freeze" worksheet formulas and must be performed before specific cells are protected using the RANGE PROTECT, UNPROTECT commands.

### TYPICAL OPERATION

1.  Retrieve the CANDY worksheet saved in Module 42.

2.  Type **/WGP**. Notice the following screen:

```
A1:[W25] 'POPULAR CANDY SALES                                    MENU
 Enable  Disable
 Turn protection on
               A              B         C          D
 1    POPULAR CANDY SALES
 2    -------------------
 3                                   SQUARES OF
 4                                   DIFFERENCE
 5         CANDY NAME      UNITS SOLD FROM MEAN   DOLLARS
 6         ----------     ---------- ----------   -------
 7    LICORICE                    28   4303.36     $50.12
 8    PEANUT BRITTLE              56   1413.76    $131.60
 9    MINT PATTIES                72    466.56     $64.08
 10   CHOCOLATE BARS             112    338.56    $140.00
 11   FRUIT GUMS                 200  11320.96    $156.00
 12
 13   TOTAL                      468
 14
 15
 16
 17
 18              MEAN           93.6              108.36
 19           MINIMUM            28               50.12
 20           MAXIMUM           200                 156
```

3.  Type **E** to "Enable" the worksheet for cell protection.

**NOTE**

The only function the WORKSHEET GLOBAL
PROTECTION command performs is to toggle on
or off the option to protect or unprotect a range
of cells using the RANGE PROTECT, UNPROTECT
commands.

4.  Quit the worksheet.

5.  Turn to Module 60 to continue the learning sequence.

# Module 65

## WORKSHEET GLOBAL RECALCULATION

**DESCRIPTION**

Lotus 1-2-3 provides several alternative methods for recalculation of worksheet values. The following table lists these methods and the functions they perform:

| METHOD | DESCRIPTION |
|---|---|
| NATURAL | Recalculate in natural order, that is, as value and formulas are encountered in the worksheet. |
| COLUMNWISE | Recalculate in columnwise order, that is column by column. |
| ROWWISE | Recalculate in rowwise order, that is row by row. |
| AUTOMATIC | Automatically recalculate after every entry. |
| MANUAL | Recalculate only by pressing F9. |
| ITERATION | Set the number of times a calculation is to be performed. |

*Lotus 1-2-3 Worksheet Global Recalculation Menu Choices*

The WORKSHEET GLOBAL RECALCULATION commands are located and used from the worksheet READY screen by typing a / (slash) and then typing the first letters of the following menu titles:

```
MENU TITLES:              USE AND USE REQUIREMENT:

Worksheet Global
   Recalculation          Set recalculation mode
Worksheet Global
   Recalculation
   Natural                When needed only
Worksheet Global
   Recalculation
   Columnwise             Recalculate columns only
```

| MENU TITLES: | USE AND USE REQUIREMENT: |
|---|---|
| Worksheet Global<br>  Recalculation<br>  Rowwise | Recalculate rows only |
| Worksheet Global<br>  Recalculation<br>  Automatic | Default recalculate after every entry |
| Worksheet Global<br>  Recalculation<br>  Manual | Recalculate by pressing 9 only |
| Worksheet Global<br>  Recalculation<br>  Iteration | Set recalculation for # of times |

## APPLICATIONS

Use the WORKSHEET GLOBAL RECALCULATION commands to set the method for mathematical recalculations for the entire worksheet. These commands are useful when typing data into a large worksheet that requires a few seconds to recalculate after each new entry. By setting the recalculation to manual, you do not have to pause in your data entry or worksheet creation while the formulas in the worksheet adjust themselves for the new information.

## TYPICAL OPERATION

1.  Retrieve the CANDY worksheet saved in Module 11.

2.  Move the cell pointer to B7 and type **/WGRM** to set worksheet recalculation to manual only.

3.  Type **100** and press **Return**. Notice the following screen:

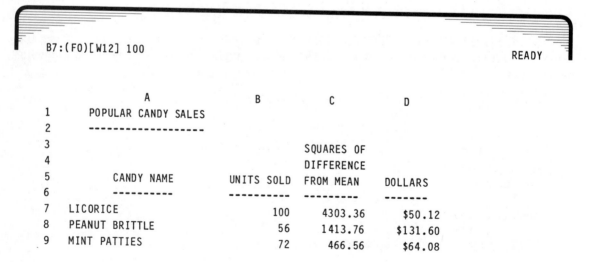

```
B7:(F0)[W12] 100                                                    READY


              A              B          C          D
    1   POPULAR CANDY SALES
    2   --------------------
    3                                SQUARES OF
    4                                DIFFERENCE
    5        CANDY NAME      UNITS SOLD FROM MEAN   DOLLARS
    6        ----------      ---------- ----------  -------
    7   LICORICE                  100    4303.36     $50.12
    8   PEANUT BRITTLE             56    1413.76    $131.60
    9   MINT PATTIES               72     466.56     $64.08
```

```
10   CHOCOLATE BARS              112      338.56    $140.00
11   FRUIT GUMS                  200    11320.96    $156.00
12
13   TOTAL                       468
14
15
16
17
18                 MEAN         93.6                 108.36
19              MINIMUM           28                  50.12
20              MAXIMUM          200                    156
                                                   CALC
```

Notice the small "CALC" displayed in the lower right-hand section of the screen. When manual recalculation is set, this reminder tells you that a value has been typed into the worksheet and that manual recalculation is required.

    4.   Press **F9**.

Notice that all values in the worksheet are recalculated. Use the F9 function key to manually recalculate worksheet values when the manual recalculation option is set.

    5.   Type **/WGRA** to set recalculation back to automatic.

    6.   Type **28** and press **Return**.

The worksheet automatically recalculates once the new value is entered.

    7.   Quit the worksheet.

    8.   Turn to Module 61 to continue the learning sequence.

# Module 66

## WORKSHEET INSERT

### DESCRIPTION

WORKSHEET INSERT commands insert one or more blank rows or columns into a worksheet.

The WORKSHEET INSERT commands are located and used from the worksheet READY screen by typing a / (slash) and then typing the first letters of the following menu titles:

```
MENU TITLES:              USE AND USE REQUIREMENT:

Worksheet Insert          Insert a column or row
Worksheet Insert
  Column                  Insert column(s) Specify range
Worksheet Insert Row      Insert row(s) Specify range
```

### APPLICATIONS

Once a worksheet is developed, there is often a need to have additional rows or columns inserted for information. Use the WORKSHEET INSERT commands to add rows or columns in between existing columns or rows that contain information. Often, you find you need an additional column of information in the middle of a worksheet after creating it. Using this command saves you the effort of having to recreate a large worksheet just to accomodate the new column.

### TYPICAL OPERATION

1.  From the worksheet READY screen, retrieve the worksheet used in Module 47.

2.  Move the cell pointer to B3 and type **/WI**.

3. Select "C" to insert a column. The screen displays the following:

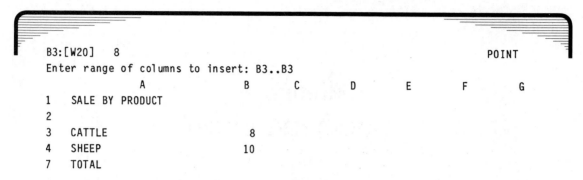

```
B3:[W20]   8                                              POINT
Enter range of columns to insert: B3..B3
                A               B       C       D       E       F       G
1   SALE BY PRODUCT
2
3   CATTLE                      8
4   SHEEP                      10
7   TOTAL
```

As with many Lotus 1-2-3 commands, a range must be specified.

4. Press **Return** to select one column to insert to the left of column B. Notice the following screen:

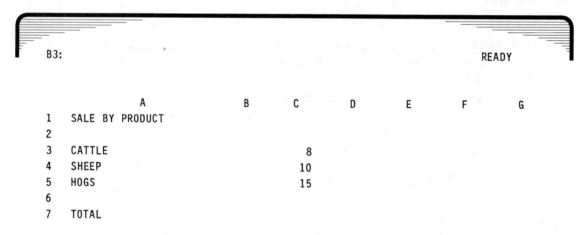

```
B3:                                                       READY


                A               B       C       D       E       F       G
1   SALE BY PRODUCT
2
3   CATTLE                              8
4   SHEEP                              10
5   HOGS                               15
6
7   TOTAL
```

Lotus 1-2-3 inserts a blank column in place of column B and moves all columns one column to the right of the new column. Notice that the new column is only nine characters wide. Lotus 1-2-3's "Insert" command always creates a new column using the default value for the column width.

5. Quit the worksheet.

6. Turn to Module 58 to continue the learning sequence.

# Module 67
## WORKSHEET PAGE

**DESCRIPTION**

The WORKSHEET PAGE command sets a page break within a worksheet. Similar to the ability of most word processors to set a page break at any location within a document, this new Release 2.01 command performs the same function within a Lotus 1-2-3 worksheet.

The WORKSHEET PAGE command is located and used from the worksheet READY screen by typing a / (slash) and then typing the first letters of the following menu titles:

```
MENU TITLES:            USE AND USE REQUIREMENT:

Worksheet Page          Insert a page break above the cell pointer
```

**APPLICATIONS**

Use the WORKSHEET PAGE command to set a page break at any location within a Lotus 1-2-3 worksheet. This command is very useful when setting up a large worksheet for printing. The use of a page break within the worksheet itself overrides the page length settings specified using the PRINT PRINTER OPTIONS commands. This command allows you to "see" what worksheet information will be on a single page before printing it.

**TYPICAL OPERATION**

1. Retrieve the CANDY worksheet saved in Module 11.

2. Move the cell pointer to A3 and type **/WP** to set a page break.

Notice the following screen:

```
B7:(F0)[W12] 100                                                    READY


                    A              B         C          D
     1      POPULAR CANDY SALES
     2      -------------------
     3   ::
     4                                    SQUARES OF
     5                                    DIFFERENCE
     6          CANDY NAME      UNITS SOLD FROM MEAN    DOLLARS
     7          ----------      ---------- ---------    -------
     8   LICORICE                      28    4303.36    $50.12
     9   PEANUT BRITTLE                56    1413.76   $131.60
    10   MINT PATTIES                  72     466.56    $64.08
    11   CHOCOLATE BARS               112     338.56   $140.00
    12   FRUIT GUMS                   200   11320.96   $156.00
    13
    14   TOTAL                        468
    15
    16
    17
    18
    19               MEAN           93.6               108.36
    20            MINIMUM             28                50.12
```

A double colon (::) appears in cell A3 and the worksheet information below A3 moves down one row. When this worksheet is printed, the printer automatically moves to the next page when the double colon is encountered. Do not type any other information into the page break row.

3.  Type **/WDR** and press **Return**.

To eliminate a page break, type over the double colon or delete the line that contains it.

4.  Quit the worksheet.

5.  Turn to Module 42 to continue the learning sequence.

# Module 68
## WORKSHEET STATUS

**DESCRIPTION**

The WORKSHEET STATUS command displays the status of the worksheet default values set using the WORKSHEET GLOBAL RECALCULATION, WORKSHEET GLOBAL FORMAT, WORKSHEET LABEL-PREFIX, WORKSHEET COLUMN-WIDTH, and WORKSHEET GLOBAL PROTECTION commands.

The WORKSHEET STATUS command is located and used from the worksheet READY screen by typing a / (slash) and then typing the first letters of the following menu titles:

```
MENU TITLES:            USE AND USE REQUIREMENT:

Worksheet Status        Display all worksheet settings
```

**APPLICATIONS**

Use the WORKSHEET STATUS command to display all worksheet status settings. This is particularly useful when you want to know what the current worksheet settings are before changing them.

**TYPICAL OPERATION**

1. From the worksheet READY screen, type **/WS**. Notice the following screen:

```
                                                                    STAT



     Available Memory:
        Conventional..... 344800 of 344800 Bytes (100%)
        Expanded........ (None)

     Math Co-processor: (None)
```

```
Recalculation:
  Method.......... Automatic
  Order........... Natural
  Iterations....... 1

Circular Reference: (None)

Cell Display:
  Format.......... (G)
  Label-Prefix..... '
  Column-Width..... 9
  Zero Suppression. Off

Global Protection:  Off

02-Jan-88  02:15 AM
```

2.  Press **Esc** to return to the worksheet menu.

3.  Quit the worksheet.

4.  Turn to Module 67 to continue the learning sequence.

# Module 69

## WORKSHEET TITLES

### DESCRIPTION

Use the WORKSHEET TITLES commands to designate one or more columns to the left of the cell pointer or one or more rows above the cell pointer as title information for the worksheet. Also use this command to clear all title designations or to set both the horizontal (row) and vertical (column) titles at the same time. Once a title is designated, the cell pointer is effectively "locked-out" of the designated cells.

The WORKSHEET TITLES commands are located and used from the worksheet READY screen by typing a / (slash) and then typing the first letters of the following menu titles:

```
MENU TITLES:              USE AND USE REQUIREMENT:

Worksheet Titles          Create worksheet titles
Worksheet Titles Both     Create vertical and horizontal titles
Worksheet Titles
  Horizontal              Create horizontal titles
Worksheet Titles
  Vertical                Create vertical titles
Worksheet Titles Clear    Remove all titles
```

### APPLICATIONS

Use the WORKSHEET TITLES commands to permanently designate both rows and columns of worksheet information as titles for the worksheet. These title designations will print on every page of a worksheet. Typically, this command is used to set permanent title blocks for a series of worksheet ranges, for example, setting one title for a business' income statement worksheet even though the worksheet contains information for several months. Using this command eliminates the need to repeat the title information within the worksheet and saves time and space.

### TYPICAL OPERATION

1. From the worksheet READY screen, type **TITLE1** and press **Return**.

2. Move the cell pointer to cell reference A3, type **TITLE2** and press **Return**.

3. Move the cell pointer to B2 and type **/WT**. The following screen displays:

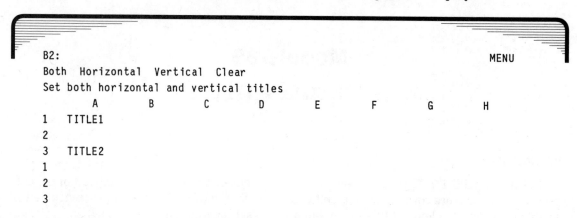

```
B2:                                                      MENU
Both  Horizontal  Vertical  Clear
Set both horizontal and vertical titles
          A         B         C         D       E       F       G       H
1    TITLE1
2
3    TITLE2
1
2
3
```

4. Press **Return** and then try to move the cell pointer to A1.

Notice that Lotus 1-2-3 prevents the cell pointer from entering an area designated as a title.

5. Type **/WTC** and move the cell pointer to A1.

Using the WORKSHEET TITLES CLEAR command removes the title area designations.

6. Quit the worksheet.

7. Turn to Module 50 to continue the learning sequence.

# Module 70

# WORKSHEET WINDOW

## DESCRIPTION

Use the WORKSHEET WINDOW commands to split the display screen either vertically (up and down) or horizontally (from side to side). Additionally, you can synchronize each window resulting from a screen split. *Synchronize* means that the information in one window is always displayed while the information in the other moves with the cell pointer. Finally, use these commands to unsynchronize windows or to clear them entirely from the screen.

The WORKSHEET WINDOW commands are located and used from the worksheet READY screen by typing a / (slash) and then typing the first letters of the following menu titles:

```
MENU TITLES:            USE AND USE REQUIREMENT:

Worksheet Window        Create windows in worksheet
Worksheet Window
   Horizontal           Create horizontal window at cell pointer location
Worksheet Window
   Vertical             Create vertical window at cell pointer location
Worksheet Window
   Sync                 Synchronize information displayed in windows
Worksheet Window
   Unsync               Unsynchronize information displayed in windows
Worksheet Window
   Clear                Remove all windows
```

## APPLICATIONS

When the screen display for a worksheet that exceeds the Lotus 1-2-3 display character limits moves to the right, one or more columns disappear from the left-hand side of the monitor. Generally, row descriptions for the worksheet disappear with it. The WORKSHEET WINDOW commands are used to split a window that contains the descriptive information for columns or rows. Typically, this command is used to split out financial information headings or column descriptions.

## TYPICAL OPERATION

1.  Retrieve the CANDY worksheet saved in Module 18.

2. Move the cell pointer to B1 and type **/WW**. Study the following display:

```
B1:[W12]                                                        MENU
Horizontal  Vertical  Sync  Unsync  Clear
Split the screen horizontally at the current row
                  A              B        C           D
 1    POPULAR CANDY SALES
 2    -------------------
 3                                     SQUARES OF
 4                                     DIFFERENCE
 5         CANDY NAME        UNITS SOLD FROM MEAN   DOLLARS
 6         ----- ----       ---------- ---------   -------
 7    CHOCOLATE BARS            112       338.56    $140.00
 8    LICORICE                  28       4303.36     $50.12
 9    FRUIT GUMS               200      11320.96    $156.00
10    MINT PATTIES              72        466.56     $64.08
11    PEANUT BRITTLE            56       1413.76    $131.60
12
13    TOTAL                    468
 |
18                  MEAN       93.6                  108.36
19               MINIMUM       28                     50.12
20               MAXIMUM       200                       156
```

3. Type **V** to create a vertical window between columns A and B. Look at the following screen:

```
A1:[W25] ^POPULAR CANDY SALES                                  READY


                  A              1      B        C           D
 1    POPULAR CANDY SALES        1
 2    -------------------        2
 3                               3           SQUARES OF
 4                               4           DIFFERENCE
 5         CANDY NAME            5   UNITS SOLD FROM MEAN   DOLLARS
 6         ----------            6   ---------- ---------   -------
 7    CHOCOLATE BARS             7      112       338.56    $140.00
 8    LICORICE                   8      28       4303.36     $50.12
 9    FRUIT GUMS                 9      200      11320.96   $156.00
10    MINT PATTIES              10      72        466.56     $64.08
11    PEANUT BRITTLE            11      56       1413.76    $131.60
```

| 12 | | 12 | | |
|---|---|---|---|---|
| 13 | TOTAL | 13 | 468 | |
| 18 | MEAN | 18 | 93.6 | 108.36 |
| 19 | MINIMUM | 19 | 28 | 50.12 |
| 20 | MAXIMUM | 20 | 200 | 156 |

Notice that the cell pointer automatically moved to column A. You always know which window contains the stationary screen by finding the cell pointer. The window containing the cell pointer is the window which allows its movement within the screen and is called the *active* window. The window which does not contain the cell pointer is called *inactive*.

4.  Press **F6** to transfer the cell pointer to the window in which you want to move (the right-hand window).

The cell pointer moves to the right-hand window making it active.

Pressing F6 activates another of Lotus 1-2-3's function key features. Many of these function keys act as *toggles*. You use them like a switch to turn on or off a specific Lotus 1-2-3 feature. The table below lists and describes other Lotus 1-2-3 function key features.

| FUNCTION KEY | DESCRIPTION |
|---|---|
| F1 | PRESSING F1 ALWAYS DISPLAYS A LOTUS 1-2-3 HELP SCREEN |
| F2 | PRESSING F2 TOGGLES THE TO/FROM EDIT MODE FOR THE WORKSHEET ENTRY. |
| F3 | PRESSING F3 DISPLAYS A MENU OF WORKSHEET CELL RANGE NAMES. |
| F4 | PRESSING F4 TOGGLES THE MAKE/UNMAKE ABSOLUTE FEATURE FOR A WORKSHEET CELL OR CELLS. |
| F5 | PRESSING F5 MOVES THE CELL POINTER TO A PARTICULAR CELL. |
| F6 | PRESSING F6 MOVES THE CELL POINTER FROM ONE WINDOW TO ANOTHER. |
| F7 | PRESSING F7 REPEATS THE MOST RECENT DATA QUERY OPERATION. |
| F8 | PRESSING F8 REPEATS THE MOST RECENT DATA TABLE OPERATION. |
| F9 | PRESSING F9 RECALCULATES ALL WORKSHEET FORMULAS, OR IF IN THE VALUE AND EDIT WORKSHEET MODES, IT CONVERTS FORMULAS TO THEIR NUMERICAL VALUES. |
| F10 | PRESSING F10 DRAWS A GRAPH USING THE CURRENT GRAPH SETTINGS. |

*Lotus 1-2-3 Function Keys*

5. Move the cell pointer to E25.

Notice that the inactive window remains unchanged as you move the cell pointer down the cells in the column. After you reach the end of the worksheet (E20), the inactive window is still displayed as if the row numbers on the inactive window matched the rows on the active window. This happens because the two windows are not synchronized.

6. Press **Home** and then type **/WWS** to synchronize the two windows.

7. Move the cell pointer to E35 again.

The two windows follow one another, linking the correct row descriptions in the inactive window with the information contained in the corresponding row/column locations in the active window. The default for Lotus 1-2-3 is now synchronized.

8. Type **/WWC** to clear the window from the worksheet.

### NOTE
Worksheet windows are saved as part of the worksheet and automatically display when the worksheet is retrieved for use at a later session.

9. Quit the worksheet.

10. Turn to Module 11 to continue the learning sequence.

# Appendix A

## LOTUS 1-2-3 REL. 2.01 MENU PATHS

**MENU PATH**                                                  **FUNCTION**

Worksheet                                                      [Set worksheet items]
Worksheet Global                                              [Set for entire worksheet]
Worksheet Global Format                                       [Set display forms]
Worksheet Global Format Fixed                                 [# decimal places]
Worksheet Global Format Scientific                            [Scientific notation]
Worksheet Global Format Currency                              [# decimal places for $'s]
Worksheet Global Format General                               [Default toggle]
Worksheet Global Format + / −                                 [ + / − graph]
Worksheet Global Format Percent                               [# decimal places for %]
Worksheet Global Format Date                                  [Set date display]
Worksheet Global Format Date 1 (DD-MM-YY)                     [Display date as noted]
Worksheet Global Format Date 2 (DD-MM)                        [Display date as noted]
Worksheet Global Format Date 3 (MM-YY)                        [Display date as noted]
Worksheet Global Format Date 4 (Long Int'l)                   [Display date as noted]
Worksheet Global Format Date 5 (Short Int'l)                  [Display date as noted]
Worksheet Global Format Time 1 (HH:MM:SS
   AM/PM)                                                     [Display time as noted]
Worksheet Global Format Time 2 (HH:MM AM/PM)                  [Display time as noted]
Worksheet Global Format Time 3 (Long Int'l)                   [Display time as noted]
Worksheet Global Format Time 4 (Short Int'l)                  [Display time as noted]
Worksheet Global Format Text                                  [Display formulas instead of values]
Worksheet Global Format Hidden                                [Hide text within a worksheet]
Worksheet Global Label-Prefix                                 [Set justification of text]
Worksheet Global Label-Prefix Left                            [Left justify]
Worksheet Global Label-Prefix Right                           [Right justify]
Worksheet Global Label-Prefix Center                          [Center text]
Worksheet Global Column-Width                                 [Set column width in # of characters]
Worksheet Global Recalculation                                [Set recalculation mode]
Worksheet Global Recalculation Natural                        [When needed only]
Worksheet Global Recalculation Columnwise                     [Recalculate columns only]
Worksheet Global Recalculation Rowwise                        [Recalculate rows only]
Worksheet Global Recalculation Automatic                      [Default recalculate after every entry]
Worksheet Global Recalculation Manual                         [Recalculate by pressing 9 only]
Worksheet Global Recalculation Iteration                      [Set recalculation for # of times]
Worksheet Global Protection                                   [Set protected cells feature]
Worksheet Global Protection Enable                            [Can protect cells]
Worksheet Global Protection Disable                           [Can not protect cells]
Worksheet Global Default                                      [Set default settings]
Worksheet Global Default Printer                              [Set default settings for printer]

| MENU PATH | FUNCTION |
|---|---|
| Worksheet Global Default Printer Interface | [Set interface type] |
| Worksheet Global Default Printer Interface 1 | [Parallel] |
| Worksheet Global Default Printer Interface 2 | [Serial] |
| Worksheet Global Default Printer Interface 3 | [Parallel] |
| Worksheet Global Default Printer Interface 4 | [Serial] |
| Worksheet Global Default Printer Auto-LF | [Set automatic line feeding] |
| Worksheet Global Default Printer Auto-LF Yes | [Automatic line feed] |
| Worksheet Global Default Printer Auto-LF No | [No automatic line feed] |
| Worksheet Global Default Printer Left | [Set left margin in # of characters] |
| Worksheet Global Default Printer Right | [Set right margin in # of characters] |
| Worksheet Global Default Printer Top | [Set top margin in # of characters] |
| Worksheet Global Default Printer Bottom | [Set bottom margin in # of characters] |
| Worksheet Global Default Printer Page-Length | [Set page length in # of characters] |
| Worksheet Global Default Printer Wait | [Set pause between pages feature] |
| Worksheet Global Default Printer Wait No | [Do not pause between each page] |
| Worksheet Global Default Printer Wait Yes | [Pause between each page] |
| Worksheet Global Default Printer Setup | [Set default setup string] |
| Worksheet Global Default Printer Quit | [Quit default printer settings menu] |
| Worksheet Global Default Directory | [Set program start-up directory] [Specify new directory] |
| Worksheet Global Default Status | [Display default settings] |
| Worksheet Global Default Update | [Save default settings to a configuration file] |
| Worksheet Global Default Quit | [Quit default menu] |
| Worksheet Insert | [Insert a column or row] |
| Worksheet Insert Column | [Insert column(s)] [Specify range] |
| Worksheet Insert Row | [Insert row(s)] [Specify range] |
| Worksheet Delete | [Remove columns and rows] |
| Worksheet Delete Column | [Remove column(s)] [Specify range] |
| Worksheet Delete Row | [Remove row(s)] [Specify range] |
| Worksheet Column | [Set width of column(s)] |
| Worksheet Column Set Width | [Set width of column in # characters] [Specify range] |
| Worksheet Column Reset Width | [Set width of all columns in # of characters for entire worksheet] |
| Worksheet Column Hide | [Hide the information in a column of cells] [Specify column range] |
| Worksheet Column Display | [Display the information in a column of cells] [Specify column range] |
| Worksheet Erase | [Erase entire worksheet] |
| Worksheet Erase No | [Do not erase entire worksheet] |
| Worksheet Erase Yes | [Do erase entire worksheet] |
| Worksheet Titles | [Create worksheet titles] |
| Worksheet Titles Both | [Create vertical and horizontal titles] |
| Worksheet Titles Horizontal | [Create horizontal titles] |
| Worksheet Titles Vertical | [Create vertical titles] |
| Worksheet Titles Clear | [Remove all titles] |
| Worksheet Window | [Create windows in worksheet] |
| Worksheet Window Horizontal | [Create horizontal window at cell pointer location] |
| Worksheet Window Vertical | [Create vertical window at cell pointer location] |
| Worksheet Window Sync | [Synchronize information displayed in windows] |
| Worksheet Window Unsync | [Unsynchronize information displayed in windows] |
| Worksheet Window Clear | [Remove all windows] |
| Worksheet Status | [Display all worksheet settings] |
| Worksheet Page | [Insert a page break above the cell pointer] |

| MENU PATH | FUNCTION |
|---|---|
| Range | [Settings for a range only] |
| Range Format | [Set display form] |
| Range Format Fixed | [# decimal places] [Specify range] |
| Range Format Scientific | [Scientific notation] [Specify range] |
| Range Format Currency | [# decimal places for $'s] [Specify range] |
| Range Format General | [Default toggle] [Specify range] |
| Range Format +/− | [+/− graph] [Specify range] |
| Range Format Percent | [# decimal places for %] [Specify range] |
| Range Format Date | [Set date display] |
| Range Format Date 1 (DD-MM-YY) | [Display date as noted] |
| Range Format Date 2 (DD-MM) | [Display date as noted] |
| Range Format Date 3 (MM-YY) | [Display date as noted] |
| Range Format Date 4 (Long Int'l) | [Display date as noted] |
| Range Format Date 5 (Short Int'l) | [Display date as noted] |
| Range Format Time 1 (HH:MM:SS AM/PM) | [Display time as noted] |
| Range Format Time 2 (HH:MM AM/PM) | [Display time as noted] |
| Range Format Time 3 (Long Int'l) | [Display time as noted] |
| Range Format Time 4 (Short Int'l) | [Display time as noted] |
| Range Format Text | [Display formulas instead of values] |
| Range Format Hidden | [Suppress the display of a range of cells] [Specify the cell range] |
| Range Format Reset | [Clear all format settings in entire worksheet] |
| Range Label-Prefix | [Set justification of text] |
| Range Label-Prefix Left | [Left justify] [Specify range] |
| Range Label-Prefix Right | [Right justify] [Specify range] |
| Range Label-Prefix Center | [Center text] [Specify range] |
| Range Erase | [Erase a range of cells] |
| Range Name | [Name a range of cells] [Specify range] |
| Range Name Create | [Range name] [Specify range] |
| Range Name Delete | [Range name] |
| Range Name Labels | [Use labels to create names] |
| Range Name Labels Right | [Specify range of cells to the right of labels] |
| Range Name Labels Down | [Specify range of cells below the labels] |
| Range Name Labels Left | [Specify range of cells to the left of labels] |
| Range Name Labels Up | [Specify range of cells above the labels] |
| Range Name Reset | [Delete all names] |
| Range Justify | [Set automatic margin justification for a range of cells] [Specify range] |
| Range Protect | [Protect from change a range of cells] [Specify range] |
| Range Unprotect | [Unprotect from change a range of cells] [Specify range] |
| Range Input | [Specify a range of cells for keyboard entry] [Specify range] |
| Range Value | [Copy cell values without the formulas] [Specify the copy "from/to" range] |
| Range Transpose | [Copy cells from columns to rows & vice versa] [Specify copy "from/to" range] |
| Copy | [Copy from a range of cells to a range of cells] [Specify from/to range] |
| Move | [Move a range of cells to a range of cells] [Specify from/to range] |
| File | [Manipulate Lotus files] |
| File Retrieve | [Load a .WKS file into the worksheet] [Specify file name] |
| File Save | [Save a .WKS file on diskette] [Specify file name] |

## MENU PATH

File Combine
File Combine Copy
File Combine Copy Entire File
File Combine Copy Named Range

File Combine Add

File Combine Add Entire File

File Combine Add Named Range

File Combine Subtract

File Combine Subtract Entire File

File Combine Subtract Named Range

File Xtract

File Xtract Formulas

File Xtract Values

File Erase
File Erase Worksheet
File Erase Print
File Erase Graph
File List
File List Worksheet
File List Print
File List Graph
File Import
File Import Text
File Import Numbers
File Directory
Print
Print Printer
Print Printer Range

Print Printer Line
Print Printer Page
Print Printer Options
Print Printer Options Header
Print Printer Options Footer
Print Printer Options Margins
Print Printer Options Margins Left
Print Printer Options Margins Right
Print Printer Options Margins Top
Print Printer Option Margins Botttom
Print Printer Options Borders
Print Printer Options Borders Columns
Print Printer Options Borders Rows

## FUNCTION

[Combine one worksheet file with another]
[Copy one worksheet to another]
[Copy complete file] [Specify file name]
[Copy named range only] [Specify range name] [Specify file name]
[Add numeric data or formulas from one worksheet to another]
[Add numbers and formulas from entire file] [Specify file name]
[Add #'s or formulas from named range] [Specify range and file name]
[Subtract numeric data or formulas from one worksheet to another]
[Subtract numbers or formulas from entire file] [Specify file name]
[Subtract #'s or formulas from named range] [Specify range and file name]
[Extract information from the current worksheet to a worksheet]
[Extract formulas] [Specify "extract to" file name] [Specify range]
[Extract formula values] [Specify "extract to" file name] [Specify range]
[Delete Lotus files]
[Delete a .WKS file] [Specify file name]
[Delete a .PRN file] [Specify file name]
[Delete a .PIC file] [Specify file name]
[List all files on current directory diskette]
[List .WKS files]
[List .PRN files]
[List .PIC files]
[Copy a text file to a worksheet]
[Copy text only] [Specify file name]
[Copy text and numbers as numbers] [Specify file name]
[Change file directory] [Specify new directory]
[Print a file]
[Print a file to the printer]
[Set the range of cells within the file to print] [Specify range]
[Advance one line on the printer]
[Advance one page on the printer]
[Set printed worksheet options]
[Create header for printed worksheet] [Type header]
[Create footer for printed worksheet] [Type footer]
[Set margins]
[Set left margin] [Specify margin in # characters]
[Set right margin] [Specify margin in # characters]
[Set top margin] [Specify margin in # characters]
[Set bottom margin] [Specify margin in # characters]
[Set printed worksheet borders]
[Use column headings as borders]
[Use row descriptions as borders]

| MENU PATH | FUNCTION |
|---|---|
| Print Printer Options Setup | [Create setup string] [Specify string] |
| Print Printer Options Page-Length | [Set page length] [Specify length in # lines] |
| Print Printe Options Other | [Set miscellaneous print options] |
| Print Printer Options Other As-Displayed | [Print worksheet as displayed on monitor] |
| Print Printer Options Other Cell-Formulas | [Print cell formulas] |
| Print Printer Options Other Formatted | [Print with all printer settings] |
| Print Printer Options Other Unformatted | [Print ignoring printer settings] |
| Print Printer Options Quit | [Quit options menu] |
| Print Printer Clear | [Erase printer settings] |
| Print Printer Clear All | [Erase all printer settings] |
| Print Printer Clear Range | [Erase the range setting only] |
| Print Printer Clear Borders | [Erase the borders setting only] |
| Print Printer Clear Format | [Erase the format setting only] |
| Print Printer Align | [Align paper in printer] |
| Print Printer Go | [Print worksheet] |
| Print Printer Quit | [Quit printer menu] |
| Print File | [Print worksheet to a disk file] [Specify .PRN file name] |
| Graph | [Create a graph from worksheet information] |
| Graph Type | [Set the type of graph to create] |
| Graph Type Line | [Set line graph] |
| Graph Type Bar | [Set bar graph] |
| Graph Type XY | [Set XY graph] |
| Graph Type Stacked-Bar | [Set stacked-bar graph] |
| Graph Type Pie | [Set pie graph] |
| Graph X | [Specify data range for X data] |
| Graph A | [Specify data range for A data] |
| Graph B | [Specify data range for B data] |
| Graph C | [Specify data range for C data] |
| Graph D | [Specify data range for D data] |
| Graph E | [Specify data range for E data] |
| Graph F | [Specify data range for F data] |
| Graph Reset | [Delete data ranges] |
| Graph Reset Graph | [All data ranges] |
| Graph Reset X | [X data range only] |
| Graph Reset A | [A data range only] |
| Graph Reset B | [B data range only] |
| Graph Reset C | [C data range only] |
| Graph Reset D | [D data range only] |
| Graph Reset E | [E data range only] |
| Graph Reset F | [F data range only] |
| Graph Reset Quit | [Quit reset menu] |
| Graph View | [Display graph on monitor] |
| Graph Save | [Save .PIC file on diskette] [Specify name] |
| Graph Options | [Set graph options] |
| Graph Options Legend | [Create data legends] |
| Graph Options Legend A | [Create legend for A range data] [Type legend] |
| Graph Options Legend B | [Create legend for B range data] [Type legend] |
| Graph Options Legend C | [Create legend for C range data] [Type legend] |
| Graph Options Legend D | [Create legend for D range data] [Type legend] |
| Graph Options Legend E | [Create legend for E range data] [Type legend] |
| Graph Options Legend F | [Create legend for F range data] [Type legend] |
| Graph Options Format | [Set display format for graphs] |

| MENU PATH | FUNCTION |
|---|---|
| Graph Options Format Graph | [Set display format for entire graph] |
| Graph Options Format Graph Lines | [Display lines connecting data points] |
| Graph Options Format Graph Symbols | [Display symbols for data points] |
| Graph Options Format Graph Both | [Display lines connecting and symbols for data points] |
| Graph Options Format Graph Neither | [Do not display lines connecting or symbols for data points] |
| Graph Options Format A | [Set display format for A range only] |
| Graph Options Format A Lines | [Display lines connecting data points] |
| Graph Options Format A Symbols | [Display symbols for data points] |
| Graph Options Format A Both | [Display lines connecting and symbols for data points] |
| Graph Options Format A Neither | [Do not display lines connecting or symbols for data points] |
| Graph Options Format B | [Set display format for B range only] |
| Graph Options Format B Lines | [Display lines connecting data points] |
| Graph Options Format B Symbols | [Display symbols for data points] |
| Graph Options Format B Both | [Display lines connecting and symbols for data points] |
| Graph Options Format B Neither | [Do not display lines connecting or symbols for data points] |
| Graph Options Format C | [Set display format for C range only] |
| Graph Options Format C Lines | [Display lines connecting data points] |
| Graph Options Format C Symbols | [Display symbols for data points] |
| Graph Options Format C Both | [Display lines connecting and symbols for data points] |
| Graph Options Format C Neither | [Do not display lines connecting or symbols for data points] |
| Graph Options Format D | [Set display format for D range only] |
| Graph Options Format D Lines | [Display lines connecting data points] |
| Graph Options Format D Symbols | [Display symbols for data points] |
| Graph Options Format D Both | [Display lines connecting and symbols for data points] |
| Graph Options Format D Neither | [Do not display lines connecting or symbols for data points] |
| Graph Options Format E | [Set display format for E range only] |
| Graph Options Format E Lines | [Display lines connecting data points] |
| Graph Options Format E Symbols | [Display symbols for data points] |
| Graph Options Format E Both | [Display lines connecting and symbols for data points] |
| Graph Options Format E Neither | [Do not display lines connecting or symbols for data points] |
| Graph Options Format F | [Set display format for F range only] |
| Graph Options Format F Lines | [Display lines connecting data points] |
| Graph Options Format F Symbols | [Display symbols for data points] |
| Graph Options Format F Both | [Display lines connecting and symbols for data points] |
| Graph Options Format F Neither | [Do not display lines connecting or symbols for data points] |
| Graph Options Format Quit | [Quit format menu] |
| Graph Options Titles | [Create graph titles] |
| Graph Options Titles First | [Create first line of graph titles] [Type text] |
| Graph Options Titles Second | [Create second line of graph titles] [Type text] |
| Graph Options Titles X-Axis | [Create description for X axis on graph] [Type text] |
| Graph Options Titles Y-Axis | [Create description for Y axis on graph] [Type text] |
| Graph Options Grid | [Display grids on graph] |
| Graph Options Grid Horizontal | [Set horizontal grid] |
| Graph Options Grid Vertical | [Set vertical grid] |
| Graph Options Grid Both | [Set both vertical and horizontal grids] |
| Graph Options Grid Clear | [Erase grid display] |
| Graph Options Scale | [Set scale for X axis and Y axis on graph] |
| Graph Options Scale Y Scale | [Set Y-axis scale] |
| Graph Options Scale Y Scale Automatic | [Let Lotus automatically scale based upon Y-axis values] |
| Graph Options Scale Y Scale Manual | [Manually scale Y axis] |
| Graph Options Scale Y Scale Lower | [Set lower limit of Y-axis values] |
| Graph Options Scale Y Scale Upper | [Set upper limit of Y-axis values] |

**MENU PATH**

**FUNCTION**

| Menu Path | Function |
|---|---|
| Graph Options Scale Y Scale Format | [Set display format for Y-axis scale numbers] |
| Graph Options Scale Y Scale Format Fixed | [# decimal places] |
| Graph Options Scale Y Scale Format Scientific | [Scientific notation] |
| Graph Options Scale Y Scale Format Currency | [# decimal places for $'s] |
| Graph Options Scale Y Scale Format General | [Default toggle] |
| Graph Options Scale Y Scale Format + / − | [ + / − graph] |
| Graph Options Scale Y Scale Format Percent | [# decimal places for %] |
| Graph Options Scale Y Scale Format Date | [Set date display] |
| Graph Options Scale Y Scale Format Date 1 (DD-MM-YY) | [Display date as noted] |
| Graph Options Scale Y Scale Format Date 2 (DD-MM) | [Display date as noted] |
| Graph Options Scale Y Scale Format Date 3 (MM-YY) | [Display date as noted] |
| Graph Options Scale Y Scale Format Date 4 (Long Int'l) | [Display date as noted] |
| Graph Options Scale Y Scale Format Date 5 (Short Int'l) | [Display date as noted] |
| Graph Options Scale Y Scale Format Time 1 (HH:MM:SS AM/PM) | [Display time as noted] |
| Graph Options Scale Y Scale Format Time 2 (HH:MM AM/PM) | [Display time as noted] |
| Graph Options Scale Y Scale Format Time 3 (Long Int'l) | [Display time as noted] |
| Graph Options Scale Y Scale Format Time 4 (Short Int'l) | [Display time as noted] |
| Graph Options Scale Y Scale Format Text | [Display formulas instead of values] |
| Graph Options Scale Y Scale Quit | [Quit the Y-axis menu] |
| Graph Options Scale X Scale | [Set X-axis scale] |
| Graph Options Scale X Scale Automatic | [Let Lotus automatically scale based upon X-axis values] |
| Graph Options Scale X Scale Manual | [Manually scale X axis] |
| Graph Options Scale X Scale Lower | [Set lower limit of X-axis values] |
| Graph Options Scale X Scale Upper | [Set upper limit of X-axis values] |
| Graph Options Scale X Scale Format | [Set display format for X-axis scale numbers] |
| Graph Options Scale X Scale Format Fixed | [# decimal places] |
| Graph Options Scale X Scale Format Scientific | [Scientific notation] |
| Graph Options Scale X Scale Format Currency | [# decimal places for $'s] |
| Graph Options Scale X Scale Format General | [Default toggle] |
| Graph Options Scale X Scale Format + / − | [ + / − graph] |
| Graph Options Scale X Scale Format Percent | [# decimal places for %] |
| Graph Options Scale X Scale Format Date | [Set date display] |
| Graph Options Scale X Scale Format Date 1 (DD-MM-YY) | [Display date as noted] |
| Graph Options Scale X Scale Format Date 2 (DD-MM) | [Display date as noted] |
| Graph Options Scale X Scale Format Date 3 (MM-YY) | [Display date as noted] |
| Graph Options Scale X Scale Format Date 4 (Long Int'l) | [Display date as noted] |
| Graph Options Scale X Scale Format Date 5 (Short Int'l) | [Display date as noted] |

**MENU PATH**

**FUNCTION**

Graph Options Scale X Scale Format Time 1
(HH:MM:SS AM/PM)

[Display time as noted]

Graph Options Scale X Scale Format Time 2
(HH:MM AM/PM)

[Display time as noted]

Graph Options Scale X Scale Format Time 3
(Long Int'l)

[Display time as noted]

Graph Options Scale X Scale Format Time 4
(Short Int'l)

[Display time as noted]

Graph Options Scale X Scale Format Text | [Display formulas instead of values]
Graph Options Scale X Scale Quit | [Quit the X-axis menu]
Graph Options Scale Skip | [Set skip factor for X axis] [Specify skip #]
Graph Options Color | [Display graph in color]
Graph Options B&W | [Display graph in black and white]
Graph Options Data-Labels | [Create labels for data points]
Graph Options Data-Labels A | [Create label for A data points] [Type label]
Graph Options Data-Labels B | [Create label for B data points] [Type label]
Graph Options Data-Labels C | [Create label for C data points] [Type label]
Graph Options Data-Labels D | [Create label for D data points] [Type label]
Graph Options Data-Labels E | [Create label for E data points] [Type label]
Graph Options Data-Labels F | [Create label for F data points] [Type label]
Graph Options Data-Labels Quit | [Quit data-label menu]
Graph Options Quit | [Quit options menu]
Graph Name | [Create/use a name for a graph]
Graph Name Use | [Use the graph under specified name] [Specify name]
Graph Name Create | [Name the current graph in worksheet] [Specify name]
Graph Name Delete | [Delete a named graph] [Specify name]
Graph Name Reset | [Delete all named graphs]
Graph Quit | [Quit the graph menu]
Data | [Manipulate worksheet data]
Data Fill | [Fill a table with data] [Specify data range]
Data Table | [Create a data table]
Data Table 1 | [Create data table 1] [Specify range]
Data Table 2 | [Create data table 2] [Specify range]
Data Table Reset | [Erase all data table settings]
Data Sort | [Sort worksheet data]
Data Sort Data-Range | [Specify range of all data to be sorted]
Data Sort Primary-Key | [Specify range of the first sorting key]
Data Sort Secondary-Key | [Specify range of the second sorting key]
Data Sort Reset | [Erase all sorting parameters]
Data Sort Go | [Sort the worksheet]
Data Sort Quit | [Quit the sort menu]
Data Query | [Interrogate a range of worksheet values]
Data Query Input | [Specify range of data to query]
Data Query Criterion | [Specify the query parameters]
Data Query Criterion Output | [Specify a range of cells for answers to query]
Data Query Criterion Find | [Find a specific value in queried range]
Data Query Criterion Extract | [Extract a specific value in queried range]
Data Query Criterion Unique | [Find a unique value in queried range]
Data Query Criterion Delete | [Delete a query range]
Data Query Criterion Delete Cancel | [Cancel deletion]
Data Query Criterion Delete Delete | [Delete settings]
Data Query Reset | [Clear all query settings]

| MENU PATH | FUNCTION |
|---|---|
| Data Query Quit | [Quit query menu] |
| Data Distribution | [Specify values range] [Specify bin range] |
| Data Matrix Invert | [Invert a range as a square matrix] [Specify the range of cells to invert] |
| Data Matrix Multiply | [Multiply cells in two ranges times one another using matrix multiplication to produce third matrix of the products] [Specify multiplier and output ranges] |
| Data Regression | [Perform regression analysis on a range of numerical information] |
| Data Regression X-Range | [Set the independent variable(s) of the X range] [Specify range] |
| Data Regression Y-Range | [Set the dependent variable for the Y range] [Specify range] |
| Data Regression Output-Range | [Set output range for the results of regression analysis] [Specify range] |
| Data Regression Intercept Compute | [Compute the intercept] |
| Data Regression Intercept Zero | [Force intercept at origin] |
| Data Regression Reset | [Clear all regression ranges and the intercept option] |
| Data Regression Go | [Perform the regression analysis] |
| Data Regression Quit | [Quit the regression menu] |
| Data Parse | [Split a column of labels into separate ranges]Data Parse Format-Line Create [Create a format line (Parse split) at the current cell] |
| Data Parse Format-Line Create | [Create a format line at (parse split) at the current cell] |
| Data Parse Format-Line Edit | [Edit the format line at the current cell] |
| Data Parse Input-Column | [Specify the range of labels to parse] [Specify range] |
| Data Parse Output-Range | [Specify the output range for the parsed labels] [Specify range] |
| Data Parse Reset | [Cancel all parse input and output ranges] |
| Data Parse Go | [Perform the parse] |
| Data Parse Quit | [Quit the parse menu] |
| System | [Exit to DOS] |
| Quit | [Quit the worksheet] |
| Quit No | [Do not quit the worksheet] |
| Quit Yes | [Do quit the worksheet] |

# Appendix B
## LOTUS 1-2-3 FUNCTIONS

| LOTUS @ FUNCTION | DESCRIPTION |
|---|---|
| **MATHEMATICAL FUNCTIONS** | |
| @ABS(x) | Absolute value |
| @INT(x) | Integer part |
| @MOD(x,y) | X mod Y |
| @PI | Pi |
| @RAND | Random # between 0 and 1 |
| @SQRT(x) | Square root |
| @ROUND(x,digits) | Rounded-off value |
| @LOG(x) | Log base 10 |
| @LN(x) | Log base e |
| @EXP(x) | Exponential |
| @SIN(x) | Sine |
| @COS(x) | Cosine |
| @TAN(x) | Tangent |
| @ASIN(x) | Arc sine |
| @ACOS(x) | Arc cosine |
| @ATAN(x) | 2-quadrant arc tangent |
| @ATAN2(x,y) | 4-quadrant arc tangent |
| **SPECIAL FUNCTIONS** | |
| @NA | The value NA (not available. |
| @ERR | The value ERR (error). |
| @CHOOSE(t,v0,v1,v2,...,vn) | Select value from list: if t = 0, selectv0, if t = 1, select v1, etc. |
| @HLOOKUP(x,table_range,row#) | Table lookup with index row. |
| @VLOOKUP(x,table_range,column#) | Table lookup with index column. |
| @@ (cell address)  (Rel.2.01 only) | The contents of the cell referenced by the cell address. |
| @CELL(attribute,range)  (Rel.2.01 only) | The code representing the attribute of the specified range. |
| @CELLPOINTER(attribute) (Rel.2.01 only) | The code representing the attribute of the highlighted cell. |
| @COLS(range)  (Rel.2.01 only) | The number of columns in a range. |
| @INDEX(range,column,row)  (Rel.2.01 only) | The value of the cell located at the intersection of the specified column and row within the specified range. |
| @ROWS(range)  (Rel.2.01 only) | The number of rows in a range. |

| LOTUS @ FUNCTION | DESCRIPTION |
|---|---|

## FINANCIAL FUNCTIONS

| | |
|---|---|
| @NPV(x,range) | Net present value. |
| @IRR(guess,range) | Internal rate of return. |
| @PMT(prn,int,term) | Payment. |
| @FV(pmt,int,term) | Future value. |
| @PV(pmt,int,term) | Present value. |
| @CTER(int,fv,pv)   (Rel.2.01 only) | The number of compound interest periods for an investment of pv to reach a future value of fv at a rate of interest of int. |
| @DDB(cost,salvage,life,period) (Rel.2.01 only) | Computes double declining balance depreciation. |
| @RATE(fv,pv,term)   (Rel.2.01 only) | The interest rate required for the present value pv to grow to the future value fv during the term. |
| @SLN(cost,salvage,life)   (Rel.2.01 only) | Computes straight line depreciation. |
| @SYD(cost,salvage,life,period) (Rel.2.01 only) | Computes the sum-of-the-year's digits depreciation. |
| @TERM(pmt,int,fv)   (Rel.2.01 only) | The number of payment periods required to pay the future value fv of an investment at a specified interest rate int with payment amounts pmt. |

## CONDITIONAL LOGIC FUNCTIONS

| | |
|---|---|
| @FALSE | The value 0 (meaning FALSE). |
| @TRUE | The value 1 (meaning TRUE). |
| @ISNA(x) | The value 1 (TRUE) if x = NA; otherwise, the value 0 (FALSE). |
| @ISERR(x) | The value 1 (TRUE) if x = ERR; otherwise, the value 0 (FALSE). |
| @IF(x,true_value,false_value) | If-then-else statement: If x is non-0 (TRUE), the value "true-value." If x is 0 (FALSE), the value "false-value." |
| @ISSTRING(x)   (Rel.2.01 only) | The value 1 (TRUE) if x = a string value; otherwise, the value 0 (FALSE). |
| @ISNUMBER(x)   (Rel.2.01 only) | The value 1 (TRUE) if x = a numeric value; otherwise, the value 0 (FALSE). |

## STATISTICAL FUNCTIONS

| | |
|---|---|
| @COUNT(list) | Counts the number of argument values. |
| @SUM(list) | Adds together all the argument values. |
| @AVG(list) | Adds together all the argument values and divides the sum by the number of argument values. |
| @MIN(list) | Locates and displays the minimum argument value. |
| @MAX(list) | Locates and displays the maximum argument value. |
| @STD(list) | Calculates the standard deviation of all the argument values. |
| @VAR(list) | Calculates the variance of all the argument values. |

## STATISTICAL DATABASE FUNCTIONS

| | |
|---|---|
| @DCOUNT(inp_rng,offset,crit_rng) | Field count |
| @DSUM(inp_rng,offset,crit_rng) | Field sum |
| @DAVG(inp_rng,offset,crit_rng) | Field average |
| @DMIN(inp_rng,offset,crit_rng) | Field minimum |
| @DMAX(inp_rng,offset,crit_rng) | Field maximum |
| @DSTD(inp_rng,offset,crit_rng) | Field standard deviation |
| @DVAR(inp_rng,offset,crit_rng) | Field variance |

| LOTUS @ FUNCTION | DESCRIPTION |
| --- | --- |

## DATE AND TIME FUNCTIONS

| | |
| --- | --- |
| @DATE(yr,mnth,dy) | Serial number of day (1 = 01-Jan-00...73049 = 31-Dec-2099). The arguments must be single values within these ranges: yr: 0-199, mnth: 1-12, dy: 1-31 days in month. |
| @NOW   (Rel.2.01 only) | Replaces Rel.1A's @TODAY function. @DATE value of entry you made at Enter new date prompt when you started the computer. |
| @DAY(x) | The day (1-31), month (1-12), and year |
| @MONTH(x) | (0-199) of the day whose serial number |
| @YEAR(x) | is 'x'. The argument value must be between 1 and 73049 (01-Jan-1900 to 31-Dec-2099). |
| @DATEVALUE(date string)   (Rel.2.01 only) | The date number of the specified date string. |
| @TIME(hr,min,sec)   (Rel.2.01 only) | The time number of the specified hour hr, minute min, and second sec. |
| @TIMEVALUE(time string)   (Rel.2.01 only) | The time number of the specified time string. |
| @HOUR(time number)   (Rel.2.01 only) | The hour number of the time number. |
| @MIN(time number)   (Rel.2.01 only) | The minute number of the time number. |
| @SEC(time number)   (Rel.2.01 only) | The second number of the time number. |

## STRING FUNCTIONS   (ALL RELEASE 2.01 ONLY)

| | |
| --- | --- |
| @CHAR(x) | The ASCII character that corresponds to the number x. |
| @CODE(x) | The ASCII number that corresponds to the character x. |
| @EXACT(string1,string2) | The value 1 (TRUE) if string1 = string2; otherwise, the value 0 (FALSE). |
| @FIND(search string,string,start number) | The postition at which the first occurence of search string begins in string. |
| @LEFT(string,n) | The first n characters in string. |
| @RIGHT(string,n) | The last n characters in string. |
| @LENGTH(string) | The number of characters in string. |
| @LOWER(string) | Sets all characters in string to lower-case. |
| @UPPER(string) | Sets all characters in string to upper-case. |
| @MID(string,start number,n) | Extracts n characters from the string beginning with start number. |
| @N(range) | The numeric value of the upper left-hand corner of the specified range. |
| @PROPER(string) | Sets all words in a string with the first letter in upper-case and all the remaining letters in lower-case. |
| @REPEAT(string,n) | Duplicates string n number of times. |
| @REPLACE(original string,start number,n,new string) | Removes n characters from original string beginning at the start number, and then inserts the new string. |
| @S(range) | The string value of the upper left-hand corner of the specified range. |
| @STRING(x,n) | Sets the numeric value of x to string value with n decimal places. |
| @TRIM(string) | Strips all leading, trailing and consecutive spaces from a string. |
| @VALUE(string) | Sets a string number to a true numeric value. |

# Appendix C

## LOTUS 1-2-3, RELEASE 2.01 EXERCISES

1. *About This Book*
   a. What type of computer hardware do you need to run Lotus 1-2-3, Release 2.01?

2. *LOTUS 1-2-3, Release 2.01 Overview*
   a. Name three new features of Lotus 1-2-3, Release 2.01 not found in Lotus 1-2-3, Release 1A.
   b. Define the term worksheet.
   c. At the DOS prompt, type _____ and then press the Return key to load Lotus 1-2-3's Access System into the computer.
   d. Pressing the F1 function key displays Lotus 1-2-3 _____ screens.
   e. Type _____ to quit a Lotus 1-2-3 worksheet.

3. *Recommended Learning Sequence*
   a. Why would you follow the recommended learning sequence for Lotus 1-2-3, Release 2.01?

4. *Copy*
   a. Type _____ to use Lotus 1-2-3's Copy command.
   b. With Lotus 1-2-3, marking the upper left-hand cell for the "Copy To" range is the same as _____ the entire range.

5. *Data Distribution*
   a. Define the term interval (bin range).
   b. The Data Distribution command tests a range of cells for a specified _____ distribution.

6. *Data Fill*
   a. You can/cannot use the Data Fill command to create a Data Distribution bin range?
   b. With a skip factor of 9, what is the next number that the Data Distribution command would create in the following series?   18, 27, _____.

7. Data Matrix
   a. Define the phrase "inverse of a square matrix."
   b. The Data Matrix Multiply command can multiply any two matrices. True or false?

8. *Data Parse*
   a. Use the Data Parse command to _____ a text file imported into a Lotus 1-2-3 worksheet.
   b. Type _____ to use the Data Parse command.

9. *Data Query*
   a. Give an example of why the Data Query commands would be useful.
   b. The value against which the test range of cells is evaluated is known as the _____ range.

10. *Data Regression*
    a. The Data Regression commands are used to _____.
    b. A maximum of _____ independent variables can be used with the Data Regression commands.

11. *Data Sort*
    a. Explain the difference between the Data Sort command's data range and sorting key ranges.
    b. Lotus 1-2-3 can sort data in _____ and in _____ order.

12. *Data Table*
    a. Type _____ to use the Data Table commands.
    b. Give an example where using the Data Table commands would be useful.

13. *File Combine*
    a. Two worksheet can be combined by _____ or _____ or _____ a range of cells or the entire worksheet into another worksheet.
    b. Before you can combine a range of cells from one worksheet into another, the range must be _____.

14. *File Directory*
    a. Use the File Directory command to _____.

15. *File Erase*
    a. Using the File Erase command deletes the specified file from _____.
    b. _____, _____, _____, and other file types can be erased using the File Erase command.

16. *File Import*
    a. Type _____ to use the File Import command.
    b. Files imported by Lotus 1-2-3 can treat the imported information as _____ or as _____.

17. *File List*
    a. Why would the File List command be useful?

18. *File Save, Retrieve*
    a. Lotus 1-2-3 automatically assigns the file name extension _____ when a worksheet file is saved for the first time.
    b. Type _____ and then specify the file name to retieve a Lotus 1-2-3 worksheet file.

19. *File Xtract*
    a. Explain the major difference between the File Extract and the File Combine commands.
    b. When extracting information from one worksheet into another, care must be taken not to _____ the extracted information on top of information in the current worksheet.

20. *Formulas - Advanced*
    a. Define the phrase "conditional transfer statement."
    b. In the formula @IF(A7 > 25,1,0), the A7 > 25 is the _____ to be met.

21. *Formulas - Primer*
    a. Define the term argument.
    b. The use of @ functions saves a great deal of _____ when creating formulas.
    c. What is wrong with the following @ formula? @SUM(B17.B25)
    d. The use of a $ in a formula _____ the cell reference.

22. *Graph Options B&W, Color*
    a. Type /GO and then _____ to set a color monitor to display in color.

23. *Graph Name*
    a. Naming a graph is the same thing as saving it. True or false?
    b. Type _____ to name a graph.

24. *Graph Options Data*
    a. Graph data labels are used to identify the _____ _____ on a graph.
    b. You must specify the _____ for data labels you want to display in your graph.

25. *Graph Options Format*
    a. Use the Graph Format commands to display the numbers on a graph in different ways. True or false?
    b. You can set the format for an entire graph for _____ graph ranges.

26. *Graph Options Grid*
    a. The Graph Options Grid command can/can not be used on a pie chart.
    b. Give an example of why a grid would be useful on a graph display.

27. *Graph Options Legend*
    a. What is the difference between a graph legend and a graph data label?
    b. The Graph Options Legend commands are reached by typing _____.

28. *Graph Options Scale*
    a. The Graph Options Scale commands allow you to manually set the scale and the _____ for graphs.
    b. Why would you want to manually set a graph's scale?

29. *Graph Options Titles*
    a. The Graph Options Title command allows 2 lines for a graph title and _____ line for the X and Y axis.
    b. A graph title can have up to _____ characters.

30. *Graph Reset*
    a. Using the Graph Reset command always erases all graph settings for a worksheet. True or false?

31. *Graph Save*
    a. Saving a graph creates a Lotus 1-2-3 _____ file.
    b. Saving a graph automatically names it. True of false?

32. *Graph Type*
    a. Lotus 1-2-3 can create _____ different types of graphs.
    b. What is the difference between a bar and a stacked bar graph?

33. *Graph View*
    a. Type _____ to view on the screen a graph you have created.

34. *Graph Quit*
    a. After finishing all work with graph parameters, you type _____ to leave the graph menu.

35. *Graph X, A, B, C, D, E, F*
    a. Lotus 1-2-3 can plot _____ data type for the X axis of a graph and up to _____ data types along the Y axis.
    b. You must mark the _____ for the information that a graph plots.

36. *Macros*
    a. A macro is actually a _____ _____ that performs a series of worksheet commands when it is executed.
    b. It is always a good idea to _____ the worksheet steps you want to perform before writing a macro for them.
    c. What is the difference between the {GOTO} macro instruction and the /XG macro instruction?
    d. What function does the tilde perform in a macro?
    e. Before a macro can be executed, it must be _____ .

37. *Move*
    a. Explain the difference between the Move command and the Copy command.
    b. Type _____ to use the Move command.

38. *Print File*
    a. Using the Print File command creates a _____ diskette file.
    b. Why would you want to print a worksheet to a diskette file?

39. *Print Printer Align, Line, Page*
    a. The Print Printer Align, Line and Page commands are useful to _____ .

40. *Print Printer Clear All*
    a. Use the Print Printer Clear command to clear _____, _____, _____, and _____ .

41. *Print Printer Options*
    a. A header or footer can have up to _____ characters.
    b. The _____ symbol is used to insert a page number in a header or footer.

42. *Print Printer Range*
    a. Type _____ to specify the area of a worksheet to print.
    b. The print range set for a worksheet is not permanent. True or false?

43. *Print Printer Go, Quit*
    a. When you are ready to print a worksheet you must type _____ to start the process.
    b. To compress print a worksheet you must provide Lotus 1-2-3 with a _____ _____ for your particular printer.

44. *PrintGraph*
    a. For what is Lotus 1-2-3's PrintGraph program used?
    b. To see what default settings you have for printing graphs, you must look at the PrintGraph _____ screen.
    c. For a graph to be selected for printing you must have saved it to a _____ file.

45. *Quit*
    a. Type _____ to leave a Lotus 1-2-3 worksheet.

46. *Range Erase*
    a. The Range Erase command is the same as the Erase command. True or false?

47. *Range Format*
    a. How many decimal places can be set using the Range Format commands?

48. *Range Input*
    a. Type _____ to specify a range of worksheet cells for input only.

49. *Range Justify*
    a. Define the term justify.

50. *Range Label - Prefix*
    a. The Range Label commands are used to _____, _____, and _____ justify text.
    b. Typing _____ before text causes that text to be centered in the column.

51. *Range Name*
    a. How would the Range Name Table command be useful?

52. *Range Protect, Unprotect*
    a. Why would want to protect a range of worksheet cells?

53. *Range Transpose*
    a. To convert a row of numbers into a line of numbers you type _____ and then mark the appropriate input and _____ ranges.

54. *Range Value*
    a. Type _____ to copy formula values from one cell location to another.

55. *System*
    a. How would you access your computer's DOS operating system from inside a worksheet?

56. *Translate*
    a. Can Lotus 1-2-3 translate a dBase II file into a dBase III file?

57. *Worksheet Column*
    a. _____ is the default column width for Lotus 1-2-3 worksheet columns.
    b. Why would you want to hide a worksheet column?

58. *Worksheet Delete*
    a. Type _____ to delete a worksheet column or row.

59. *Worksheet Global Column - Width*
    a. Using the Worksheet Global Column-width command sets the column widths for specified ranges. True or false?

60. *Worksheet Erase*
    a. The Worksheet Erase command erases the displayed worksheet even if cells have been protected within it. True or false?

61. *Worksheet Global Default Printer*
    a.  The Worksheet Default commands are important because _____?
    b.  Type _____ to set a new default directory at startup.

62. *Worksheet Global Format*
    a.  The Worksheet Global Format commands are the same as the Range Format commands except that they _____.

63. *Worksheet Global Label - Prefix*
    a.  Type _____ to center all the text in a worksheet.

64. *Worksheet Global Protection*
    a.  The Worksheet Global Protection command must be used before a _____ of cells can be protected.

65. *Worksheet Global Recalculation*
    a.  Why would you want to set worksheet recalculations to manual?

66. *Worksheet Insert*
    a.  When inserting a new column into a worksheet, the cell pointer should be on the _____ to the right where the new column is to appear.

67. *Worksheet Page*
    a.  Type _____ to set a page break within a worksheet.

68. *Worksheet Status*
    a.  Why would you want to know the status of a worksheet?

69. *Worksheet Titles*
    a.  Once a range of columns or rows has been specified as a worksheet title, the _____ is prevented from moving into those cells.

70. *Worksheet Window*
    a.  Define the phrase "synchronize windows."
    b.  Press the _____ key to move the cell pointer from its location in the current window to the other window.

# Appendix D
## GLOSSARY

**Absolute cell reference**  A reference that pertains to a permanent cell location within a worksheet by specifying the exact location of that cell. An absolute cell reference is specified by inserting dollar signs before the column and row coordinates such as in the reference $C$15. Copying such a cell reference does not change its absolute coordinates. (See relative cell reference.)

**Address**  The location of a worksheet cell expressed as column and row coordinates.

**Argument**  The individual pieces of information that are operated upon by mathematical operators.

**Cells**  Areas within a worksheet where text, formulas, and numbers are placed.

**Cell coordinate**  The column and row position of a worksheet cell.

**Cell pointer**  The highlighted area of a worksheet screen that indicates the worksheet cell location where additions, changes, and deletions to text, and formulas, and numbers are made.

**Character**  Any letter, number, or symbol which can be displayed on the monitor.

**Column width**  The number of spaces from the left edge of a column to the right edge of a column.

**Database**  A collection of information about one or several subjects.

**Default value**  The assumed parameter settings for any computer device such as a printer, worksheet, etc.

**Diskette**  A 5¼-inch diameter disk which accepts and stores electromagnetic charges that carry informational content.

**DOS**  The acronym for "disk operating system." DOS tells the computer how to arrange information on the system diskettes.

**Edit mode**  The status of a worksheet where previous entries are changed.

**Error message**  A display which indicates that an error has been made in a worksheet command. Usually accompanied by a "beep" from the computer.

| | |
|---|---|
| **File** | A named collection of information such as the Lotus 1-2-3 Program, a worksheet saved to diskette, etc. |
| **File name** | The name given to a file. With MS-DOS and PC-DOS, this name must be no more than eight characters in length. |
| **Font** | A character set used in printing such as italic, block, pica, etc. |
| **Format** | The way in which information is displayed such as scientific, dollars and cents, etc. |
| **Formula** | The solution to a problem expressed as a series of logical operators applied to the arguments of the problem. (See argument.) |
| **Function** | A Lotus feature which uses symbols to represent complicated sets of instructions such as the @ functions. |
| **Function key** | F(number) key used to execute a specific worksheet command such as Lotus's F1 that displays the Help screen. |
| **Help** | The Lotus feature that displays a screen filled with information about commands by pressing F1. |
| **Left justified** | The display of information flush with the left-hand margin. |
| **Menu** | A list from which a selection is made. Menus make it possible for a series of functions to be performed without the need to memorize a non-mnemonic set of instructions. |
| **Point mode** | The status of a worksheet when data ranges are specified. |
| **Prompt** | Any symbol displayed on the monitor that require a response from the computer user before executing further instructions. |
| **Range** | The coordinates of two worksheet cells which enclose the contents of all cells in between. Cell ranges indicate that all information within the range is a valid argument for Lotus functions such as printing, graph creation, etc. |
| **Ready mode** | The status of a worksheet when entries are made to cells. |
| **Relative cell reference** | A reference that pertains to a dynamic (changing) cell location within a worksheet by specifying the location of that cell relative to another cell(s). Copying such a cell reference does change its column/row reference. (See absolute cell reference.) |
| **Right justified** | The display of information flush to the right-hand margin. |
| **Toggle** | A function that is enabled or disabled like an ON/OFF switch. |
| **Value** | Any number or formula typed into a worksheet. |
| **Window** | The sectioning of a worksheet into two areas in which one window remains static (the information displayed within it does not change) and the information in the other is dynamic. |

# Appendix E

## INSTALLATION OF LOTUS 1-2-3, RELEASE 2.01 MONITOR AND PRINT DRIVERS

As it comes from the package, the Lotus 1-2-3, Release 2.01 System diskette allows you to create worksheets, but does not allow you to print worksheets, view on your screen any graphs created with the program or print your graphs. To print worksheets or view and print graphs, a special file must be created containing the appropriate settings for the unique combination of equipment that your computer system contains. This special set of specifications is called a *hardware driver* and is usually contained in a Lotus 1-2-3 file called 123.set.

Perform the following steps to create a typical 123.set hardware driver file that contains all the settings necessary to print worksheets, graphs and to view graphs on the screen if the computer system has graphic display capability.

**NOTE**

If your computer system hardware does not match that used in these instructions, you will want to substitute the names for your own equipment where required.

1.  From the DOS prompt A>, insert the Lotus 1-2-3 Install Utility diskette into drive A.

2.  Type **Install** and then press **Return**. Notice the following screen:

```
                        1-2-3 Install Program

                           Copyright 1986
                     Lotus Development Corporation
                          All Rights Reserved
                            Release 2.01



        The Install program lets you tell 1-2-3 what equipment you have.  You
        choose your equipment from a list of options by moving a highlight bar
        (the menu pointer) to your choice and pressing [RETURN].  You can start
        1-2-3 without using the Install program first, but you will not be able
        to see graphs or use a printer.

        If you need more information to make a particular choice, press [F1] to
        see a Help screen.  If you are a new user, make sure you have filled in
        the Hardware Chart in your 1-2-3 package before you begin.


                    Press [RETURN] to begin the Install progrm.
```

The installation program contains many helpful explanations as to how it is used.

3. Press **Return**. The following screen displays:

```
Install needs some information from the Install Library Disk.


IF YOU STARTED INSTALL FROM A DISKETTE:

  • Remove the Utility Disk and place the Install Library Disk
    in drive A.

  • Close the disk drive door and press [RETURN] to continue.


IF YOU STARTED INSTALL FROM A HARD DISK:

  • Some of the files that Install needs are not in this directory.

  • Press [ESCAPE] to return to the operating system, copy all the
    1-2-3 files into the same directory, and start Install from
    that directory.
```

4. Remove the Install Utility Diskette from drive A, insert the Install Library diskette, and then press **Return**.

The computer works for a few moments, and then displays another diskette swapping screen.

5. Replace the Install Library diskette with the Lotus 1-2-3 System diskette and then press **Return**. The following screen displays:

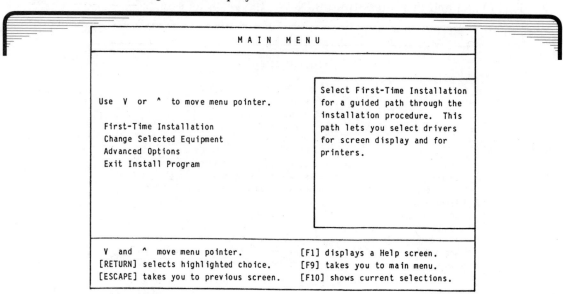

```
                        M A I N   M E N U

                                        Select First-Time Installation
                                        for a guided path through the
                                        installation procedure.  This
Use  V  or  ^  to move menu pointer.    path lets you select drivers
                                        for screen display and for
  First-Time Installation               printers.
  Change Selected Equipment
  Advanced Options
  Exit Install Program



  V  and  ^  move menu pointer.        [F1] displays a Help screen.
  [RETURN] selects highlighted choice. [F9] takes you to main menu.
  [ESCAPE] takes you to previous screen. [F10] shows current selections.
```

Use the up and down arrow keys to move from one selection to another while using the Install program.

6. Press **Return** to select the first-time installation choice.

The Install program asks you a series of questions about your computer system. The answers let it know how to configure the 123.set file.

7. Press **Return** to indicate that your computer system can display graphs.

**NOTE**
Your computer system must have a graphics display card installed before the monitor can display Lotus 1-2-3 graphs.

8. Press **Return** to select one monitor and notice the following screen:

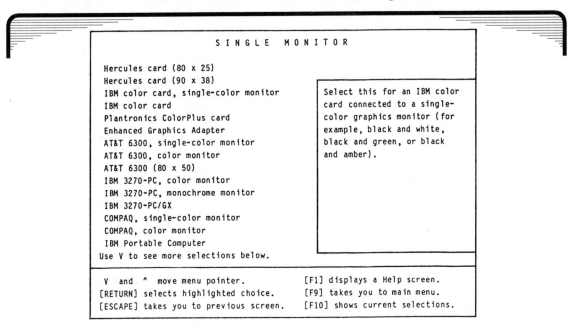

```
                        S I N G L E   M O N I T O R

    Hercules card (80 x 25)
    Hercules card (90 x 38)
    IBM color card, single-color monitor        Select this for an IBM color
    IBM color card                              card connected to a single-
    Plantronics ColorPlus card                  color graphics monitor (for
    Enhanced Graphics Adapter                   example, black and white,
    AT&T 6300, single-color monitor             black and green, or black
    AT&T 6300, color monitor                    and amber).
    AT&T 6300 (80 x 50)
    IBM 3270-PC, color monitor
    IBM 3270-PC, monochrome monitor
    IBM 3270-PC/GX
    COMPAQ, single-color monitor
    COMPAQ, color monitor
    IBM Portable Computer
    Use V to see more selections below.

    V  and  ^  move menu pointer.           [F1] displays a Help screen.
    [RETURN] selects highlighted choice.    [F9] takes you to main menu.
    [ESCAPE] takes you to previous screen.  [F10] shows current selections.
```

9. Select the type of computer monitor (or graphics card) your system contains and then press **Return**.

10. Press **Return** to select a text printer. Notice that the Install program lists available printers with which it works.

11. Select the text printer your system uses and then press **Return**.

The Install program requires the specific make for the printer you are using.

12. Select the specific type of printer your system contains and then press **Return**.

Notice that the Install program asks if you have another text printer. The program repeats each section of information requests until you have answered them for all equipment types connected to your system. For example, you may have another printer that you use with your system.

13. Select **No**.

The Install program displays a series of screens for each type of equipment you might have in your computer system. Answer the questions as appropriate. Once you have specified all the equipment, the following screen displays:

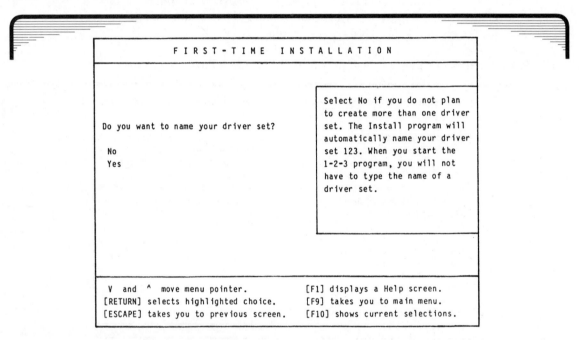

```
                    F I R S T - T I M E   I N S T A L L A T I O N


                                              Select No if you do not plan
                                              to create more than one driver
     Do you want to name your driver set?     set. The Install program will
                                              automatically name your driver
       No                                     set 123. When you start the
       Yes                                    1-2-3 program, you will not
                                              have to type the name of a
                                              driver set.




     V  and  ^  move menu pointer.         [F1] displays a Help screen.
     [RETURN] selects highlighted choice.  [F9] takes you to main menu.
     [ESCAPE] takes you to previous screen. [F10] shows current selections.
```

You can create different hardware driver sets and name each differently. This feature is useful if you set-up your computer system differently depending on the use to which it is to be put and require a different driver for each configuration.

14. Select **No** and press **Return**.

The 123.set file is created by the Install program and saved to the Lotus 1-2-3 System diskette.

15. Perform the diskette swapping procedures noted on the screen to save the 123.set file to the other diskettes in the Lotus 1-2-3 package. When you finish, press **Esc** and select **Yes** to exit the Install program.

Your Lotus 1-2-3 System diskette is now able to print worksheets and display graphs and your PrintGraph diskette is able to print and display graphs.

# Appendix F

## CONVERSION OF LOTUS 1-2-3, RELEASE 1A, FILES TO LOTUS 1-2-3, RELEASE 2.01, FILES

Use the procedures described in Module 56 of this book to convert Lotus 1-2-3, Release 1A, worksheet files to Lotus 1-2-3, Release 2.01, worksheet files.

After you select the Release 1A to be converted to Release 2.01, the following screen displays:

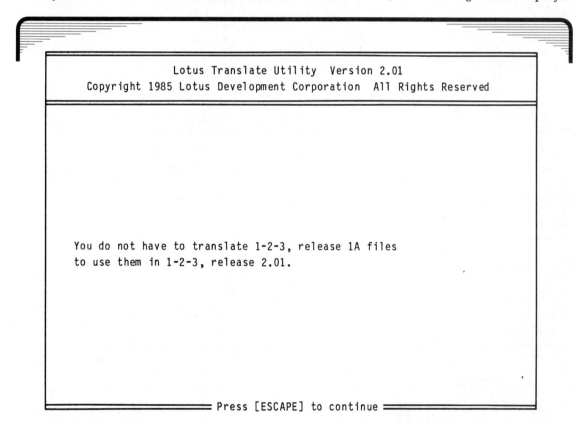

```
                    Lotus Translate Utility   Version 2.01
         Copyright 1985 Lotus Development Corporation   All Rights Reserved




          You do not have to translate 1-2-3, release 1A files
          to use them in 1-2-3, release 2.01.




                      ═══ Press [ESCAPE] to continue ═══
```

One of the outstanding features of Lotus 1-2-3, Release 2.01, is that no special conversion is necessary to use all the worksheets you created using the prior versions of the program.

# Index